**Second Edition**

# 100

# B E S T

# Ranch Vacations
# in North America

### THE TOP GUEST AND RESORT RANCHES
### WITH ACTIVITIES FOR ALL AGES

## Gavin Ehringer

The
Globe
Pequot
Press

GUILFORD, CONNECTICUT

Copyright © 2004, 2007 Morris Book Publishing, LLC

Text design by Nancy Freeborn

Photos pages i, 1, 193, and 207 © Photos.com; spot art throughout © Bob Woodall/ FocusProductions.com for Triangle C Ranch

ISSN 1933-9771
ISBN 978-0-7627-4391-9

Manufactured in the United States of America
Second Edition/First Printing

The prices and rates listed in this guidebook were confirmed at press time. We recommend, however, that before traveling you call establishments to obtain current information.

# CONTENTS

# INTRODUCTION

The horse is a vehicle that not only can carry us but also can carry us back to a simpler time. For many that journey begins at a guest ranch.

The guest ranch experience dates back more than a century and a half, when well-to-do easterners and foreign guests would travel to the sparsely populated environs of the western United States to view its scenic wonders and enjoy its open spaces. Many came West to share in the great adventure of the cowboy, an American icon whose mythology was already being written even as these rugged men were still driving cattle up the trails out of Texas.

Teddy Roosevelt was one of those early "dudes," and he often credited his days spent out West for transforming him from a pale, sickly individual into a robust man with abundant health and self-confidence. Doubtless, the modern guest doesn't anticipate such a dramatic makeover. But still, spending a week's vacation outdoors, participating in rigorous activities, or just lazing along a sunny fishing stream not only has a certain restorative value but a transformative one, too.

I know, because dude ranches played a big role in my life. For several years I worked as a guest ranch wrangler in the Colorado Rockies. My experiences spanned

Guest ranches offer a restorative experience and escape from daily stresses.

the entire range of adventures one can find among the huge variety of guest ranches. At one extreme was a ranch at which guests stayed in a century-old bunkhouse with neither electricity nor indoor plumbing and dined on meals cooked on an authentic woodstove. That was real cowboy stuff.

At the other extreme I spent a season working at the C Lazy U Guest Ranch (featured in this book), a five-star, five-diamond resort facility with a top-shelf bar, chef-prepared meals, a spa, indoor pool, an extensive western art collection, and its own tennis pro.

Whether your idea of the perfect guest ranch vacation includes sleeping on a bedroll underneath the stars or resting your head on a goosedown pillow beneath a hand-stitched quilt, chances are you'll find your kind of place in these pages.

No two guest ranches are alike. Most are family-owned, and much of the owners' personalities are invested in their properties. My goal was to select a broad variety of guest ranches so that you might find one tailored to your interests and inclinations.

I've picked traditional working ranches where guests ride herd side-by-side with real cowboys. New age ranches are also included, where you can luxuriate in full-service spas or focus on activities to enhance the body, mind, and soul. For the adventurous there are ranches that emphasize thrilling activities like river rafting, rock climbing, and mountain biking. There are sportsmen's ranches and ranches with championship golf courses. Ranches for gourmands and ranches that serve home-raised beef cooked on an open fire outdoors. Ranches on both coasts, in the scenic Rockies, and in Canada and Mexico.

One thing that ties all these places together is their hosts' hospitality and dedication to service. The guest ranch tradition grew out of the Code of the West, where the doors were always open to strangers and a place was set at the table. That same spirit pervades today's guest ranches, which offer a vacation experience unlike any other and second to none.

## Being a good dude

The word "dude" might at first seem uncomfortable to wear, but it will soon fit you like an old flannel shirt. In the Old West to be a dude simply meant that you were an urbanite or an Easterner. There's no shame in that: As one ranch hand aptly said, "We were all pilgrims once."

But there are good dudes and bad dudes. Remember, you're there to share in the ranch lifestyle, and the more willing you are to take an active role with enthusiasm and a sense of adventure, the more likely you will enjoy the experience.

Ease into the experience during the first few days. You've probably got some stress to unload before you begin to properly enjoy your vacation. Get a feel for how things are done, the pace and rhythm of the guest ranch. As you become a part of the place, you can step up your level or interaction. But at first, take things slow and easy.

One thing about ranchers and cowboys: They aren't too sympathetic to whining. After a day in the saddle, you're likely to be sore. Don't be surprised when the ranch wrangler tells you that riding the next day is the best way to get the kinks out. He's right.

While some ranches are set up to pamper their guests, many are not. You may be expected to learn to saddle and unsaddle your own horse or take part in camp chores. "Hands-on" can be a wonderful and enriching experience, so don't pass on such opportunities.

Furthermore, you might want to leave the modern devices you're accustomed to

There are many different types of guest ranches, but they all have one thing in common: horses!

using behind. A guest who is constantly yapping on his cell phone or a kid who spends his entire vacation playing video games on his personal console rather misses the point of the ranch vacation. I once took a family from Florida to a beautiful mountain valley in the Rockies and was somewhat startled when, having set up camp, the father sat down to watch a handheld television set. I was quite pleased that there was no reception in this remote wilderness, and it wasn't long before he'd turned his attention to the herd of elk streaming across the mountainside just a few hundred yards from camp.

## What to Pack

Nearly every guest ranch has its own list of suggested items to bring for your trip, particularly if you're going on a pack trip, where weight and bulk are considerations.

Of course, weather is a factor too. Your packing list for a fall trip in Wyoming will be considerably different from a spring trip in Arizona.

Still, there are basic items that nearly every guest should plan to bring.

• **Riding boots.** Many ranches require that guests wear flat-soled cowboy boots for riding, as a safety measure. The cowboy boot heel is designed to keep your foot from slipping through the stirrup, while the sole helps maintain good contact with the stirrup. Buy quality cowboy boots for everyone in the family, and be sure to allow a week or two to break them in so that you won't develop sore feet on your trip.

In addition to the traditional leather-soled cowboy boots, many western-wear stores offer crepe-soled cowboy boots, which are more comfortable to stand and walk in. If you have back or leg problems, these might be worth investing in.

- **Cowboy hats.** Although you don't need a cowboy hat, you do need some sort of head covering. Remember, you'll be spending a good portion of the day outdoors, often at high altitudes where solar rays can be intense. A baseball cap or a floppy-brimmed golfers' hat may serve you well.

That said, a cowboy hat is ideal. Its broad brim shadows the face and neck and serves as a personal umbrella in a rain shower. In summer an inexpensive straw hat will serve you well. For spring and fall trips, you might prefer a wool or animal-fur felt hat, which provides greater warmth. You may also wish to add a "stampede string," a thin chin strap that will keep your hat from flying away during a sprited gallop or if the wind kicks up.

- **Rainwear.** Mountain weather can be unpredictable, so be prepared with light-weight, quality rainwear. Some ranches provide guests with riding slickers or rain suits, but having your own is a good idea.

- **Jeans.** Jeans are the standard riding pants in the West, and you'll want to pack several pair. Buy "boot cut" styles to fit over your riding boots, and buy them 2 to 3 inches longer than normal, because while riding they tend to hike up your leg. You want them to have a few wrinkles above your boot, and the hem should reach your boot heel when you're standing. Buying jeans that are loose in the seat will make mounting and dismounting easier.

Cotton jeans can be worse than useless when they get wet. Consider taking along some wool pants (excellent varieties can be found in military surplus stores, as well as at outdoor outfitting shops). They'll keep you warm even when wet.

- **Layering.** Weather can change considerably in the mountains, from near-freezing temperatures in the morning to 90-degree heat at midday. Having several layers of light clothing is the best way to adjust to changing climate. Lightweight pile sweaters, undershirts, vests, and rainproof shell overcoats should all be included in your suitcase.

- **Sun protection.** Take along a good sunblock—you'll need it.

- **Sunglasses.**

- **Insect repellent.** One that contains DEET is recommended.

- **Skin-care lotion, lip balm, and essential toileteries.**

If you plan to take part in specific recreational activities, such as river rafting, fishing, or mountain biking, you should find out what clothing and gear will be needed.

## What Not to Pack

- **Spurs and riding chaps.** Most guest ranchers frown on inexperienced riders using spurs, which can be irritating or downright dangerous to horses when used incorrectly. As for chaps (leather leggings worn by riders), they do offer great leg protection, but in most cases will not be necessary.

## Selecting a Guest Ranch

First, get your priorities in order. Is your heart set on visiting Yellowstone National Park during your guest ranch odyssey? Or is getting in several rounds of golf important? Will your children be happy in structured, age-appropriate activities, or would you rather they spend as much time sharing experiences with you as your vacation will allow? Do you want to ride herd on a cattle drive, or would you prefer spending more leisure time poolside?

Look over the various listings and photos; these will give you an idea of whether the ranch leans in the direction of a posh resort or is more "down home"—or somewhere in between.

Be attentive to the activities. Horseback riding is the center of nearly every guest ranch experience, but many ranches also offer a broad palette of others things to do. Some ranches have structured recreational programs, while others leave guests to explore and plan their day on their own schedules.

If you have children, you'll want to look at ranches with kids' programs or teen programs. Day care is offered (and noted) at several facilities; others may require that you bring a nanny. Some ranches are for adults or mature teens only.

I've tried to provide an index of costs associated with your guest ranch stay. Although prices are listed on a per-day rate, the general practice is to offer multiday packages. In most cases the ranches listed in this book follow the American plan, which includes food, lodging, and activities. Others offer a modified American plan, which generally includes meals and lodging, with activities charged separately, or a European plan, which is an a la carte approach. The type of payment plan is noted for each listing. Prices, however, are subject to change, and factors such as length of stay, accommodations, extra activities, transportation, and more can affect the price you actually pay. Be sure to get specifics about your costs and what is and isn't included in those costs.

## Price Index

| | |
|---|---|
| $ | Less than $100 per person, per day |
| $$ | 100–199 per person, per day |
| $$$ | 200–299 per person, per day |
| $$$$ | 300–399 per person, per day |
| $$$$$ | More than $400 per person, per day |

## Some common questions to ask about your ranch stay

### Rates

What are the rates, and what do they include?

What are your policies on tipping and gratuities?

Do you offer discounted off-season rates?

Do you offer senior or children's discounts?

What is the preferred method of payment?

Is there a deposit, and if so, when is payment required?

What happens to my deposit if I am forced to cancel?

### Horse programs

What learning opportunities do you provide?

Will we be allowed to groom and saddle our horses?

Are individuals assigned one horse for their stay?

Are there opportunities to trot, canter, and gallop?

Is there any arena instruction?

Can you accommodate English riding?

What is your policy for children riding?

Are riding helmets available or provided? Are they required?

Are there opportunities to be involved with cattle work?

What safety training do your wranglers have?

How do you address emergency situations, and how far is the nearest medical facility?

Can I bring my own horse?

How much time each day can we expect to spend riding?

What are your weight limits for riders?

### Activities

What activities, besides horseback riding, are offered?

Which activities carry extra fees?

What equipment does the ranch provide?

What cultural or sightseeing opportunities are available near the ranch?

## Children

Describe the children's program, if available.

How old must my kids be to ride?

What child care is available?

Can kids take part in adult activities?

Do children dine separately?

What are the qualifications of child care providers?

What activities can families participate in together?

## Cattle work

Does a ranch stay include participation in cattle work?

Do you offer opportunities to do such things as branding or roping?

Do you have arena activities, such as roping or team penning contests?

Describe any programs you have for trail herding.

## Backcountry packing

Do you offer backcountry pack trips?

If so, what are the costs?

Where do your pack trips go, and how many days are they?

What type of accommodations do you provide for pack trips?

What clothing and gear do you suggest for pack trips?

How many guests are allowed per pack trip?

What emergency evacuation plan do you have for guests if they are injured on a pack trip?

What type of camp food do you serve?

## General

Do you have an activities planner to help with off-site arrangements?

Do you have staff or visiting naturalists?

Do you provide off-site transportation, or should I plan on bringing a rental car?

What is the ranch elevation, and do I need to take any health or safety precautions due to altitude?

I have family members who don't wish to ride or fish. Will there be other things for them to do?

What are your policies on liquor?

Can you accommodate special diets?

What is your smoking policy? Do you have non-smokers' rooms?

Can you provide guest references?

# UNITED STATES

# CIRCLE Z RANCH

## Patagonia, Arizona

Circle Z Ranch is the southernmost ranch in Arizona, just 15 miles from the Mexican border. It is also the oldest continuously operating guest ranch in Arizona, having welcomed dudes since 1926. The ranch is something of an aviary super highway for migrating birds from Central America, and astute bird-watchers may encounter any of fifteen species of hummingbirds! (Special feeders are scattered around the ranch grounds to help coax the birds within easy seeing range of guests.)

The ranch is nestled in the foothills of the Santa Rita mountain range, which provide a scenic backdrop to this historic high-desert ranch. Guests get a sense of stepping back in time, as this region hasn't changed much since the days when Apache Indians and Spanish conquistadors rode these hills. One reason the area was considered vital to both groups is Sonoita Creek. Bordered on both sides by ancient cottonwood trees, the waterway forms a desert oasis. Much of the land surrounding the 5,500-acre spread has been set aside for preservation: The ranch is rimmed by the Coronado National Forest, a Nature Conservancy preserve, a state park, and several large cattle ranches.

Although the Circle Z is an actual working cattle ranch, the focus of its managers, Jim and Ginny Cosbey, is clearly on their guests. Attention to meeting the needs and expectations of visitors is one reason why more than 80 percent of the Circle Z guests are return customers.

Riding is the main emphasis of the activities at Circle Z. The horses here are gentle and well-bred, and the majority are born, raised, and trained right on the ranch. Careful attention is paid to matching horse to rider, and in most cases, once you've been assigned a horse and gotten familiar with it, you remain paired with that mount for the remainder of your stay. Experienced wranglers lead small groups of riders on twice-daily rides. More experienced riders may opt for a ground-covering excursion, whereas beginners participate in a slower-paced tour. It's your option to ride in the morning, the afternoon, or both.

A seemingly endless network of trails provides a great deal of scenic variety. One day, you may find yourself exploring colorful red-rock canyons; the next day's ride may take you through rugged mountain terrain, or you might explore the gentle, rolling range land or take a ride along the ever-flowing Sonoita Creek. No matter where on the ranch you go, you're likely to encounter a variety of native flora and fauna. The land here is populated by stands of cacti and pine forests and is home to a variety of desert and woodlands animals—deer, wild boar, bobcats, rabbits, quail, and coatimundi (a small tree mammal similar to a raccoon)—that thrive in this environment. Be sure to take along a pair of binoculars.

If some of the scenery seems strangely familiar to you, that may be because the Circle Z has been a favorite location for several Hollywood films, including the John Wayne films *Red River* and *Broken Lance,* and for the television series *Gunsmoke.*

Although the ranch cocktail hour is strictly BYOB, you may be invited to partake of a "saloon ride" to historic Patagonia, where you can enjoy a glimpse of the West as it once was. Just remember, you've got to ride home at the end of the day!

For the saddle sore, there are a number of other recreational choices including tennis, swimming in the heated outdoor pool, fishing in Lake Patagonia, and an 18-hole championship golf course nearby. Children will find plenty of amusements, too: Ping-Pong, pool, shuffleboard, horseshoes, basketball, and their own favorite meeting place, the Kid's Cantina. Although no specific children's programs are held at the Circle Z, children over age six can ride with their parents. The ranch has no nursery, however.

Overall, the Circle Z is a great choice for people who want to spend their vacation enjoying great desert scenery and wild animals, warm, sunny weather, and a lot of quality time in the saddle on the ranch's 165 miles of trails.

---

**Circle Z Ranch**
P.O. Box 194
Patagonia, AZ 85624
Phone: (888) 854–2525
Fax: (520) 394–2058
E-mail: info@circlez.com
Web site: www.circlez.com

**Managers:** Jim and Ginny Cosbey

**Accommodations:** 7 adobe cottages provide lodging for 40 guests; 27 separate rooms, each with its own bathroom. A variety of bed sizes and arrangements provide flexibility for guests. Wood-floored rooms open to porches or patios.

**Meals:** The emphasis here is on healthy foods rather than the typically heavy guest-ranch fare. Fresh vegetables and home-made breads and desserts complement main courses such as mesquite-grilled steaks and regional southwestern dishes. Meals are served in the dining room or patio of the main lodge, affording a beautiful panoramic view of the nearby hills.

**Activities:** Riding on an endless variety of trails is the outstanding feature at the Circle Z. Twice-daily rides except Sunday, when rides go out only on holidays. Experienced and friendly wranglers lead small groups of riders. You may choose rides for the morning, afternoon, or both at the pace with which you are most comfortable. Unstructured activities include birding and nature hikes. Side trips to nearby Patagonia, ghost towns, old mining sites, the Old West tourist towns of Tombstone and Bisbee, and the border shopping town of Nogales can be arranged. Fishing in Lake Patagonia. Golf at an 18-hole course in Patagonia.

**Amenities:** Outdoor heated pool, all-weather tennis court, recreation room, Kid's Cantina, adult piano lounge, and a variety of table games and outdoor games—pool, Ping-Pong, shuffleboard, basketball, horseshoes

**Special Programs:** No specific children's programs, although children are welcome. Weekly overnight pack trips, off-ranch trailered rides, lunch and breakfast rides, team penning, and games on horseback are scheduled regularly.

**Rates:** $$–$$$ American plan. Reduced rates for preteens and toddlers under 6. Off-season discounts.

**Credit Cards:** Visa, MasterCard. Personal checks accepted.

**Season:** November to May

**Getting There:** Nearest major airport is Tucson International, also Nogales International in Mexico. Located off Highway 82, 60 miles south of Tucson and 15 miles north of the Mexico/U.S. border.

**What's Nearby:** Old West towns of Tombstone and Bisbee. Mining ruins, artisan village, ghost towns, Spanish mission, and border shopping in Nogales. The Nature Conservancy maintains a preserve adjacent to the ranch.

# GRAND CANYON
# BAR 10 RANCH
Wash, Arizona

Imagine not only being able to enjoy a gratifying ranch vacation but also being able to do so on the rim of one of the world's greatest natural wonders, the Grand Canyon. That, in a nutshell, summarizes the Bar 10 Ranch experience.

The Bar 10 may qualify as one of the most remote ranches in the "lower 48": It's an 80-mile trip from St. George, Utah, the nearest sizable town, down a dirt road to this northern Arizona desert oasis. Most visitors fly in, and the Bar 10 originally got into the dude-ranch business as an adjunct to its main business: providing air service to Grand Canyon visitors.

For those of you who don't mind spending time off the main highway, the seclusion of the Bar 10 Ranch may be just your style. The ranch serves as a jumping-off point and a destination for excursions into America's mightiest canyon. A typical guest will opt to take a scenic rafting trip down the Grand or to explore the chasm via a helicopter ride. Pack trips are another option. Regardless of the mode of transportation, nobody misses the opportunity to get an up-close-and-personal view.

Back on the ranch, however, one can find more than enough activities to fill the time. In addition to daily horseback rides, guests can participate in numerous activities that include skeet shooting, horseshoes, volleyball, and desert hiking. In the evenings, the ranch entertainment includes country/western entertainers (complete with dance-hall girls) and boisterous conversation around the large fireplace "pit."

A unique feature of the ranch is the sleeping arrangements: In addition to dormitory-style lodging in the six large sleeping rooms of the main lodge, guests can also choose to sleep out under the cover of their very own Conestoga wagon! A total of thirteen wagons provide an unusual experience that will have folks back home marveling in disbelief. Each wagon sleeps two adults.

Because so many of the guests use the Bar 10 as a jumping-off or pickup point for Grand Canyon trips, the guest list is highly variable. Although extended stays are common, it is also possible to make your stay an overnighter, one that will leave you rested, refreshed, and ready to tackle the gorge. The ranch will make all arrangements for extended horse pack trips, river-rafting excursions lasting from three to nineteen days, and aerial tours of the region.

But the Bar 10 is far more than a way station for eager adventurers; it is a real working ranch with close to 250,000 acres of territory that is home to 1,400 head of Bar 10 cattle. When not managing ranch affairs, the Heaton family can inform guests on the day-to-day travails and triumphs of actual working cattle ranchers. If you wish to play cowboy, you can take part in scheduled cattle gatherings. If motorized transportation is more your preference, the ranch also offers ATV trips lasting from two hours to an entire day.

In the evenings, staff members provide homegrown entertainment in the form of a patriotic Wild West show that includes singing, dancing, country fiddlin', humorous cowboy poetry, even a gunfight. A slide show that recounts the historic development of the Bar 10 is another favored part of the evening festivities.

## Home on the Range

The Bar 10 is hidden in a side canyon of the Grand Canyon known as Whitmore Wash. Explorer John Wesley Powell, the namesake of Lake Powell,  was the first man to negotiate the Colorado River through the Grand Canyon. Powell came across the wash in the 1870s. He learned from an early Mormon mercenary that it had been the site of a massacre involving three Anglos who'd gone awry of the local Native Americans. One of those would-be settlers was James Whitmore, whose memory was honored by Powell when he gave the area the name Whitmore Wash. Sandwiched between the Utah border and the north rim of the Grand Canyon, which isolates the land from the rest of that state, the stretch of land here came to be known as the "Arizona Strip."

The Heaton family's rich history on the Arizona Strip runs deep. Their story begins in the late 1800s, when an itinerant cowhand named George Lytle was assigned the task of overseeing the Mormon Church's cattle-ranching operations here. Lytle's daughter married Gilbert Heaton, whose father had walked all the way from Illinois seeking a new life out west. Gilbert and his bride settled in southeastern Nevada, but the pull of the Arizona strip proved strong. Their son, Tony, moved to St. George and fell in love with a fellow schoolteacher named Ruby. Ranching ran deep in both of their souls, and eventually they returned to found the Bar 10 in the very place where the Heaton family had laid down roots a half century before.

Given the ranch's remote location, nearly all guests opt to arrive and depart in small aircraft. When planning your trip, the Heatons can advise you on how best to coordinate your travel. The ranch has its own airstrip, suitable for light planes and helicopters, most of which fly out of Las Vegas. For some guests, getting to this remote and secluded ranch is an adventure all its own!

If serenity and proximity to the Grand Canyon coupled with plenty of adventure sound like your kind of vacation, your only choice is the Grand Canyon Bar 10 Ranch.

---

**Grand Canyon Bar 10 Ranch**
P.O. Box 910088
St. George, UT 84791
Phone: (800) 582–4139; (435) 628–4010
Fax: (435) 628–5124
E-mail: reservations@bar10.com
Web site: www.bar10.com

**Owner/Manager:** Gavin Heaton

**Accommodations:** Choose from bunkhouse-style rooms (4 persons to a room) or opt for the privacy and uniqueness of sleeping in the West's original mobile home—a Conestoga Wagon! The Bar 10 can accommodate 45 to 60 guests, with larger groups able to participate in day tours.

**Meals:** Meals are served buffet style. Dinner is prepared in Dutch ovens. A typical dinner consists of tender beef, potatoes, fresh vegetables, rolls, and a homemade dessert. A plentiful sandwich bar and "cowboy breakfast" of eggs, sausages, toast, and so on, keep the troops fueled for the day's activities. No alcoholic beverages are served; guests may bring their own, however.

**Activities:** Active outdoor action is the essence of the Bar 10 experience. Tour packages and ranch activities include white-water rafting on the Colorado River, cattle drives, horseback rides, ATV treks, horseback pack trips, and scenic flights in the Grand Canyon region. On the ranch, guests enjoy evening shows, skeet shooting, hiking, and a variety of recreational sports.

**Amenities:** Able to host conference groups and engage participants in challenging outdoor activities. The main ranch includes The Trading Post, a gift shop where guests can find such necessary items as sunscreen and river supplies, as well as the usual T-shirts, snacks, and souvenir items. The ranch serves as an important aviation destination in the area and has the facilities to refuel and provide service for light aircraft.

**Special Programs:** Numerous different packages allow guests to custom-tailor their own adventure. Tour packages include river rafting, ATV trekking, horseback riding, horse pack trips, and more. No specific children's programs, although children may participate in most activities (kids under 8 are discouraged from river rafting, however).

**Rates:** $$$ American plan, plus a la carte activities for day guests. Packages all-inclusive except for airfare and helicopter tours. Inquire about package rates, off-season rates.

**Credit Cards:** Visa, MasterCard

**Season:** Open year-round

**Getting There:** Most guests fly in on small chartered planes or helicopters. The ranch reservationist will help arrange travel from Las Vegas, Nevada, a 50-minute flight one way, or the Bar 10 can provide an interpretive van tour from either St. George, Utah, or Las Vegas. Driving, which involves a 2½-hour, 80-mile drive over dirt roads from St. George, is not recommended for those travelers without high-clearance, 4-wheel-drive vehicles.

**What's Nearby:** Most trips originate in Las Vegas, the entertainment capital of the West. The main draw is, of course, the Grand Canyon.

# HIDDEN MEADOW RANCH
## Greer, Arizona

In most people's minds, Arizona calls to mind the endless and sparsely vegetated environs of the Sonoran Desert. However, Hidden Meadow Ranch will certainly add new pictures to your mental scrapbook: pine forests, mountain streams, deer and elk, and large stands of aspen that color the mountains in vivid yellow patches in the fall.

Hidden Mountain Ranch, residing at 8,500 feet in Arizona's Apache National Forest's White Mountain Range, shares more in common with its kin folk in New Mexico and the Colorado Rockies than with

its other Arizona guest ranch brethren. Expect the unexpected: warm summer days that cool rapidly in the evening as the dry air dissipates the heat of the day and winters with generous snowfall that allows guests to enjoy a variety of winter sports. This is Arizona?

Yes, indeed. Just not the Arizona of oppressive summer heat and green desert golf courses best played in the dead of winter!

First impressions of the Hidden Meadow Ranch are shaped by the spectacular main lodge, a multistory log and stone structure

Hidden Meadow Ranch, Arizona

Hidden Meadow Ranch, Arizona

that recalls the grand lodges of Yosemite, Yellowstone, Crater Lake, and Mt. Rainier. It is truly an impressive building, and one where you will enjoy many great meals and conversations by the huge stone fireplace.

After a get-acquainted meet-and-greet with a ranch staff member, you can get comfortable in your cabin. Frankly, "cabin" hardly seems accurate; these are more like log vacation homes, whose outward rusticity cloaks the opulence and comfort found inside. Each cabin is unique, based on a theme that borrows from the local flora and fauna, or from the traditions of Native American tribes and of Arizona cowboys. But some things are standard décor—such as the pillowtop mattresses or featherbeds, handcarved wood furniture, and fine art and antiques that add a distinction to every room.

Because of its relatively small size, guests have the freedom to choose their own schedules and activities. One can do as little, or as much, as one likes. This informality is reflected in the weekly lineup of special events—which one week might include a visit from Apache dancers, the next, a seminar on nature photography with a professional shooter. A daily newsletter, laid at your doorstep in the morning, details the various special events that are scheduled to take place.

Flexibility also characterizes a guest's stay. You will not be locked into a rigid Monday-to-Sunday, seven-day vacation. Instead, you can arrive and stay for as long, or as little, time as your vacation allows. This scheduling is reinforced with the recent creation of second-home cabin sites, which will allow individuals to actually buy and own their own time-share cabins at Hidden Mountain Ranch. (If having a vacation home time-share adjacent to a guest ranch interests you, you can find out more on the Hidden Meadow Web site.)

One of the best features of the ranch is its namesake meadow. A fifty-acre open space, the meadow provides grazing for the ranch's horse herd. But it is also an important wildlife corridor for elk, deer, wild turkey, coyotes, foxes, raccoons, brown bears, the endangered Mexican gray wolf, and other wildlife. Early risers have the best chance of seeing these animals, and if that interests you, you might even plan a morning spent with a hot pot of coffee and a spotting scope.

If you just aren't up to rising before the crack of dawn, you'll nevertheless awaken to the meadow's amazing display of colorful wildflowers, especially in the spring. It may not be what you expected when you think about Arizona, but Hidden Meadow Ranch is certainly someplace very special.

---

**Hidden Meadow Ranch**
620 County Road 1325/P.O. Box 300
Greer, AZ 85927
Phone: (866) 333–4080; (928) 333–1000
Web site: www.hiddenmeadow.com

**Owners:** Tim and Casey Bolinger, Gary and Jeanne Herberger

**Accommodations:** Guest capacity, 30. Guests stay in 10 luxurious log cabins, each with a unique decor evoking Northern Arizona's natural and cultural attributes. Each hand-built cabin features a living room/dining room with wood-burning stone fireplace, mini-fridge, bar sink, microwave oven, and coffeemaker. Each cabin has a covered porch with meadow view, master bedroom, and upstairs sleeping loft. Also, a powder room and separate downstairs bath with slate countertops and custom soaking bathtub. Wheelchair-accessible Strawberry Canyon cabin.

**Meals:** Hidden Meadow features a seasonal menu inspired by regional foods and customs. Three meals served daily, with trailside lunches. Two seatings for dinner allow parents to either dine informally with their children or enjoy a more formal and intimate late-night dining experience. A sample dinner menu includes a duck confit appetizer served on saffron rissoto; a variety of salad and soups selections, and a main course selection of herb-grilled lamb chops, pan-seared trout medallions, marinated elk tenderloin, and New York prime rib steak. Needless to say, meals are a gourmand's dream.

**Activities:** A concierge helps plan your daily activities. With 975 miles of trails in the Apache-Sitgreaves National Forest, there is a great deal to explore. Hiking, fly fishing on the ranch's stream-fed pond, and trail riding on horseback are the mainstays of the ranch vacation itinerary. Guests also enjoy canoeing, rock climbing, archery, and mountain biking. Winter visitors can downhill ski off-site, snowmobile, cross-country ski, ice fish, or take the family or partner for a ride on the horse-drawn sleigh. Snowcat tours of the winter backcountry also available at additional charge. Finally, the ranch offers a variety of special activities, such as wildlife and nature photography classes, Apache dances and storytelling, antiquing tours, and more, so inquire about what is planned when booking your stay, or check the daily newsletter for details of available activities.

**Amenities:** Meeting facilities with communications and audiovisual technology for executive retreats and small corporate groups; central ranch house with dining room, lounge, and library; ranch mercantile store

**Special Programs:** Kids' "Dude Ranch" with camp program featuring scheduled special dining events such as picnics, barbecues, and S'mores by a campfire; children's horseback riding, arts, crafts, games, and more. For children of all ages. Seasonal special events, e.g., October Halloween at the ranch, November "wine weekend," etc. Inquire for special events or check the Web site, which is updated frequently.

**Rates:** $$$$$ American plan. Some off-site activities at additional charge. Children's rates.

**Credit Cards:** Visa, MasterCard, American Express, Discover. Traveler's checks and cash also accepted.

**Season:** Open year-round

**Getting There:** Located in the mountains of northeastern Arizona, the ranch is approximately 10 miles from the town of Greer. Guests generally fly into Phoenix or Tucson and make the four-hour drive via rental car. Another option is to drive from Albuquerque, a long but scenic route that takes one through the Datil Mountains and the volcanic landforms of El Malpais National Monument. Private or chartered aircraft to Springerville Airport, approximately twenty-five-minute drive from Hidden Meadow via ranch shuttle (by request only). Request directions for your point of departure.

**What's Nearby:** Winter alpine skiing at Sunrise Ski Resort

# RANCHO DE LOS CABALLEROS
## Wickenburg, Arizona

It's very name honors an ages-old tradition of the Southwest: "caballero" literally means "a gentleman on horseback." The word calls to mind a person of skillful horsemanship, style, and substance. This historic 20,000-acre property lives up to its name in every way.

Rancho de los Caballeros owes some of its legacy to another property in this book, Bishop's Lodge in New Mexico. During the 1930s Dallas Gant managed that landmark guest ranch, which is where he met his wife, Edie. The couple returned to Wickenburg following their wedding in 1941, managing guest ranches in the area. With the help of

two winter guests, they opened Rancho de los Caballeros in 1947. The ranch continues to be run by Rusty Gant, Dallas and Edie's son.

Here, one can explore the serenity of the Sonoran Desert. Anyone who is an aficionado of the classic black-and-white Hollywood westerns will feel a warm familiarity with the rolling, wide-open countryside forested with the majestic Saguaro cactus, which are indigenous only to this area of the world. It is no wonder that many Hollywood films were made in the truly wonderful and distinct Sonoran wilderness.

While there is the Wild West allure, to be sure, Rancho de los Caballeros is a refined experience. The ranch has its own golf course, a beautiful 72-par, 18-hole championship course that will challenge even the most avid golfer. The front nine offers broad fairways and rolling hills of emerald grass amid the dry desert landscape, while the back nine is more hilly and calls for the golfer to use every club in the bag. Voted "one of America's Top 75 Resort Courses" by *Golf Digest,* it is a rare gem of which the folks at Rancho de los Caballeros are understandably proud.

Even if golf isn't your game, you'll find lots to do on this gracious spread. Those who truly want to become caballeros can learn to handle cattle in the corral, participating in a favorite activity: team penning. In this contest, riders ease into a herd of steers and "cut" out a trio of numbered cattle. The riders then endeavor to move the cattle down the arena and into a pen—without causing the remaining herd to stampede. It is exciting, challenging, and fun.

Those looking for a more contemplative horseback experience can join trail rides that take them throughout the huge ranch. Saddle-sore guests can work the kinks out with guided nature hikes that explore the unique flora and fauna of the Sonoran ecosystem. Day trips to Wickenburg offer the chance to shop for Southwestern-style clothing, Indian handicrafts, art, and antiques. The posh Arizona town of Sedona is another alternative for truly different shopping experiences.

Back at the ranch, guests enjoy mastering the art of skeet and trap shooting, improve their tennis skills under the watchful eye of a tennis instructor, and get to explore even more of the ranch with Jeep tours and even hot-air balloon rides. If you have never been in a hot-air balloon, be sure to avail yourself of the opportunity. It is the ultimate way to get "the big picture" view of this amazing desert property.

Kids aren't left out of the fun, either. Rancho de los Caballeros runs an excellent kids' program. Counselors oversee their daily activities, accompanying children throughout the day and during meals. There are opportunities for children to ride, hike, swim, and participate in an endless variety of games.

After a day's activities, guests are treated to a fine dining experience rarely seen at a guest ranch. In keeping with its caballero tradition, men are asked to wear jackets or western vests to the table; women similarly are asked to dress in tasteful western fashion. A less-formal "cowboy cookout" takes place during the week. Guests gather on the Yucca Flats for a true southwestern barbecue cooked over mesquite coals and are entertained by a cowboy singer who croons the coyotes to bed.

---

**Rancho de los Caballeros**
1551 South Vulture Mine Road
Wickenburg, AZ 85390
Phone: (800) 684–5030
Fax: (928) 684–9565
E-mail: home@SunC.com
Web site: www.sunc.com

**Owner:** The Gant Family

**Accommodations:** Guest capacity, 160. 79 "casita" rooms and suites. Southwestern decor characterizes all of the accommodations at Rancho de Los Caballeros. From the original ranch rooms to the large and luxurious Sunset and Hermosa Rooms, guests are surrounded with colorful and highly textural handcrafted furniture, Native American–style rugs, and wrought-iron appointments that give this property a true sense of place. Each "casita" (little house) includes a private patio, AC, television, and telephone with data port. Larger families can be accommodated through adjoining casitas.

**Meals:** Breakfast is served buffet-style, with made-to-order omelets and egg dishes, breakfast meats and homemade biscuits; lunch is similarly served as a buffet, with poolside service available. Dinner is a fairly formal affair; one can expect a selection of soups and salads, five entrees, and, of course, dessert. Weekly cookouts with steaks, barbecue chicken, and ribs prepared over a mesquite wood fire are a special event. Another favorite tradition is gathering in The Saloon, the full-service bar, to watch the sun set over the Bradshaw Mountain Range.

**Activities:** The ranch prides itself on its horse herd and its fine golfing opportunities (the 18-hole championship course was acclaimed by *Golf Digest* as one of the five best in this golf-crazy state). But there is far more to do than teeing up or saddling up. Guests can tan by the pool or play tennis, take a spa treatment, go mountain biking, or accompany a naturalist on a hike or bird-watching outing. Or hone your shooting skills on the trap and skeet range. There is also a desert Jeep tour to abandoned mines and ghost towns and hot-air balloon excursions. In other words, this is a place for couples or families with diverse interests.

**Amenities:** 18-hole championship golf course and clubhouse; fitness center; spa with spa services; full-service bar; 4,500 square-foot Palo Verde Conference Center and 3,400 square-foot Sonoran conference room; facilities for weddings and family reunions

**Special Programs:** Caballeros Kids Program for children 5–12. Counselors accompany kids to all three meals, occupy their evenings with games, and in the morning take them swimming, hiking, and riding. Children 8 and older can enjoy trail rides, those under 8 ride in the ranch corrals. Inquire for information on all-women getaways with golfing, horseback riding, or mixed packages.

**Rates:** $$$–$$$$ modified American plan (choose from several lodging and activity packages). 15 percent gratuity charged with bill. Rates vary by accommodations. Some activities require additional payment. Weekday and off-season discounts.

**Credit Cards:** Visa, MasterCard

**Season:** October through mid-May

**Getting There:** Most guests fly into Phoenix Sky Harbor International Airport. Ground shuttle to and from resort can be arranged at extra cost. Rental cars also available. Private planes at Wickenburg Municipal Airport. Wickenburg is located 50 miles southwest of Phoenix.

**What's Nearby:** Wickenburg, with its shops, galleries, antiques stores, and acclaimed Western museum, makes for an interesting day trip. Also, plan on a day to visit Sedona, local ghost towns, or the Grand Canyon.

# TANQUE VERDE RANCH

Tucson, Arizona

Tanque Verde Ranch ranks among the most luxurious resort destinations in Arizona, making it the ideal spot for those who prefer being pampered to "roughing it." Located in the upper Sonoran Desert on the outskirts of Tucson, Tanque Verde benefits from striking views of the Rincon Mountains and the huge and majestic saguaro cactus indigenous to this region of the Southwest. The 640-acre ranch is bordered by Coronado National Forest land and by the Saguaro National Park, affording guests an unlimited opportunity for exploration.

There are any number of ways to explore this unique and fascinating natural landscape during your visit. The ranch offers miles of hiking and mountain-biking trails and features one of the largest horse herds of any Arizona guest ranch. Rides go out daily, and individuals may choose easygoing walking tours for beginners or loping trail rides for the more experienced. Other "specialty" rides are also available, including breakfast rides to the Old Homestead, half-day picnic rides that stop in a scenic grove of trees, and riding lessons that focus on improving the skills of beginners and advanced riders alike.

For those persons who prefer mounts of a more mechanical sort, the ranch offers mountain bikes, riding helmets, and gloves. The mountain-bike excursions are led by experienced biking guides who will teach you the essentials of negotiating rough terrain in safety.

Slower-paced hikes are the best way to become familiar with the fascinating Sonoran Desert environment. Staff naturalists lead guided nature walks, giving people an up-close-and-personal tour of the native flora and fauna. And if your hike doesn't reveal all of the desert creatures you'd hoped to see, you can continue your education at the ranch nature center, where many live animals are on display.

Back on the ranch, you can find facilities that rival those of most any posh resort. Tanque Verde has five Omni artificial turf tennis courts (one of them lighted for evening play) and a staff pro to help you hone your serve and volley. You can also get in a game of pickup basketball or volleyball or spend the afternoon wetting your line in a catch-and-release pond. Fitness buffs will appreciate the extensive spa facilities, which include an indoor and an outdoor pool, sauna, whirlpool baths, and fitness room.

Don't worry about bringing a bunch of extra sports equipment: Everything you need will be provided by the ranch. And did we mention golf? Guests at Tanque Verde can tee up at one of several nearby courses for an additional fee.

Although the wide variety of activities certainly encourages one to be active, inevitably you'll want to just kick back and relax. You may wish to request an in-room massage by a staff massage therapist (at an extra charge, of course) or simply relax on the broad veranda of the ranch's main lodge with a fine glass of wine (Tanque Verde maintains an extensively stocked wine cellar, along with an assortment of domestic and imported beers).

In the evenings you can become engrossed in the crystal-clear night sky while learning the constellations with a guest astronomer or listen to a lecture by one of the staff naturalist/historians. There are also country-dancing parties and a bingo night.

Kids aren't excluded from the action, as Tanque Verde offers one of the most complete supervised children's programs of any guest ranch in the country. Children from ages four to six make up the "Bucakaroos" program, whereas those aged seven to eleven make up the Wrangler Kids. The younger group participates in supervised horse riding in an arena setting, while the older kids gain proficiency on more advanced rides and on the trail. Children are also led on other activities that include tennis, swimming, nature programs, arts and crafts, and games.

---

**Tanque Verde Ranch**
14301 East Speedway
Tucson, AZ 85748
Phone: (800) 234–DUDE; (520) 296–6275
Fax: (520) 721–9426
E-mail: dude@tvgr.com
Web site: www.tvgr.com

**Owner:** The Cote Family

**Accommodations:** 72 rooms and suites, fully air-conditioned, each with telephones and full private bathrooms. Most have fireplaces and patios. Desert and mountain views. Rates vary according to room size. Smaller standard rooms with one queen-size bed or two twins are perfect for two people. Mid-priced rooms are larger, generally with two queen-size beds and a shared courtyard, but no fireplace. Large deluxe rooms have two queen-size beds or a king, fireplaces, and private patios, some of which have sitting areas with sofa sleepers. There are also 1-bedroom suites, all with fireplaces and patios.

**Meals:** Chef Mark Shelton, who in 2004 was voted Arizona chef of the year, oversees the preparation of the Tanque Verde kitchen. Meals go well beyond standard ranch fare and are more on a par with a luxury resort hotel. Guests can enjoy weekly evening cookouts and barbecue rides, fully catered. Most other dining takes place in the main dining room overlooking the outdoor pool and the Rincon Mountains. Breakfast includes typical menu items plus a buffet of chilled juices, fresh fruits, yogurts, breakfast breads, and cereals. Examples from the dinner menu include carved roast prime ribs of beef au jus, game hens tandoori, poached filet of fresh salmon with lemon and tartar sauce, vegetable-filled egg rolls, fresh steamed asparagus spears, country mashed potatoes with chives, and French onion soup. Drinks are served in The Doghouse Saloon, with wine and beer available at all meals.

**Activities:** With 120 horses, Tanque Verde has one of the largest guest strings in the state. Trail rides are divided into slow and fast rides; children ride in their own groups, although adults have the option of joining them. Advanced riding lessons available.

Mountain biking is another favorite activity, and the ranch provides all bikes, gear, and guides. Tennis with an on-site pro, swimming, fishing, hiking with resident naturalists, stargazing with an astronomer, spa services, basketball, volleyball, and golfing off-site at select Tucson courses.

**Amenities:** Historic ranch property dating from the 1860s. Spanish-style architecture. Natural history museum. Conference facility with 6,800 feet of meeting space. Gift shop. Tennis courts, outdoor and indoor pools, spa with exercise room, whirlpool baths, and saunas. Most rooms feature "kiva"-style fireplaces and patios.

**Special Programs:** Comprehensive supervised kids' program (ages 7–12) focusing on introduction to horseback riding, games, recreational activities. Pack trips available certain times of the year (inquire for dates).

**Rates:** $$$ American plan. Rates vary according to season and room size.

**Credit Cards:** Visa, MasterCard, Discover, American Express

**Season:** Open year-round

**Getting There:** Easy, quick access to Tucson International via Speedway Road. Located 15 miles east of the city on Speedway. Call to arrange shuttle service.

**What's Nearby:** Saguaro National Park, downtown Tucson

# ALISAL GUEST RANCH AND RESORT

## Solvang, California

Central California's ranching traditions date back to the earliest days of Spanish settlement. And although the heyday of big-spread cattle ranching has largely passed, the 10,000-acre Alisal Guest Ranch is a stalwart throwback to that bygone era. The rooms lack telephones and television sets, but that doesn't mean that California's premier guest ranch is lacking in creature comforts. Far from it. This is a full-service resort and conference center that stands up against some of the great resort properties throughout the world.

Two 72-par championship golf courses have been carved out of the rugged Santa Ynez Mountains and carefully tendered and developed to provide golfers an especially scenic playing experience. A shaped pool, hot tub, and brick-red patio (complete with cabanas) offer the perfect place to relax outdoors. A 100-acre lake is ideal for anglers, and one can get fly casting lessons from experienced staff. The lake is also a good place to take a sail or paddle a canoe or kayak or try sailboarding. The Alisal maintains its own flotilla of paddleboats and sailing craft as well as a few small outboard-motor-powered boats. The Alisal is further blessed with an abundance of wildlife. Equipped with a sighting lens and Alisal Field Guidebook, you can partake of a guided nature hike to the southern edge of the lake, on a trail rich with flora and fauna. Teeming with a variety of birds, deer, and wildlife, these nature walks are favorites with photographers. For the gustatory explorer, there's a winery tour that visits up to twenty-five of the region's exceptional vintners.

Horseback riding, of course, is at the center of the activities here. Each day is jam-packed with scheduled trail rides. The ranch maintains a mixed-breed herd of one hundred equines, so finding one suitable to one's riding skills is never a problem. A maximum of six people per riding group ensures personalized attention from the Alisal's expert guides. Be sure to take an early morning breakfast ride to Adobe Camp, where you'll be greeted with hot-cakes on a griddle and a singing cowboy!

Rodeo action is a popular Alisal tradition, and guests can participate in a slate of activities including team penning, cattle sorting, and pole bending. You'll also enjoy a quick-draw shooting demonstration or exhibitions by the rodeo-savvy Alisal wranglers.

Alisal Guest Ranch and Resort, California

In addition to serving individual guests, the Alisal hosts conference groups, providing activities and planning for golfing and tennis tournaments, fishing derbies, and team-building outings. If you are looking for a unique corporate or small-business getaway, the Alisal's conference advisers will go out of their way to satisfy your group's every need.

---

### Alisal Guest Ranch and Resort

1054 Alisal Road
Solvang, CA 93463
Phone: (800) 4–ALISAL; (805) 688–6411
Fax: (805) 688–2510
E-mail: sales@alisal.com
Web site: www.alisal.com

**Manager:** David Lautensack

**Accommodations:** 150–250 guests (150 conference attendees); 73 modern cottages

ranging from 1-room studios to 2-room suites, each with private covered porches. All include fireplaces and refrigerators. Daily maid service and nightly turndown service. No phones or television sets in rooms but available in public areas.

**Meals:** The Alisal's proximity to California's wine country and the sophistication of California diners are reflected in the care taken in food preparation and service. Although the menu varies daily depending on the availability of local and seasonal foods, one can expect meals to satisfy a gourmand replete with fresh seafood, aged and tender meats, fresh vegetables, and fruits. In summer, lunch is served poolside, and luncheon facilities are also available at golf clubhouses. An exceptional wine menu complements the chef-prepared meals.

**Activities:** 2-hour trail rides go out twice daily and are separated by ability. Advanced riders may schedule longer excursions, and arena riding instruction is available to riders of all levels. Biweekly breakfast rides and weekly rodeo competition for guests. Private lake suitable for fishing, boating, and windsurfing. Equipment available. 2 golf courses, the private Ranch Course and the public River Course, offer par-72 tournament-quality layouts with PGA-certified professionals available for instruction. Tennis, nature hikes, mountain biking, volleyball, game room, billiards, and outdoor recreational facilities.

**Amenities:** Heated outdoor pool and Jacuzzi; 7 tennis courts and tennis pro shop; 2 championship golf courses, clubhouse, and pro shop; 100-acre private lake; ranch rodeo arena; library; fine dining facilities (evening attire required for dinner); Oak Room Lounge with stone fireplace and comfy leather lounge chairs, cocktail service, and live music

**Special Programs:** Kid-friendly facilities include a year-round petting zoo and kid-specific riding lessons. Kids' program includes daily arts and crafts instruction, games, and evening entertainment. Special holiday events such as the Easter Egg Hunt and a visit from Santa Claus at Christmas. Extensive conference facilities (including 6,000-square-foot conference space) and special group activities and sports tournaments available. Consult with the Alisal conference planner when making plans.

**Rates:** $$$$ Includes room, breakfast, and dinner. Activities sold individually and as seasonal "activity packages." Two-night minimum stay.

**Credit Cards:** Visa, MasterCard, American Express

**Season:** Open year-round

**Getting There:** Commercial airline service to Santa Barbara, 35 miles from ranch. Also, Los Angeles International, 2½ hours by car. Inquire about ground transportation to and from the Santa Barbara Airport.

**What's Nearby:** Local wineries, shopping, art galleries, Santa Ynes Mission, and the historic Solvang Danish Community

# DRAKESBAD GUEST RANCH
## Chester, California

Do you have fond memories of a particularly special childhood camping trip? If so, the things you remember most were probably the simple ones: catching your first fish, sleeping under the stars, or spying a doe and her fawn as they grazed. Drakesbad Guest Ranch is the kind of place where memories like these are made. The ranch, which is more than a century old, is located in a place that is about as off the beaten path as you can get in the most populous state in the West.

Hidden away in a remote corner of Lassen Volcanic National Park, Drakesbad appeals simply for its simplicity. The ranch was founded by E. R. Drake, who sold the property to the Sifford family in 1900. (They named it Drakesbad for the warm waters fed by natural hot springs). At present, the ranch is operated by a concessionaire and is part of the National Parks System. Not much has changed since its creation—kerosene lamps still provide most of the ambient lighting, and the outdoor pool is still heated by the hot-springs waters.

The pace here is similarly simple, with an unstructured schedule that allows guests plenty of time to form their own explorations or simply slow down and revel in the tranquility and peacefulness of this particularly scenic mountain valley. Activities are in keeping with the "old-timey" feel of the place: horseback riding, fishing, and simple outdoor recreations such as volleyball, badminton, horseshoes, croquet, and hiking.

Drakesbad is best suited to those who wish to commune with nature, who don't need constant action and activity to find contentment, and who think that spending an hour staring at a starry sky is an hour well spent. If you are worried about your kids becoming bored, you should be forewarned that there's nary a Nintendo Game Boy nor DVD player on the place. In their stead, however, is a supervised kids' program for children under the age of twelve. The program runs three days a week when offered and includes enough activities to satisfy all but the most jaded mall-going preteens. In all likelihood, your kids will find the hiatus from the typical multiplex suburban habitat to be a wonderful growing experience.

Guests here tend to create their own nightly entertainment, too. Bring along a few good books, take time out to play some board games, and enjoy the camaraderie of an outdoor campfire. The musically inclined might want to pack along a guitar or mouth organ and stage an impromptu sing-along.

Situated at an altitude of 5,700 feet, the ranch is surrounded by stands of pine trees and aspen groves. Wildflowers abound in spring, and fall brings a particularly colorful display. Guests are advised to pack carefully, as cool weather and rainstorms are not uncommon, even during the height of summer. You'll be pleased to know that the ranch is "green certified" and maintains a rigorous program of energy conservation and resource recycling.

Overall, this historic property provides the perfect environment for a relaxing vacation unencumbered by the trappings of modern living. It harkens back to a time when life was simpler and compels its guests to clear their own minds and focus on the important things—family, friends, and the awesome beauty of unspoiled nature. Really, what more could one want?

---

**Drakesbad Guest Ranch**
Lassan Volcanic National Park
Warner Valley Road
Chester, CA 96020
Alternative (year-round) address:
2150 Main Street, Suite 5
Red Bluff, CA 96080
Phone: (530) 529–1512 ext. 120
Fax: (530) 529–4511
Web site: www.drakesbad.com

**Managers:** Ed and Billie Fiebiger

**Accommodations:** Guest capacity, 75. 13 cabins, 6 lodge rooms, some with full baths, others with half baths (a bathhouse is provided). Rooms are furnished with attractive pine furniture and have hardwood floors. Electricity is limited; kerosene lamps provide a warm, homey ambience and authentic Old West feel. Daily maid service provided.

**Meals:** Breakfast and dinner served in the main dining hall, with either a midday buffet meal or sack lunch on the trail. Menu varies according to seasonal and local availability. Emphasis is on nutritious foods, simply but carefully prepared. Special diets accommodated with advance notification.

Weekly cookouts feature steaks, ribs, and hamburgers and hot dogs for children.

**Activities:** Horseback riding is available on a daily basis: Guests must make reservations the night before the ride. Length depends on the individual's ambitions: short, 2-hour rides or all-day excursions. All rides are conducted at a walk; no "fast" rides are offered. Lake fishing, hiking, and swimming in the naturally heated hot-springs pool make up the bulk of the activities. This is a ranch best suited to the relaxation-minded and those wishing to spend unstructured time amid a tranquil wilderness.

**Amenities:** A rustic, turn-of-the-century ranch house best appreciated for its sparcity of amenities. Electricity is used sparingly, with kerosene lanterns and few electrical appliances or gadgets. Spring-fed pool and naturally heated spring water bathing. Simple but comfortable bedrooms. Modest collection of books and games are provided for guests' entertainment.

**Special Programs:** Supervised children's program for kids ages 6 to 12 available 3 days per week (ask to ensure availability)

**Rates:** $$ American plan prices include lodging and 3 daily meals; horseback riding extra. Due to limited space and high demand, guests must book their trips months in advance. Make initial inquiries in February in order to book summer dates. Reduced rates for children 2 to 11. Prices slightly higher for "bungalow" cabins and rooms with private baths.

**Credit Cards:** Visa, MasterCard. Personal checks accepted.

**Season:** Early June to October

**Getting There:** Ranch is located 120 miles south of Redding on State Highway 36, 17 miles from Chester. Commercial airline service to Reno, Redding, or Sacramento.

**What's Nearby:** Boiling Springs Lake, Devil's Kitchen, and the Pacific Crest Trail

# HOWARD CREEK RANCH
## Westport, California

While most of the ranches featured in this book cater to, and even emphasize, family vacations with children, the Howard Creek Ranch Inn has distinguished itself as a romantic getaway for adults. "This is one of the most romantic places on the planet!" wrote a reviewer in the *San Francisco Chronicle.*

Indeed, as a romantic destination, its location on the scenic Mendocino Coast of northern California is idyllic, with its craggy cliffs, sandy beaches, and high bluffs offering views of the largely unspoiled shoreline. This is the place for anyone who has ever dreamed of riding free alongside crashing ocean waves or who is seeking the perfect place to propose marriage.

Howard Creek Ranch has been in existence since 1867, when the pioneering Howard family homesteaded a substantial land grant on California's lonely northern coast. The original ranch was supported by timber, sheep, cattle, and a blacksmith shop. The current owners, Charles and Sally Grigg, have preserved and improved many of the oldest buildings, earning the ranch a nomination for the National Historic Register by Mendocino County. The original farmhouse (circa 1871) is a showcase for antiques, and each room is uniquely themed and pains-takingly decorated with lush redwood trim, carefully matched color themes, and quirky antiques and contemporary furnishings that support the essential "feel" of each room.

The overall impression is one of an utterly charming turn-of-the-century farm, augmented by well-tended flower gardens and a lush coastal landscape (a stark contrast to the arid guest ranches typical of the American West). A swinging bridge spans Howard Creek, which flows to the Pacific just 200 hundred yards away. The beach is wild and rugged, full of rough-hewn boulders and brimming with tide pools.

The activities here are leisurely as opposed to rigorous: strolling the gardens, inspecting the tide pools, whale-watching, or luxuriating in a hot tub, followed by a relaxing massage. A trip to Mendocino, one of California's more picturesque towns, is almost mandatory, as is a visit to the fabulous vineyards and wineries that have made northern California a world leader in quality wines.

Howard Creek Ranch offers a surprisingly accomplished and complete riding program, thanks to instructor Lari Shea, winner of the prestigious Tevis Cup 100-mile Endurance Race. Riders can explore the coastal highlands, visit a local cattle ranch, or opt for that once-in-a-lifetime opportunity to ride on a lovely sandy beach. In addition to standard western breeds, Appaloosas and quarter horses, Shea maintains a group of Russian-bred Arabian horses, a preferred breed for serious endurance enthusiasts, as well as Akhal-Teke horses. These sweet-faced and beautiful horses make for impressive mounts and outstanding photographs. Both Western and English tack are available for riders.

Howard Creek Ranch is quite a departure from the standard Western guest ranch but an alternative that may be just what a romantically inclined couple desires. All in all, it is the perfect haven for lovers.

---

**Howard Creek Ranch**
40501 North Highway One
P.O. Box 121
Westport, CA 95488
Phone: (707) 964–6725
Fax: (707) 964–1603
Web site: www.howardcreekranch.com

**Owners/Managers:** Sally and Charles Grigg

**Accommodations:** Capacity, 26. Lodging varies from guest rooms and suites in the Old World–style ranch house and the artistically renovated Carriage House to individual and secluded cabins, some with meadow views and two with an ocean view. Decor reflects an early California-inspired influence, with antiques and lovely embellishments. Some rooms have decks, microwave ovens, and refrigerators. Most are trimmed with redwood, and most have glass-doored wood stoves. Renovation of the historic ranch buildings continues to be an ongoing project, with Charles (Sunny), a master craftsman, doing all the work using old-growth redwood.

**Meals:** As a bed-and-breakfast, the ranch serves only that meal. Breakfast is a hearty farm meal with fresh juice, omelets, bacon, sausage, hotcakes, fried potatoes, grits, and baked apples with granola and whipped cream. Coffee is strong and early. Tea is available any time. Menus change daily. Vegetarians gladly accommodated.

The staff will be glad to assist you in making dining plans and can recommend a broad spectrum of excellent restaurants in the Mendocino area.

**Activities:** Mendocino County is a hiker's paradise, with miles of shoreline and stands of the huge and stately redwoods indigenous to the area. The staff at Howard Creek will gladly assist you in planning hikes and provide directions to popular trailheads, or you can simply spend your time exploring the 60-acre ranch or strolling the shore. Horseback riding is provided by Lari Shea, who operates the concession on an "a la carte" basis. Be sure to make reservations. Seasonal whale-watching, bird-watching, tidal-pool exploration, deep-sea fishing, hot tubbing, wine-country tours, and relaxation round out the list of activities.

**Amenities:** The ranch offers farm animals, award-winning gardens, fireplaces/wood stoves, a 75-foot swinging footbridge over Howard Creek, a hot tub, sauna, and a German masseuse by appointment. Accommodations include cabins, suites, and rooms furnished with antiques, large comfortable beds, and handmade quilts and have views of the ocean, mountains, creek, or gardens.

**Special Programs:** No children's programs or other special programs, and visits with children are not emphasized.

**Rates:** $–$$ European plan. Horseback riding is separate, as are other activities. Price varies by accommodations. Reduced winter rates available.

**Credit Cards:** Visa, MasterCard, American Express

**Season:** Open year-round

**Getting There:** The ranch is located 3 miles north of Westport, on State Highway 1. Nearest commercial airport is in San Francisco, 150 miles south. Private car or rental necessary.

**What's Nearby:** Mendocino, with quaint shops and excellent restaurants, art galleries, theater performances, and concerts; Sinkyone Wilderness (the Lost Coast), 2 miles north, offers excellent hiking. The redwood forest just a few miles north of the ranch is an excellent spot for a picnic.

# HUNEWILL CIRCLE H GUEST RANCH
## Bridgeport, California

Hunewill Circle H takes one back to the original concept of the western guest ranch: a working ranch whose owners invite "dudes" to share in their rural lifestyle. If your goal is to experience the life of a cowboy (with or without all the strenuous work that goes with it), the Hunewill Circle H Guest Ranch is your kind of place.

Hunewill Guest Ranch is located just east of Yosemite National Park, so plan on staying an extra day to explore that national treasure. The ranch itself is situated in a broad, green valley in the very heart of the rugged Sierra Nevada. The 4,500-acre working cattle ranch is family owned and operated by the Hunewills, the actual descendants of the original family that homesteaded the ranch in 1861. The Hunewills began hosting guests in the 1930s, but they never lost sight of the land's original purpose. Currently the Hunewill Ranch supports a herd of 1,200 cows and 120 horses, as well as sheep, llamas, and four pigs.

As a true working ranch, the emphasis here is on riding and cattle work, which the guests are welcome to participate in as they wish. One need not stick solely to well-trodden trails: With its huge acreage, lush meadows, and timbered woodlands, the ranch invites guests to range free and wide. It is, in short, a horseman's paradise. Horses are carefully chosen to match riders' abilities (guests may also bring their own), and groups are similarly separated so that inexperienced riders can take it slow and easy while seasoned riders can trot, lope, and canter to their heart's content.

A favorite for riders of all abilities is an early-morning breakfast ride on Robinson Creek. Those who want to spend lots of time in the saddle can take part in an all-day ride to the fringes of Yosemite National Park and the Hoover Wilderness. Anyone not acquainted with ranching will likely be fascinated just watching as young foals and yearlings are being gentled in the corral or seeing the herd of saddle horses come thundering into sight during the daily morning roundup.

Activities are traditional and, for the most part, homespun: There's a talent night, family dance night, barbecues on the creek, and fishing in the many creeks and ponds of the adjacent Toiyabe National Forest and on the ranch itself.

The Hunewills are avid fly fishermen and have been in the process of revitalizing trout habitat on the ranch. They recently opened their "ice pond" to anglers. This very special fishing hole is available by reservation only and at additional cost, and only for fly fishing with appropriate equipment. Anglers who want to experience true catch-and-release trout fishing in a pristine lake environment will definitely want to inquire about this opportunity.

Given its age and location, it is not surprising that a distinct Victorian flavor characterizes the ranch buildings. The main lodge is a stately Victorian constructed in 1880; guests are housed in simple but clean white duplex cottages, each with private baths, porches, and through-doors for large families.

Overall, the Hunewill is a great place to enjoy a real working cattle ranch and to share time with a friendly and authentic western family whose roots in this beautiful place go back six generations. So, pull on your boots and jeans, set your hat low on your head, and get ready for the time of your life, cowboy.

---

### Hunewill Circle H Guest Ranch

(winter) 200 Hunewill Lane
Wellington, NV 89444
Phone: (775) 465–2201
(summer) P.O. Box 368
Bridgeport, CA 93517
Phone: (760) 932–7710
E-mail: hunewillranch@tele-net.net
Web site: www.hunewillranch.com

**Owner/Manager:** The Hunewill Family

**Accommodations:** Capacity, 45. Duplex cabins, each unit with 2 rooms, carpeting, electric or gas heat, private bathroom, and porch

**Meals:** 3 meals served daily. Family-style dining features traditional western dishes. Twice-weekly outdoor barbecue.

**Activities:** The ranch program is centered on horseback riding. Rides go out in the morning and afternoon, with riders divided into groups of beginning, intermediate, and advanced riders. Most of the rides take place in large, open meadows. Guests may be invited to help out with cattle chores, such as moving cattle between pastures. Hayrides, roping lessons, and weekly gymkhana (games on horseback). Other activities include fishing, nature walks, and recreational games. Cross-country skiing, snowshoeing, or downhill skiing at June Mountain Ski Area in winter (guests must bring their own equipment).

**Amenities:** On-premises laundry facilities, masseuse by appointment

**Special Programs:** No formal children's programs, although kids are welcome to join in all ranch activities. Children under age 6 may be "babysat" by a kids' counselor during adult riding times and also may be led on pony rides in the corral. For those who want to get hands-on ranch experience, the ranch offers several special events guaranteed to challenge advanced equestrians. Guests learn to rope, part out a cow, track a cow and not get lost, and explore "cow logic," among other things. Fall roundup, fall cattle work, fall cattle drive, fall color ride, and spring cattle work are some of the special events offered.

**Rates:** $$$ American plan, includes 3 meals per day, lodging, and horseback riding. Discounts for children under 12 and for nonriders. Off-season reduced rates, special package rates during fall and spring cattle work.

**Credit Cards:** Visa, MasterCard, Discover. Personal checks accepted. Advance deposit required.

**Season:** May through mid-September

**Getting There:** Commercial airlines fly into Reno-Tahoe International Airport in Reno, Nevada. The drive from Reno to Bridgeport, along the scenic eastern Sierra, takes approximately 2½ hours. The ranch does not provide transportation between Reno and Bridgeport. Rental cars and bus service, however, are available in Reno. Private planes can land at the Bridgeport Airport.

**What's Nearby:** Yosemite National Park, ghost towns, hot-springs spa, and the town of Bridgeport and the resort communities of Lake Tahoe and Mammoth Lakes (each within 1 hour's drive)

# RANKIN RANCH

## Caliente, California

Southern California brings to mind sandy beaches, the teeming metropolis of Los Angeles, and the world-famous Hollywood hills. But long before it became a cultural melting pot and mecca for "the beautiful people," southern California was ranching country. The Rankin Ranch came to be in those halcyon days, way back in the 1860s. In those times, if travelers happened by the ranch, they were welcome to stop in for a meal and a bed before moving on. That was simply the way of the West. Nowadays, the Rankin Ranch remains much as it has always been: a friendly place as ideal for human habitation as for the white-faced cattle brought here by Walker Rankin Sr. more than a century ago.

Located inland from all the hubbub of the coast, the Rankin Ranch is managed by Bill and Glenda Rankin, who continue the guest-ranching tradition started by Bill's mother, Helen, in the mid-1960s. The entire Rankin family is involved in the ranch, and that family familiarity overflows to the guests who come here to stay. It's not unusual for families to return year after year, their feeling of friendship growing with each visit.

As one might expect of a place where family roots go back many generations, the Rankins are big on family values. To make guests with children more comfortable, they offer a fully supervised kids' program that includes arts and crafts projects, games, swimming, nature hikes, and visits to the petting farm, where kids can befriend new-born calves. The ranch is an ideal place for family reunions and special celebrations, and the Rankin clan will do their utmost to make those special events memorable.

The Rankin spread takes in a full 30,000 acres, making the opportunities to ride and explore quite extensive. Riding is conducted at the walk, with the exception of occasional easy lopes in the open areas. The Rankins still maintain herds of cattle, which guests enjoy seeing during ranch rides.

A typical ride will take you through meadows of wildflowers and oak-covered mountains where the white-faced Hereford cattle graze. Twice-daily rides typically last for an hour. There are also opportunities for longer rides during a weekly lunch ride and a sunrise ride.

Besides riding, the list of activities is quite varied. Of course, many guests simply enjoy hiking and exploring the land, so far removed from the noise and congestion of modern life. Others bring their mountain

bikes, which can be ridden for hours down the quiet rural byways. A 7-mile loop trail that takes in the entire valley is a favorite excursion. For the less athletic, there's a stocked fishing pond (bring your own pole and tackle), and if you bring in a fat trout, the ranch cook will prepare it for you. There's also a hot tub for soaking sore muscles, and a macadam tennis court to make them sore again. Of course, there's the obligatory hay-wagon ride, and twice-weekly outdoor barbecues featuring a haywagon ride along with a splendid spread of traditional ranch cooking. Certainly, an event to look forward to!

---

### Rankin Ranch

P.O. Box 36
Caliente, CA 93518
Phone: (661) 867–2511
Fax: (661) 867–0105
Web site: www.rankinranch.com

**Managers:** Bill and Glenda Rankin

**Accommodations:** Capacity 35–40. Guests stay in duplex-style cabins (14 rooms total), which can serve as individual units for couples and small families or as contiguous units for larger families. Cabins are air-conditioned, with wood-panel walls and carpeting. Most units have a queen, twin, and a daybed suitable for up to 5 individuals. A newly constructed cabin is somewhat roomier and more luxurious, with enough bed space for 8 people. All cabins are situated in private locations and are surrounded by beautiful oaks and pines.

**Meals:** 3 daily meals included in all-inclusive ranch price. Meals are held in the spacious Garden Room. The Rankins pride themselves on their family recipes. Weekly barbecue and hayride. Special lunch rides. Vegetarian diets served with advance request prior to arrival.

**Activities:** Horseback rides twice daily. Tennis, recreational sports (volleyball, shuffleboard, Ping-Pong, and horseshoes). Fishing in a private stocked pond. Mountain bikers should bring their bikes. Evening entertainment includes dances, pool tournaments, hayrides, barbecue, a talent show, and horse races.

**Amenities:** Hot tub, recreation room, heated swimming pool, tennis court, children's petting zoo, archery range, Ping Pong, shuffleboard, fishing, and hiking

**Special Programs:** Extensive kids' program with supervised activities. Activities include arts and crafts, swimming, nature hikes, picnics, and games. Program is for kids

between the ages of 6 and 11; babysitting for infants available with advance notice at additional charge.

**Rates:** $–$$$ American plan. Children's rates. Rates vary depending on accommodations and season, with higher rates for the deluxe "Chimo" cabin lodging.

**Credit Cards:** Visa, MasterCard, American Express, Discover

**Season:** Late March through early October

**Getting There:** Inquire for driving directions, either from LAX or from San Francisco or Sacramento.

**What's Nearby:** Gold Rush era town of Havilah; white-water rafting on the Kern River

# AMERICAN SAFARI RANCH
## Fairplay, Colorado

Infamous as the home of Kyle, Cartman, and the rest of the South Park gang, the real South Park is in fact one of the most inviting and beautiful places in Colorado. Located in Colorado's high country, South Park is a broad, green agricultural valley flanked on either side by the jagged, snow-covered peaks of the San Juan and Front Ranges of the central Rockies. The region abounds with wildlife, from pronghorn antelope to deer, elk, bighorn sheep, and the lovable marmots that inhabit the highest alpine meadows. You'll even see buffalo, as many ranchers in this region raise and nurture American bison, a healthful, low-cholesterol substitute for beef.

Set amid this fascinating and scarcely populated mountain valley is the American

Safari Guest Ranch, whose name reflects something of the flavor of this full-service dude ranch. Just as any visitor to East Africa anticipates the sighting of native species, those who come "on safari" in Colorado will be thrilled to encounter many native species as they ride through the scenic trails on the ranch and its adjoining public lands. And ride you will, with one of the best riding programs anywhere.

Voted "Best Horseback Riding in Colorado" by the *Denver Post,* American Safari actually discourages riders from going nose-to-tail on narrow trails in favor of exciting rides over varied terrain in which riders learn how to handle and guide their horses. This is real ranch riding augmented by private riding lessons, horsemanship clinics in the arena, games on horseback, and more. Guests who like to ride and want to improve their skills will truly appreciate the expert help and guidance that is part of the American Safari Ranch experience.

In addition to horseback riding, the ranch offers a wide variety of typical guest-ranch activities: barn dances and bonfires, cowboy sing-alongs, hayrides, horseshoes, and trail hiking. Located in "Colorado's Playground," the ranch also offers many nearby activities such as trout fishing in gold-medal streams and rivers, white-water rafting, fairs, festivals, and rodeos. Part of the fun of any visit to this area is the town of Fairplay, a charming mountain town with great shops and restaurants. While there, you can stop by the South Park Museum and get a feel for early Colorado history and tour the wonderful South Park Main Street, a re-created Victorian-era town with authentic clapboard sidewalks, hitching rails, and frontier-style businesses.

There's no lack of entertainment back at the ranch, either. Ranch workers keep busy creating chuckwagon barbecue cookouts, Wild West shows (with a staged shootout at the OK Corral), karaoke, Western dancing, and a variety of live entertainment.

Kids have a great time here, as there are a number of activities scheduled throughout the day. From hikes to pony rides, to games and learning activities, children will find plenty to do without having to resort to a video-game console (sorry, no Nintendo or XBox Games here!). Even the kitchen goes out of its way to accommodate kids with their favorite foods during the dining hour.

Guests to the ranch enjoy comfortable lodgings in the modern log cabins, which include private baths, oversize rooms and beds, and great mountain views. Vacationers who prefer to arrive by RV can also camp on the premises, which include twenty-five acres of camping and RV sites

(be sure to ask if this interests you). Campers who opt for horseback riding camp for free.

---

**American Safari Guest Ranch**
P.O. Box 128
Fairplay, CO 80440
Phone: (719) 836–2431
E-mail: ride@americansafariranch.com
Web site: www.americansafariranch.com

**Owner/Manager:** Stan Kopunec

**Accommodations:** Capacity, 75. Guests stay in modern log cabins, all with private baths, or in the lodge, which includes oversize hotel–style rooms, private baths; 3-bedroom suites available for large families.

**Meals:** Typical western-style fare served family style. Special requests and dietary needs accommodated with advance notice.

**Activities:** Horseback riding with trail riding, arena lessons, private lessons, games on horseback, and horsemanship clinics. Advanced riders may explore the ranch without a guide; others are accompanied by ranch wranglers, who encourage riders to really take control and learn the basics of riding in open country. A great program! A variety of outdoor recreational games (volleyball, horseshoes, etc.), evening entertainment, hiking, golf driving range, nearby fishing, river rafting, and sightseeing in historic Fairplay.

**Amenities:** Campground for tent campers and RVs (prices based on stay, with activities charged separately; campers who rent riding horses stay free). Corporate meeting facilities, with group barbecues and conference rooms.

**Special Programs:** Children's program with daily activities, pony rides, hikes, and more

**Rates:** $$–$$$ full American plan. Package price includes dining, lodging, and horseback riding. Nonriders packages available. Discounted children's rates, discounted early and late-season rates. Off-ranch activities charged separately, by arrangement. Very flexible program allows guests to custom-tailor their activities.

**Credit Cards:** Visa, MasterCard, American Express. Personal or traveler's checks accepted.

**Season:** May 1 to October 31

**Getting There:** Located 1 hour from Denver or Colorado Springs. Rental car from Denver International or Colorado Springs Airport recommended.

**What's Nearby:** Fairplay, the South Park Historical Museum, Breckenridge Resort, Colorado Springs, and Denver

# ASPEN CANYON RANCH

## Parshall, Colorado

With its log cabins, sawbuck fences, and old-timey lodge, the Aspen Canyon Ranch looks like a movie set for an old John Ford western, which, in its own way, simply adds to the charm of this rustic yet thoroughly modern guest ranch situated high up in the mountains along the Continental Divide.

Aspen Canyon Ranch borders the Arapahoe National Forest, creating a peaceful and secluded retreat well away from the hustle and bustle of a typical tourist-trap vacation. It truly is a place where getting away from it all has meaning. The Williams Fork River flows through the ranch property, creating a haven for wildlife as well as a perfect place to wet a fishing line. Located at an altitude of 8,400 feet, the ranch benefits from cool summer afternoons and evening temperatures that are just nippy enough to make a roaring campfire inviting.

A network of trails adds great variety to the horseback program at Aspen Canyon. Bridle paths meander through meadows of alpine wildflowers and stands of pine and fir trees as well as groves of quaking aspen, of course. Adventurous guests may be asked to ford streams or climb to high mountain passes that offer stunning, isolated views of the central spine of the Colorado Rockies. Rides are matched to the individual's abilities and interests, and for riders wishing to improve their equestrian skills, arena lessons are available at no additional cost. And if you want to play at being a rodeo cowboy or cowgirl, the wranglers will be glad to show you how to toss a rope or time you on a dash through the barrel-racing course. The ranch also hosts a weekly gymkhana, where guests take part in various games on horseback.

Although horseback riding is central to the Aspen Canyon experience, the menu of other activities is ample. Off-site trips include rafting on the wild white water of the Colorado River, ballooning in Grand County, and visits to the quaint former mining town of Breckenridge. One can also get some fly-fishing instruction on the banks of Lost Creek or in any of three stocked fishing ponds, or just relax in a hot tub located mere feet from your cabin—and within hearing range of the burbling river.

If shooting sports are your fancy, the ranch offers a skeet-shooting range. Rugged outdoorsmen can rough it during an overnight campout. Country-music lovers can learn the latest steps and line dances during evening get-togethers. And golfers and tennis players can avail themselves of nearby facilities, too.

Come wintertime, the ranch offers a superb family gathering place for ski trips and snowmobiling adventures. Several world-class ski resorts, including Breckenridge, Winter Park, Keystone, and Arapahoe Basin, offer skiers and snowboarders of all levels plenty of terrain to explore, while nearby Sol Vista, whose gentle slopes are ideal for instruction, is the perfect spot for first-timers.

Owned and operated by Steve and Debbie Roderick and their four kids, Aspen Canyon Ranch doesn't run on a squeaky-tight schedule but allows guests to set the agenda. By tailoring the experience to the individual, the ranch accommodates vacationers looking for high-energy adventure or low-effort relaxation. It's entirely up to you!

The Aspen Canyon Ranch is somewhat small by Colorado standards, with a capacity of 40. For persons looking for an intimate ranch vacation where you can set your own pace and enjoy scenic grandeur in a "set" befitting a John Wayne western, it may be just the place.

---

**Aspen Canyon Ranch**
13206 County Road #3, Star Route
Parshall, CO 80468
Phone: (800) 321–1357; (970) 725–3600
Fax: (970) 725–0044
E-mail: acr@rkymtnhi.com
Web site: www.aspencanyon.com

**Owners/Managers:** Steve and Debbie Roderick

**Accommodations:** 40 guests. Guests may stay in 3 4-plex log cabins situated along a bank of the Williams Fork River. Each cabin is furnished with handmade log furniture, stone fireplaces, and comfortable bedding quilts. Large families and groups may reserve the Cliff House, a spacious 3-bedroom log home tucked away into a mountainside. Conference facilities for up to 40.

**Meals:** Family-style dining takes place in the rustic main lodge, which is tastefully decorated with antiques, western art prints, log furniture, and a vast stone fireplace. Evening fare might consist of the mildly exotic such as pecan-crusted chicken breasts. For a break from the routine, guests may take part in a sunset trail ride ending in a mountaintop "cowboy" cookout.

**Activities:** Horseback riding is the center of ranch activities, and guests are encouraged to take part in grooming and saddling their own horses. Groups are separated by ability, and additional arena instruction is available at the guest's request. Other arena activities include gymkhanas and practice roping events. Guests may take part in numerous off-site activities that include golf, tennis, hot-air ballooning, river rafting, and shopping excursions to Winter Park or Breckenridge. Wintertime activities include alpine skiing, cross-country skiing, and snowmobiling. The ranch has a skeet-shooting range and several trout-fishing ponds. Fly-fishing guides are available at the guest's request. Mountain bikes are also available, or one can simply explore the area on foot. Evening activities include talent shows, country dancing, cowboy poetry, and music.

**Amenities:** Comfortable lodge with lounge (guests must bring their own liquor); streamside hot tubs; cabins with natural-gas fireplaces, refrigerators, coffeemakers, porches, and patio swings

**Special Programs:** Kid's Canyon offers a fully supervised program of activities and services for wee buckaroos. Kids 6 and over may take part in gentle trail riding, with pony rides for kids under 6. Also, arts and crafts, bicycle riding, games, fishing, panning for gold, water activities, and the kids' rodeo. Babysitting is included at no extra charge, so adults can sneak off and go golfing or river rafting.

**Rates:** $$–$$$ Reduced rates in June and September. Reduced rates for children 3–16; children under 3 are free. Reservation deposit required.

**Credit Cards:** Visa, MasterCard, Discover

**Season:** June 1 through September 27

**Getting There:** Nearest commercial airport is Denver International, where rental cars are available. Drive distance is 90 miles. Shuttle service from airport to ranch by reservation. Call for rates and a reservation form. Amtrak service is also available to Winter Park, with stops in Granby. A shuttle can pick up guests at the train station.

**What's Nearby:** Historic mining town of Breckenridge and the modern resort town Winter Park. Golf courses and tennis courts also available.

# BAR LAZY J GUEST RANCH

## Parshall, Colorado

The Bar Lazy J opened way back in 1912, which makes this quaint ranch on the banks of the Colorado River one of the West's oldest continuously run guest ranches.

At the Bar Lazy J, the old-time Western style is genuine, with nary an air of contrivance. The log cabins are authentic, right down to the chinking, as are the knotty-pine interiors and vintage western furniture. The spacious log cabin–style main lodge is adorned with real wagon-wheel chandeliers, and the wild-game trophy heads that preside over the lodge's grand dining hall are real, too.

Every guest ranch has its own character, and the Bar Lazy J is best typified as "cowboy meets river rat." Its prime location on the banks of the Colorado gives visiting anglers ample opportunity to work the eddies and pools for German and rainbow trout. You'll be hard-pressed to find better fishing habitat than the ¾ mile of private

river controlled by the Bar Lazy J. This stretch of river has been designated as Gold Medal trout-fishing habitat. A catch-and-release philosophy ensures that the fat, sassy fish you catch today will be there to challenge the next angler a week later. The fishing allure is so strong here that the cabins are named for popular fly patterns.

For those persons without an angler's patience, there is another way to enjoy the river: white-water rafting. Be sure to inquire about this thrilling activity, which is additional to the standard American plan guest rates. Golf and tennis are also available at off-site facilities and at extra charge.

Horses, however, are part of every package, and owners Cheri and Jerry Helmicki take great pride in their horse program. They offer two rides a day with groups broken up by ability. The ranch has a string of eighty-plus well-cared-for and well-trained horses that are surefooted and mountain-fit.

Each rider is assigned a horse at the beginning of the week, a practice that helps the rider to bond with his or her mount. A horse-sense orientation takes place on the first day, followed by a morning or afternoon ride. Riders can choose from a slow, sightseeing walk to a more enervating "fast" ride—or somewhere in between.

When you decide it's time to give your horse (and yourself) a rest from the trail, you can take a ride on a mountain bike or enjoy a leisurely afternoon sightseeing via the ranch tour van or opt for a more rugged tour of the backcountry via Jeep; or you can stretch your legs with a hike along the miles of trails. Your hosts will go out of the way to adapt their schedule to your wishes.

In the evenings, everyone gathers around the campfire for a sing-along or joins in the popular country-western dance class. Other evening activities include hayrides, a rodeo, and a very high quality variety show that gives the Bar Lazy J's very talented staff a chance to show off.

Of course, you may just want to relieve your aching saddle soreness by soaking in the hot tub or join other guests in a lively game of stud poker. And when the socializing gets to be too much, you can find a quiet place to yourself by the river and gaze at the stars. There are fancier guest ranches than the Bar Lazy J, but few that can match its down-home authenticity and western spirit.

---

**Bar Lazy J Ranch**
P.O. Box N
Parshall, CO 80468
Phone: (800) 396–6279; (970) 725–3437
Fax: (970) 725–0121
E-mail: BarLazyJ@rkymtnhi.com
Web site: www.barlazyj.com

**Owners/Managers:** Cheri and Jerry Helmicki

**Accommodations:** 42 guests in 12 log cabins plus the Ranch House, suitable for groups of 16. Screened porches, fireplaces, on-premise laundry, river views.

**Meals:** Family style. Vegetarian diets and other dietary needs accommodated with advance notice. All meals accompanied by homemade breads and pastries.

**Activities:** Horseback riding for all levels of riders; Jeep rides, hiking, fishing, mountain biking, and sightseeing. Additional activities at added cost include golf, tennis, and white-water rafting.

**Amenities:** Jacuzzi hot tub, children's play set, rec room, outdoor swimming pool, volleyball court, river-front lodging

**Special Programs:** Children's Ranch Fun program includes a variety of activities tailored to children's interests including hiking, fishing, arts and crafts, games, and for kids ages 7 through 12, guided trail rides. Arena horse rides for younger children.

**Rates:** $$ Reduced rates for children under 13; add $200 per person per week for Ranch House accommodations.

**Credit Cards:** Visa, MasterCard, Discover. Personal check, traveler's check, or cash preferred.

**Season:** Late May through September

**Getting There:** Located in Parshall, 15 miles west of Granby in Grand County. Driving distance from Denver International Airport, approximately 120 miles. Amtrak service from downtown Denver arrives in Granby daily. Van service from Denver International available by arrangement at additional charge.

**What's Nearby:** Lake Granby, Winter Park Ski Area, and Sol Vista Ski Resort. All offer summer recreation and some shopping.

# C LAZY U RANCH

Since 1946, the C Lazy U Ranch has set the standard for luxurious guest-ranch vacations. One point of particular pride for the owners, the Murray family, is the recognition their ranch has garnered for superlative service, facilities, activities and overall attention to guest satisfaction. The C Lazy U has consistently earned awards of distinction not only as a guest ranch but also as a world-class resort.

What makes the C Lazy U so special? Let's begin with its location. The ranch lies just west of the Continental Divide, whose soaring 14,000 peaks and lesser mountains separate the country's watersheds into distinct basins. It's said that a droplet of water that falls on the west summit of the mountains will eventually flow to the Pacific Ocean; one that falls on the east side flows all the way to the Gulf of Mexico! Some of that water meanders down through the C Lazy U, and, interestingly, the ranch derives its name from that very water course. If one stands on the broad deck of the main lodge, one can see where the Willow Creek cuts out the letters C and U.

Ranch guests are treated to outstanding views of the Indian Peaks Wilderness and Rocky Mountain National Park. The ranch can be toured on horseback or, in winter, on cross-country ski equipment furnished by the ranch. In both cases, experienced guides can be relied on to help instruct, inform, and entertain guests.

Although horses are the focus during summer months, riding is but one of a dozen scheduled activities that guests may request. Nearby Winter Park Resort affords some of the best mountain-biking trails in this bike-crazy state. You can find especially scenic hiking on or off the ranch. There's a trapshooting range, where you can test your skill at bagging clay pigeons; or the staff can arrange a tee time at one of four nearby mountainside golf courses, where you're likely to find your golf ball traveling 10 or 20 yards farther than usual, thanks to the thin mountain air.

Anglers who seek the tranquility of fly casting can practice on the banks of Willow Creek or arrange a special guided trip to several gold-medal tributaries of the mighty Colorado River. Ranch guests may also schedule wild white-water rafting trips, although these and other off-premises excursions come with an extra charge.

## Five-Star Horse Program

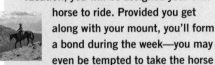

Horses form the foundation of the C Lazy U experience. At the beginning of your vacation, you will be assigned your own horse to ride. Provided you get along with your mount, you'll form a bond during the week—you may even be tempted to take the horse home with you! (You can't, of course, but the staff will do its utmost to pair you up the next time you return.)

Although western riding is the accepted standard, English equitation is an option. You can choose your ride based on your ability: slow, easy rides perfect for beginners and fast, loping rides for experts. The guest-to-wrangler ratio is low: Groups seldom number more than eight riders. Adults and children ride in separate groups except during the weekly "family ride."

If you'd rather stay put on the ranch, you can while away a few hours with the tennis pro on one of two tennis courts, or you can swim laps in the outdoor pool. A masseuse is also available to relax saddle-sore muscles.

Winter guests mainly come to avail themselves of exceptional powder skiing for which Colorado is famous. Novices will be most comfortable at the family-friendly Sol Vista Basin; intermediates can find close to one hundred trails at Winter Park, one of the most popular ski areas in the state. Adjacent Mary Jane offers challenging steeps and moguls for experts looking for a thrill. On the ranch, you can perform pirouettes on the skating pond or schuss through the native pines and spruce trees on more than 25 kilometers of groomed cross-country trails. Around dusk, the ranch team of Belgian draft horses is hitched to a sleigh and blanketed guests can tour the premises to the jangle of real sleigh bells.

As one might expect, the lodging here is simple yet sumptuous. Guests may choose from hotel-like rooms, suites, or deluxe cabins with multiple rooms that are best suited to families. Rooms do not have televisions or telephones, although most have fireplaces. Deluxe rooms feature Jacuzzi tubs and small refrigerators stocked with cold beverages.

For vacationers looking for a luxurious and pampered ranch vacation experience, the C Lazy U cannot fail to satisfy.

---

**C Lazy U Ranch**
P.O. Box 379
Granby, CO 80446
Phone: (970) 887–3344
Fax: (970) 887–3917
E-mail: ranch@clazyu.com
Web site: www.clazyu.com

**Owner:** The Murray Family

**Accommodations:** 40 total units. Rooms vary in size and décor, ranging from rooms with twin beds to multiroom suites. 75 percent include fireplaces; Jacuzzi-equipped suites also available. Guest capacity is 105; conference-group capacity is 80.

**Meals:** Dining takes place in the grand dining hall of the main lodge; outdoor barbecues held poolside twice weekly in summer. All meals served family style. A typical menu includes aged prime rib, fresh Rocky Mountain trout, rosemary rack of lamb, fresh-cooked vegetables, home-baked breads, and desserts. Special diets can be accommodated with advance notice. Wine service with dinner; bar stocked with top-shelf liquors, wine, beer.

**Activities:** More than 150 saddle horses graded and selected to suit individual riders. Trail groups are divided according to ability; children typically ride in separate groups from adults. Arena riding lessons available. Additional activities include hiking, fly fishing, tennis, swimming, skeet shooting. Off-premises activities include river rafting, mountain biking, and golf. Winter activities include cross-country skiing, telemark skiing, ice skating, indoor and outdoor horseback riding, sleigh rides, and alpine skiing at either Winter Park Resort or Sol Vista Ski Area (additional costs for off-premises activities).

**Amenities:** Indoor sauna and Jacuzzi, tennis courts, paddleboats, basketball court, exercise room, heated indoor/outdoor pool, business center, game room, bar, complimentary shuttle service to off-site activities

**Special Programs:** Activity programs for children and teens. Children seated separately for lunch, dinner. Special weeks for families with children under 3. Ask for additional details and dates.

**Rates:** $$$–$$$$ full American plan. Off-season discounts. Several off-premises activities billed separately.

**Credit Cards:** Visa, MasterCard, American Express. Personal checks, traveler's checks accepted.

**Season:** Summer, June through September; winter, mid-December through February

**Getting There:** Located 97 miles west of Denver/Denver International Airport (DIA), approximately 30 miles from Kremmling Airport (private planes only), and 10 miles from Granby Airport (private planes only). There are many airline and ground transportation options for guests of C Lazy U, including private shuttle services serving Winter Park/Sol Vista and Amtrak rail service to Granby.

**What's Nearby:** Winter Park Ski Resort offers some of the best skiing in North America and includes shopping, restaurants, ski instruction, and ski equipment. Nearby Sol Vista provides a host of winter and summer activities.

# DROWSY WATER RANCH
## Granby, Colorado

Nestled in a protected valley amid pine, fir, and aspen trees, Drowsy Water Ranch pretty much defines the ideal of what a western dude ranch should be: tranquil and secluded, with spectacular vistas, and just enough luxury to make "roughing it" pretty darn comfy.

Picturesque red-roofed outbuildings flank the rustic main lodge, affording guests great privacy despite everything being within a moment's walk. The staff is chosen for their cheerfulness, skill, and variety of talent, giving the ranch an upbeat and friendly ambience. And the variety of barnyard pets and a playground make this a children's paradise.

Owners Ken and Randy Sue Fosha and their two sons, Justin and Ryan, are hands-on ranch managers who take great pride in their 640-acre spread, conveniently bordered by thousands of acres of the Arapahoe National Forest. They've remodeled the cozy ranch cabins, which are located near the banks of Drowsy Water Creek. Guests tend to congregate at the main lodge, a log-style great house with a huge stone fireplace and decorative southwestern accents. It's a good place for card playing or just getting acquainted with one of the books in the ranch library collection.

Drowsy Water offers a typical program of horseback riding, steak fries, western dancing parties, Jeep trips, hayrides, and evening staff entertainment get-togethers. Those persons who enjoy river rafting or golf can partake of those activities by special arrangement. Other activities include boating and lake fishing at one of several high-country lakes and reservoirs.

If you enjoy fly fishing, you can work the pools of Drowsy Water Creek, which abounds with brook and rainbow trout, or you can schedule a trip to the mighty Colorado River, which offers scenic stretches of gold-medal trout habitat. During the fall hunting season, the ranch is open for big-game mule deer and elk hunts in the adjacent Elk Mountain and Cabin Creek areas. Confer with the ranch for information on game licenses and hunt camps.

The horse program is second to none, with more than one hundred horses available. Riders are matched to their mounts according to skill level and are given opportunities for daily instruction in the arena and on the trail. Riders can break out of the "head-to-tail" monotony of some guest ranches, and the better riders are given opportunities to trot and gallop during guided trail rides.

Children are attended to and entertained by handpicked counselors, most of them college-age students with an interest in child development and education. After an activity-filled day, children and teens are reunited with their parents for scheduled evening activities such as dances, hayrides, fireside marshmallow roasts, and staff shows.

---

**Drowsy Water Ranch**

P.O. Box 147
Granby, CO 80446
Phone: (800) 845–2292; (970) 725–3456
Fax: (970) 725–3611
Web site: www.drowsywater.com

**Owners:** Ken and Randy Sue Fosha

**Accommodations:** Capacity, 53. Guests stay in newly renovated cabins featuring covered porches. Cabins accommodate anywhere from 2 to 9 individuals; each has its own bathroom. The sleeping lodge includes an additional 8 rooms, all with private bathrooms.

**Meals:** Many opportunities for trailside dining, as well as group dining in the main lodge. Meals vary from western favorites to gourmet creations and include a lavish salad bar and homemade breads, pastries,

and desserts. Special diets accommodated with advance notice.

**Activities:** Lake and river fishing, Jeep tours, chuckwagon meals on the trail, horseback riding and instruction, rec room, arts and crafts for kids, evening dances and staff shows, nature hikes, and kids' gymkhana rodeos with games on horseback. Off-site activities include river rafting, golf, tennis, guided fly fishing, and boating and giant waterslide, some at additional cost.

**Amenities:** Outdoor hot tub, outdoor pool, petting zoo, children's playground, and comfortable main lodge with entertainment hall

**Special Programs:** One of the best children's programs in the country, offering a wide variety of supervised activities with special program for children 5 and under. Seasonal hunting trips available. Adults-only season in early September.

**Rates:** $$$$ Special weekly rates. Reduced rates for children and for additional guests based on double occupancy. Off-season rates 15 to 20 percent lower than peak-season rates.

**Credit Cards:** Visa, MasterCard. Personal checks, traveler's checks, and cash accepted.

**Season:** June to September 14

**Getting There:** Nearest commercial airport, Denver International, approximately 120 miles. Limousine service from airport available by reservation. Amtrak train service from downtown Denver to Granby, with a shuttle pickup available to and from the ranch.

**What's Nearby:** 4 18-hole golf courses, watersports in nearby lakes, shopping and dining in Winterpark and Granby. Close to Rocky Mountain National Park.

# THE HISTORIC PINES RANCH

Westcliffe, Colorado

Situated at the base of Colorado's Sangre de Cristo range, the Historic Pines Ranch benefits from a scenic backdrop that rivals Wyoming's Jackson Hole. Fortunately, the small, quaint ranching and farming town of Westcliffe, Colorado, remains relatively undiscovered. You can always find a parking place on Main Street, even on a "crowded" weekend afternoon. And yet there's still plenty to see and do, with a full summer schedule of arts and crafts fairs, rodeos, and a highly regarded jazz festival.

The Historic Pines Ranch is very much a part of the friendly Westcliffe community, having served as an inviting destination for more than one hundred years. The original lodge was built in the 1890s. Guests will be amazed to learn that this large and comfy building was actually ordered from a Montgomery Ward catalog at an original price of $900 (not an unusual order prior to the turn of the twentieth century). The lodge remains true to that period with Victorian antiques and decor. The renovated guest cabins befit a region of mixed settlement and history: Design themes include Victorian, Southwest/Spanish, Western, and the "catch-all" style, Country. Most of the rooms offer mountain or valley views.

This lovely little ranch benefits tremendously from its Southern Colorado location, which ranks among the premier tourism destinations in the West. Using the ranch as a base, guests can take a white-water rafting adventure on the mighty Arkansas River or embark on a pack trip in the majestic sawtooth Sangre de Cristo Mountains, whose peaks tower thousands of feet above the valley floor and reach altitudes in excess of 14,000 feet.

In addition, tours can be arranged to the Great Sand Dunes National Monument, a fascinating geological site whose dunes are among the tallest in the world. Other interesting side trips include visits to the Royal Gorge, a steep and impressive chasm formed by the Arkansas River, and the Gold Rush town of Cripple Creek, whose gingerbread Victorian buildings now house an active casino-gambling scene. Finally, one can enjoy Colorado's second-largest city, Colorado Springs, which is home to the famous U.S. Air Force Academy, the Broadmoor Hotel, the United States Olympic Training Center, and scenic Garden of the Gods Park. Many people stay an extra day in Colorado Springs (90 miles from the ranch) as a way to commence or wrap up their Colorado dude-ranch vacation.

Of course, one need not ever leave the Pines Ranch to have a perfectly wonderful and memorable vacation. Equine activities take precedence here. The ranch has more than seventy horses to ensure that each guest is matched to a cooperative mount. They will proudly tell you that more than one-third were raised and trained right on the ranch. Typically, one can rub the adorable ears of a recently born colt or filly.

Extra care is taken to orient the rider to horseback riding before a mount is selected. The riding program progresses gradually, allowing riders to work up to the all-day trip to the alpine Lakes of the Clouds, a high-altitude alpine excursion that is truly breathtaking and unforgettable. Guests may be separated by ability and are welcome to help with the grooming, feeding, and saddling of the animals. Guests wanting additional riding practice and instruction can request lessons at no additional charge.

## Genuine Western Ghost Town

Custer County, Colorado, has a peculiar and fascinating history, one you'll surely learn more about at the Pines Ranch.

Briefly, the valley was settled by a colony of German immigrants who set off from Chicago to make a better life for themselves. Soon after their establishment, silver was discovered in the valley. A silver rush ensued. In 1880 in Custer County alone, close to $2 million in silver was mined. Things could not have looked brighter. Silver Cliff, with a population of 5,040, was the third-largest town in Colorado, falling behind only Denver (with 35,629 residents) and Leadville (14,820). But when the U.S. government changed to a gold standard, silver prices plummeted, and the town was nearly abandoned.

Nearby Westcliffe was founded as the terminus of a railroad spur—a wealthy individual owned the land west of Silver Cliff, and the rail line ensured its development. To this day, the two towns (which are side by side and virtually indistinguishable) maintain separate governments and identities.

Among the oddities in Custer County is a purportedly haunted cemetery. Visitors describe floating lights of different colors that can be seen at night. The cemetery was featured in a 1963 *National Geographic* article and remains a favorite "haunt" for area residents and visitors.

Arena activities allow further equestrian-skills enhancement. A favorite activity is team penning, a competition in which riders try to separate a group of cattle from the group and herd them into a pen. For persons truly interested in cattle work and "the cowboy experience," inquire about the special four-day Cow Camp trips in the Sangre de Cristo.

Back at the Pines, guests can fish in a stocked pond, join in evening square-dance and country-swing lessons, take part in the campfire sing-along, and enjoy a staff talent show and even join in the performances, if they wish. The ranch offers an indoor, heated swimming pool and hot-tub baths for relaxation.

---

**The Historic Pines Ranch**
P.O. Box 311
Westcliffe, CO 81252
Phone: (800) 446–9462; (719) 783–9261
Fax: (719) 783–2977
E-mail: howdy@historicpines.com
Web site: www.historicpines.com

**Owner/Manager:** Dean Rusk

**Accommodations:** Guest capacity, 40. The renovated 1890s lodge has 4 guest rooms that are well-suited to couples or singles, providing a "bed-and-breakfast" atmosphere amid Victorian decorations and antiques. In addition, there are 4 guest cabins built on a duplex design, all newly decorated. Each cabin quarters includes a private bath, television/VCR, and living room.

**Meals:** Buffet-style chuckwagon meals served 3 times daily. A typical dinner meal might be chicken-fried steak, homemade mashed potatoes, cooked vegetables, and carrot cake. Well-stocked salad bar. Snacks and the "endless cookie jar" available throughout the day. Weekly breakfast ride. BYOB, nonalcohol bar. The Sundance Saloon serves as a soda fountain where guests can enjoy sodas, floats, and milkshakes. Special dietary needs accommodated with advance notice.

**Activities:** 70+ saddle horses, many raised and trained on the ranch. Guests are encouraged to get involved in grooming, saddling, feeding. Daily trail rides, arena practice, advanced instruction on request. Overnight and extended pack trips in the Sangre de Cristo Mountains. Pond and stream fishing, guest rodeo competition, evening dances, and staff talent show, "tea time" with local storyteller, campfire sing-along. River-rafting packages. Ranch employees available to help plan unaccompanied sidetrips to various southern Colorado tourist sites. Shopping in nearby Westcliffe and Silvercliffe.

**Amenities:** Historic ranch buildings. Indoor swimming pool, hot tub, and saunas. Riding arena. Victorian tearoom. Daily maid service. In-room television with VCR and video collection. On-premises laundry.

**Special Programs:** Children's programs for kids aged 2 to 8 include counselors and activities including scavenger hunts, nature hikes, and arts and crafts. Pony rides in a controlled arena environment; children age 8 and older may participate in adult rides.Other programs: high-country pack trips, river-rafting trips, special singles weeks, and Cow Camp, a backcountry cattle-herding trip. Inquire for details.

**Rates:** $$–$$$ American plan. Off-season and group discounts. Children's rates. Packages of 2-, 3-, 5-, and 7-day stays.

**Credit Cards:** Visa, MasterCard, Discover, American Express

**Season:** May through October

**Getting There:** Located 90 miles south and west of Colorado Springs near the town of Westcliffe. Most guests rent cars at the Colorado Springs Airport; ground transportation to the ranch available at extra cost.

**What's Nearby:** Arkansas River rafting, Royal Gorge, Great Sand Dunes National Monument

# THE HOME RANCH
Clark, Colorado

The Home Ranch is truly a place where riders learn to be horsemen. Horses here don't plod along nose-to-tail, and the wranglers work throughout rides to help riders gain more mastery over their mounts. In addition to riding tips, your guide may engage you in various games on horseback amid the spacious meadows or put riders to work helping to herd cattle. With close to ninety horses from which to choose, wranglers are able to tailor the abilities of the riders to the personalities of their horses.

For visitors who simply want a pleasant guest-ranch experience, The Home Ranch offers great daily trail riding. During orientation at the barn, you'll learn some basic horse-savvy safety lessons before being paired with a mount matched to your skills and even your personality. Half-day and all-day trail rides, which are scheduled throughout the week, will take you into the Routt National Forest, a million-acre forest preserve featuring high-country meadows and scenic vistas.

No matter what your goals, ranch manager Johnny Fisher's enthusiasm is bound to spill over to your attitude toward horses. Johnny took over management of The Home Ranch in the fall of 2002. He was raised in the ranching business and brings his wealth of experience to all facets of The Home Ranch. His wife, Joannie, and daughters Casey and Laura all take an active part in daily ranch life. All are accomplished riders, well accustomed to hard work and the guest ranch lifestyle. Johnny, of course, is an able horseman and goes out of his way to welcome guests and take time out to chat or to give horsemanship tips.

But exceptional horses and instructors aren't the only things that make The Home Ranch special. Guests can also enjoy fishing, hiking, and alpine skiing and snowshoeing treks, depending on the season. The cabins are amply appointed with woodburning stoves, small refrigerators, and hot tubs on the porches. For guests who prefer individual rooms in the lodge, there's a sauna, hot tub, and swimming pool. Formerly recognized by the now-defunct Mobil 4-Star Award, The Home Ranch has joined the prestigious Relais & Châteaux travel service's list of superior resort properties. It is one of only two such properties in Colorado (the other is the Little Nell Hotel in Aspen) and the only such recognized guest ranch in the United States.

With such a prestigious distinction, one fully expects high standards in its dining room. Home Ranch's head chef, Clyde Nelson, is recognized as one of the nation's best. Every meal, from sit-down dinners in the dining room to breakfast buffets and outdoor cookouts, is guaranteed to satisfy the most discriminating tastes.

The entertainment is down-home, warm, and welcoming. Johnny Fisher performs with his friends, and a live band is brought in for the barn dance. There's a staff talent show and a hayride dinner. You can also enjoy western music around the campfire, a regular Saturday-night feature. With nightly entertainment, you'll seldom bed down before the stars overhead have been twinkling for hours!

---

**The Home Ranch**
P.O. Box 822
Clark, CO 80428
Phone: (970) 879–1780
Fax: (970) 879–1795
E-mail: info@homeranch.com
Web site: www.homeranch.com

**Owners:** Steve and Ann Stranahan

**Manager:** Johnny Fisher

**Accommodations:** Capacity, 45. Well-appointed log cabins located in a grove of aspens create a feeling of privacy. Each has a woodstove, hot tub, and covered deck. A main lodge houses guests on 2 levels. There are also 3 cabins. Nightly turndown service, robes, and fresh flowers.

**Meals:** A true gourmet experience—head chef Clyde Nelson came to the ranch in 1989 and has been featured in *Food and Wine, Bon Appetit, Travel and Leisure, Gourmet,* and *Condé Naste Traveller.* The ranch employs a full-time baker whose ovens produce fresh breads, pastries, and desserts. All meals are served family style at a set time in the dining room or, in summer, at the location of the day's activity. If you are leaving the ranch for a day of fishing, hiking, or riding, your sack lunch will be made to order. Children generally are served in a separate dinner seating. Fully stocked bar.

**Activities:** Natural horsemanship is an important part of Johnny Fisher's horse program. Trail rides in neighboring Routt National Forest, along with cattle work.

Fishing and fly casting in a stocked pond on the ranch or on the Elk River, along with all-inclusive fly-fishing instruction. Hiking is a favorite summer activity. Off-site tennis and golf can be arranged. In winter, guests may take part in cross-country skiing more than 25 kilometers of groomed trails, snowshoeing, and winter sports activities at the world-famous Steamboat Springs Resort.

**Amenities:** The Home Ranch is simply a beautiful place, with lovely details such as fresh flowers in vases and cozy lounge furniture. Individual cabins have their own hot tubs, while a hot tub and sauna serve lodge guests. Each room has a minifridge and coffeemaker as well as bottle openers, glasses, and ice.

**Special Programs:** Children can become Kiddie Wranglers as part of the all-day children's activity program (age 6 and older). In spring and fall, the Home Ranch facility is host to many equine-related clinics including colt starting and natural horsemanship. For more detailed information and a list of the current clinic offerings, visit The Home Ranch Web site, www.homeranch.com.

**Rates:** $$$$ American plan. Children's rates available.

**Credit Cards:** Visa, MasterCard, American Express, Discover. Personal checks accepted.

**Season:** Open year-round, except during the slow months of November and April

**Getting There:** Located 18 miles from Steamboat Springs. Closest airport at Hayden, Colorado, with wintertime commuter connections from Denver, Salt Lake City, Houston, Chicago, and Minneapolis. In summer, plan on a 4-hour drive by rented car from Denver International Airport.

**What's Nearby:** The ranching/resort community of Steamboat Springs, with shopping, restaurants, winter-sports activities, spas, and a host of cultural events and activities. Summertime rodeo June through August, with shuttle service from The Home Ranch to the rodeo arena.

# KING MOUNTAIN RANCH

## Granby, Colorado

Located on the fringes of Rocky Mountain National Park and surrounded by nearly one million acres of public land, the King Mountain Ranch is an oasis of gentle, rolling parklands amid stands of pine and blue-spruce forests. When one thinks of Colorado, chances are this is the kind of scenic mountain ranch that comes to mind.

Ranch architecture reflects the Rocky Mountain aesthetic. A huge gambrel-roofed barn and wood-rail corral are the epicenter of the horse activities, while a stately lodge with huge lodgepole-pine supports provides a social center befitting, well, a king. Guests stay in the comfortable, if not opulent, guest apartments and guest rooms of two large, hotel-like buildings adjacent to the main lodge.

It's not likely you'll be spending much time in your room, however, as the ranch offers a smorgasbord of activities from horseback riding to fishing to river rafting, tennis, and golf. There's even an on-site bowling alley.

Despite its remote location, the ranch is but a twenty-minute drive from the myriad attractions of Grand County, one of the most heavily touristed areas in the state. Golfers can loosen up at either of two world-class courses: the Pole Creek Golf Club or the Grand Lake Golf Club. These courses cut their way through stands of pines trees and feature mountain streams and unsurpassed views. Pole Creek was rated as "The #1 place to play golf in Colorado" by the prestigious *Golf Digest* magazine.

If you prefer putting around the ranch, there are plenty of other recreational options. Among King Mountain's many amenities are an indoor swimming pool, trap- and skeet-shooting range, and billiard and Ping-Pong tables. Fishing is another option. Guests can choose to angle in the well-stocked ranch ponds or venture farther afoot and access some of the Gold-Medal trout habitats of area streams. Either way, you'll have plenty of opportunities to wet your line and collect scrapbook photos of the fat trout you caught (you'll need a camera, as the ranch supports the catch-and-release philosophy of fishing).

At the center of the King Mountain experience is the horse program. The ranch is surrounded by miles and miles of trails, ensuring that each day's ride affords new vistas and opportunities for wildlife viewing. Rides are broken down by ability and confidence, so you can be assured of spending trail time with individuals of similar abilities.

Vacationers wishing to play cowboy may take part in arena sports like team penning, an exciting test of riding skills in which riders sort and pen cattle. All guests are welcome to take a riding lesson and hone their horsemanship in the ranch's ample riding arena.

King Mountain offers an extensive children's program for dudes twelve and under.

Called The Foxes Den, the program includes activities such as treasure hunts, horseback riding, swimming, arts and crafts, cookouts, and rodeo-related activities for budding buckaroos. Kids may also take part in guided nature walks and hikes.

The action doesn't stop at sunset, either. Campfire sing-alongs, fly-fishing lessons, karaoke and line-dancing parties, talent shows, and the highly enjoyable Western Ball are just a sampling of the evening lineup. In addition to being an excellent guest ranch choice, the King Mountain Ranch also caters to corporate events and weddings. Check with their planner for details.

---

### King Mountain Ranch
P.O. Box 497
Granby, CO 80446
Phone: (800) 476–KING (5464); (970) 887–2511
Fax: (970) 887–9511
E-mail: hosts@kingmtnranch.com
Web site: www.kingmtnranch.com

**Manager:** Marci Smith

**Accommodations:** Capacity, 79. Large rooms in multistory buildings, all with king or two double beds and private bathrooms. Western-style decor. Most rooms open onto decks with views. Groups or large families may inquire about The King House, a secluded lodge with 8 bedrooms on 3 levels suitable for groups of 16 or more.

**Meals:** Opulent spreads typify King Mountain Ranch meals. Breakfast diners may choose made-to-order omelets, fresh fruits, cereals, and breads. Lunches feature hearty soups, salads, and sandwiches. Dinners begin in the Trail's End Lounge, where appetizers are served, followed by meals in the dining room overlooking the ranch corrals, lake, and evening sunset.

**Activities:** Horses are at the center of ranch action, and guests may choose trail rides of varying lengths and rides for all levels of skill. Extra credit can be earned via riding lessons in the ranch arena or via cattle working. On-site activities include indoor swimming, basketball, fly fishing, hiking, mountain biking, tennis, and shooting sports. There is also a full-service spa and a bowling alley. Off-site activities include golf, guided fly fishing, white-water rafting, canoeing, hot-air balloon rides, 4-wheel tours, and in winter, skiing or guided snow-mobiling.

**Amenities:** 2 lighted tennis courts, indoor pool, Jacuzzi, basketball court, bowling alley, rec room, video library and big-screen television, shooting range, water-sports equipment, fishing lake. Group conference facilities also available.

**Special Programs:** Kids' program, The Foxes Den, includes a full schedule of activities for kids 12 and under. Occasional overnight pack trips. Breakfast and lunch rides and chuckwagon rides. Combination fly fishing/horseback rides.

**Rates:** $$–$$$ Seasonal rates, with off-season reduced rates available. Minimum stay of 2 nights, except in winter, when 1-night stays are possible. Reduced children's rates, with reduced rates for nannies. Specially discounted rates sometimes available on short notice.

**Credit Cards:** Visa, MasterCard, Discover, American Express. Personal checks preferred.

**Season:** Open year-round

**Getting There:** Closest international airport, Denver International (approximately 125 miles). Rentals available at airport. Shuttle-bus services carry passengers to Grand County/Granby. Amtrak train service is also available but requires that plane passengers obtain ground transport to downtown Denver. Once in Granby, a ranch shuttle will be dispatched.

**What's Nearby:** Granby and the well-established vacation village of Winter Park. Grand County offers a wide variety of diversions, from winter skiing (alpine and cross country) and snowmobiling to summer fishing, golfing, festivals, rodeos, hot-air ballooning, and, of course, shopping.

# LATIGO RANCH
## Kremmling, Colorado

If there's one thing that sets the Latigo Ranch apart from many, it's the feeling of intimacy. With a mere thirty-five-guest capacity, the ranch is small by western standards. And that's a distinct advantage. Latigo's well-trained staff makes its guests feel like valued family members, and by week's end, strong bonds of friendship invariably form.

The ranch is owned by two couples: Randy and Lisa George and Jim and Kathie Yost. Their attention to detail is profound, from the simple-yet-elegant cloth table covers in the dining room to the process of carefully matching horse to rider down at the corral. And their taste in decorating the ranch is simply exquisite. Comfortably ensconced in a plush leather couch in front

Latigo Ranch, Colorado

of a massive stone fireplace, you'll feel as though you are staying in a private home rather than a guest ranch—albeit a private home with true western style and kingly proportions.

Located in a remote part of Colorado, 55 miles southeast of Steamboat Springs, the Latigo resides at an altitude of 9,000 feet and offers excellent views of the Continental Divide. The ranch is open year-round, with emphasis on horseback riding in summer and cross-country skiing in winter.

Latigo offers a plethora of summer activities including river rafting, guided fly fishing, evening cookouts, and evening dance lessons where guests can learn the latest line dance or traditional square dance. There's also a fully supervised kid's program, a recreation center and library, hayrides, and hot tub. In fall experienced riders may take part in a special "roundup,"

helping a local rancher gather and move cattle to winter pasture. The ranch also offers team penning, an exciting arena competition involving cattle.

One of the greatest benefits of the Latigo ranch is the owners' interest in nature education. Be sure to take a guided nature hike; you'll be amazed at your guide's depth of knowledge. Latigo's all-inclusive package price means you won't be surprised when it comes time to settle up.

**Latigo Ranch**
P.O. Box 237
Kremmling, CO 80459
Phone: (800) 227–9655; (970) 724–9008
Fax: (970) 724–9009
E-mail: info@latigotrails.com
Web site: www.latigotrails.com

**Owners/Managers:** Randy and Lisa George, Jim and Kathie Yost

**Accommodations:** Modern log cabins, fully carpeted with electric heat; 1- and 3-bedroom units, each with a sitting room and fireplace or wood-burning stove, refrigerator, and daily maid service.

**Meals:** The ranch kitchen provides a varied menu of cuisine, planned with your entire week in mind. For today's health-conscious guest, the ranch offers light fare along with hearty items at each meal.

**Activities:** More than 80 horses provide guests with "tailor-fit" mounts. Riders wishing to groom and saddle horses may do so, with expert assistance. Fly-fishing lessons and pond fishing, river-rafting trips, guided nature hikes, overnight pack trips, evening dances, and recreational activities. Experienced riders should ask about the fall roundup, a great chance to experience genuine cattle work. In winter the ranch offers cross-country skiing.

**Amenities:** Recreation room, library, hot-tub

**Special Programs:** Fall Cattle Roundup: Help a local rancher find, gather, and move hundreds of cattle from the high-mountain summer pastures. Long but rewarding days in the saddle. Experienced riders only. Similarly, ask about overnight campouts. Supervised kids' program with activities.

**Rates:** $$$–$$$$ American plan, all-inclusive. Children's rates, seasonal rates available. Overnight pack trip and river rafting included in price.

**Credit Cards:** Visa, MasterCard

**Season:** Late May to October (summer), mid-December to early April (winter)

**Getting There:** 130 miles northwest of Denver, 55 miles southeast of Steamboat Springs. Airline service to Denver International Airport or Hayden, Colorado. Inquire about ground transportation arrangements.

**What's Nearby:** Kremmling, a secluded ranching community, offers limited shopping and entertainment and the occasional rodeo or equestrian event. Steamboat, an hour's drive away, offers world-class alpine skiing, a variety of shops and restaurants, and a myriad of entertainment opportunities.

# SAN JUAN GUEST RANCH
## Ridgway, Colorado

It's hard to get away from superlatives when talking about the scenic settings of Rocky Mountain guest ranches, but it's particularly hard not to gush when speaking of a place like the San Juan Guest Ranch. The ranch is located in the San Juan Mountain Range, known as "the Switzerland of America," due to its abundance of 14,000 peaks and craggy, splendid mountain geology. It is so scenic that when renowned clothing designer Ralph Lauren decided to build a showcase ranch, he picked land just outside Ridgway, not far from the San Juan Guest Ranch.

This guest ranch would be notable for its location alone, but it is also one of the most complete guest ranches listed in this or any other guidebook. The list of activities is impressive: Jeep tours to abandoned ghost towns, fishing, trap and rifle shooting, off-site tennis and nearby natural hot-springs bathing, and hot-air ballooning. The winter menu is no less tasty: sleigh rides, cross-country skiing, snowshoeing, tobogganing, and excursions to the world-class ski village at Telluride.

Owner Scott MacTiernan runs a tight but fun ship; his exceptional talent as a host has earned him the honor of being chosen Outfitter of the Year by the Outfitters Association of America. The MacTiernan family opened their ranch in 1970 on the banks of the Uncompahgre River, and the entire family embraced the guest-ranch lifestyle and set about a rigorous program of expanding their skills and know-how to better serve their guests. Scott, for instance, is a certified riding instructor, and he imparts his knowledge to his carefully chosen staff of college-age ranch hands. That ensures a safe and thorough program of riding instruction in which guests learn sound riding technique and horsemanship. One comes away with an even greater appreciation of the fine horses that make up the backbone of the San Juan Guest Ranch experience.

In addition, Scott has created a photographic program in which intrepid shutter-bugs can capture the outstanding fall foliage in this preternaturally beautiful corner of Colorado. Sharpshooters, be sure to ask about this special program.

Skiers may be intrigued to learn that their host is also an expert instructor, with years of experience teaching in the world-famous Aspen Ski and Snowboard School. In fall the ranch provides guided deer and elk hunting trips both on the ranch and in the high country. Groups are limited to eight hunters, with a guest-to-guide ratio of 2 to 1.

The San Juan Ranch is big on hospitality but small in size. A maximum of thirty guests is accommodated, meaning that everyone gets personalized attention and a chance to get to know the entire MacTiernan clan. Such small size allows the ranch to do special things, such as overnight pack trips to particularly scenic mountain campsites.

---

### San Juan Guest Ranch

2882 County Road 23
Ridgway, CO 81432
Phone: (800) 331–3015; (970) 626–5360
Fax: (970) 626–5015
E-mail: Howdy@sanjuanranch.com
Web site: www.sanjuanranch.com

**Owners/Managers:** Patricia, Scott, and Kelly MacTiernan

**Accommodations:** 30. Guests stay in a 2-story lodge with individual apartments with twin-, queen-, and king-size beds, depending on the unit. Capacity is 2 to 6 people. Rates depend on accommodations. All units have coffeemakers, sitting areas, and carpeted floors, with minifridges in most units. The San Juan Cottage, adjacent to the ranch, offers 1,600 feet of floor space for groups of 8 people and includes a kitchen, 2 full bathrooms, and 4 bedrooms.

**Meals:** Family-style dining served 3 times daily and features many locally grown and organic fruits, vegetables, and meats. Guaranteed to satisfy the most ravenous or discerning appetites. Those with special dietary demands should advise the staff prior to arrival.

**Activities:** A carefully structured riding program designed by a certified riding instructor. Rides by the hour, half day, or full day. Weekly cattle herding excursion. Jeep trips to abandoned mines and ghost towns.

Nature hikes. Fishing in the Uncompaghre River or local ponds. Trap shooting and rifle range (ammo extra). Volleyball, horseshoes, and horse-drawn hayrides. Visits to natural hot springs and tennis courts in nearby Ouray, a quaint mountain town with excellent shopping and restaurants. Fall photo workshops. Winter snowshoeing, tobogganing, sleigh rides, and cross-country skiing. Alpine skiing at nearby Telluride Mountain Resort (45 minutes).

**Amenities:** 8-person hot tub, local artist's exhibit in main lodge, book and video library, comfortable leather sofas in main lodge, huge lodge fireplace, trap and rifle ranges

**Special Programs:** Limited private hunting trips in fall and winter. Fall nature-photography workshops. Supervised children's program includes a petting zoo and activities. Optional balloon rides at additional expense.

**Rates:** $$–$$$ American plan. Children's off-season and group rates available. 6-day minimum, except in winter, when a daily "bed-and-breakfast" stay is available. Rates vary according to level of accommodations. Certain special activities such as skiing or balloon rides are extra.

**Credit Cards:** Visa, MasterCard. Personal checks accepted.

**Season:** June through September (summer); adults-only stays in fall; winter bed-and-breakfast. Open Christmas.

**Getting There:** 5 miles north of Ouray, 42 miles east of Telluride. Airport service to either Montrose or Telluride. Denver International Airport, approximately 6 hours drive north and east.

**What's Nearby:** Picturesque mountain villages of Ouray and Telluride, a world-class resort center with skiing, golf, shopping, exceptional restaurants, spas, and some art galleries

# VISTA VERDE RANCH
## Steamboat Springs, Colorado

Steamboat Springs has a unique reputation: It's a place that combines true western cattle ranching country with a world-class resort destination, a thriving Olympic winter sports tradition, and a community where the phrase "family values" is more than just a political slogan.

Vista Verde Ranch, located 25 miles north of this thriving Colorado town, shares these same attributes. A 500-acre working ranch located on the edge of the Zirkel Wilderness, the Vista Verde is also one of the most acclaimed resort properties in this

book. Furthermore, it is a ranch that truly lives up to vacationers' expectations for outstanding summertime recreation and winter sports activities.

Summer, of course, is the most popular time for visiting. Given its high-altitude location (7,800 feet), the weather during the summer months is refreshingly warm and welcoming without being hot. You'll undoubtedly be inspired to spend nearly every waking hour out-of-doors, enjoying the Vista Verde's excellent horse riding program, taking a hot-air balloon adventure, river rafting, or trying the challenging sport of rock climbing with an experienced and safety-minded guide. The ranch also offers guided hiking with a staff naturalist, mountain biking, fly fishing, and nature photography.

Kids, too, will find this place offers no end of outdoor adventures. A full kids' and teens' program is offered, with different activities based on age. They will not soon forget rides in the ranch haywagon, swimming in Steamboat Lake, and overnight campouts with their newfound friends. And if they do, you can pop in a video (made by the children) to remind them of their vacation!

For those few who grow weary of the outdoors (or who are especially interested in the epicurean arts), the ranch offers a cooking class and wine tasting with its culinary school–trained staff chefs. There's also a barn dance popular among all ages and a special trip to Steamboat Springs to see the town's famous pro rodeo competition.

For winter adventurers, Vista Verde offers a wide variety of activities, both on the ranch and off-site. The cross-country skiing in Colorado's high country is perhaps the finest on the globe; high altitudes and cold temperatures result in snow that is light and dry—making the work lots easier. Ski guides take small, individualized tours into the backcountry and on roughly 18.6 miles of groomed trails. You can also choose to go snowmobiling, dog sledding, ice climbing, or hot-air ballooning. And of course, downhill skiing at world-class Steamboat Resort, in the town which has produced more U.S. Winter Olympic competitors than any other village in the country.

Vista Verde offers a pleasant blend of privacy and community. Nine log cabins provide the perfect choice for families, while the main lodge offers three deluxe guest rooms ideal for couples. The rooms and cabins don't have the nondescript feel of a hotel; instead, they are warm and comfy, with down comforters, wood ranch furniture, and antiques that pay homage to the ranches' authentic cattle-raising tradition. Private balconies in the ranch lodge offer spectacular panoramic views of the Colorado Rockies.

Certainly one of the most feature-filled and inviting, upscale ranch properties in this book, the Vista Verde is a good bet for couples and families seeking an authentic cattle ranching experience with all the comforts of home—and then some.

---

**Vista Verde Ranch**
P.O. Box 770465
Steamboat Springs, CO 80477
Phone: (800) 526–7433; (970) 879–3858
Fax: (970) 879–6814
E-mail: reservations@vistaverde.com
Web site: www.vistaverde.com

**Owner:** The Throgmartin Family

**Accommodations:** Guest capacity, 40. Guests either stay in lodge rooms or in luxurious log cabins ranging from 1 to 3 bedrooms with living rooms, wood stoves, and hot tubs. Lodge rooms have sitting areas and balconies with mountain views. Amenities include snack bars, coffeemakers, hair dryers, and more. Daily maid service.

**Meals:** Meals vary from casual family-style cookouts on the trail or sundeck to elegant white-tablecloth dinners served in the main lodge. Families eat together for most meals except for nights when the kids have their own "Dine'n'Dash" dinner while adults enjoy a leisurely fine-dining experience. Weekly cooking class with wine tasting also offered.

**Activities:** Cattle gathering and team penning on horseback, trail riding, guided fishing trips (gear included), river rafting, guided hiking, mountain biking, haywagon rides, shooting sports (at additional cost), swimming on the "Fountain Deck" and in Steamboat Lake, rock climbing, nearby golf and tennis. Overnight pack trips at additional charge. Winter cross-country skiing on ranch, snowshoeing, sleigh rides. Off-ranch activities such as snowmobiling, dog sledding, and alpine skiing at Steamboat Resort can be arranged at additional charge.

**Amenities:** Whirlpool spa, wine and beer bar, Internet access, wheelchair access, on-site massage (at additional charge)

**Special Programs:** Well-organized programs for kids and teens, from ages 3 to 18. Families may participate together or let their children spend time with newfound friends. Inquire about special "adults only" vacation dates.

**Rates:** $$$$$ American plan. Off-season rates available. Winter rates are considerably lower.

**Credit Cards:** None. Accepted payment by personal check, cash, or money order.

**Season:** June to October; December to March

**Getting There:** Located 25 miles north of Steamboat Springs. Closest airport in Steamboat Springs or Hayden, Colorado. Ground transportation to ranch via ranch shuttle or rental car.

**What's Nearby:** Steamboat Springs, a wonderful western ranching community with a world-class winter ski resort, fine dining and casual restaurants, nightclubs, shopping, and much more

# WAUNITA
# HOT SPRINGS RANCH
Gunnison, Colorado

While we hope every ranch in this book has a uniqueness all its own, the Waunita Hot Springs Ranch has a feature that truly sets it apart: that is, of course, its own natural hot spring. This upwelling of geothermic water keeps the huge pool at an amazing 95 degrees and also supplies all the heating needs for the lovely guest lodges that are home to its seasonal guests.

For some people, a vacation is not complete without a visit to a relaxing hot springs resort. That's a big draw here, of course, but there is far more to the Waunita Hot Springs Ranch than its fortunate location atop this geothermic treasure. A friendly ranch with a Christian emphasis, the Waunita Hot

Springs has been owned and operated by the Pringle family for more than forty years. This family has grown up with the guest ranch tradition, and they work hard to improve their considerable know-how with each passing season.

The Pringles are not absentee owners; adults and children work in harmony to make their guests feel like welcome family members. You won't likely find a more accommodating bunch; their passion for sharing the guest ranch life is truly warm and genuine. One of the areas that they particularly enjoy is entertaining; several of the family members have great musical skills, and they revel in performing at weekly music shows.

Western Colorado is one of the most beautiful areas of this favorite vacation state; those familiar with the geography know that the world-renowned ski resort at Crested Butte is but a short drive from Gunnison. A high-altitude ranch (8,946 feet), the Waunita enjoys lovely vistas of the local mountain ranges and provides an ideal, pristine environment ideal for its wide variety of traditional guest ranch activities.

Kids are particularly welcome here, making it perfect for young families and families with teens. The program here is quite active, with scheduled raft trips, trail rides, evening campfires, hayrides, scenic tours in 4x4s, a square dance session, and local fishing. There are also a great many informal activities such as softball games, movie nights, horseshoe matches, and more. Clearly, you won't have to work hard to find things to fill your vacation!

Of course, you'll want to set aside some time to soak in the fabulous hot springs pool. Many people pay large sums to visit such an attraction, but your natural spa therapy is included in the price. If the pool doesn't do enough to sooth your sore muscles, you can employ the services of a masseuse to put your aches to rest.

Waunita Springs Ranch is located at the edge of the forest overlooking Tomichi Dome and a high alpine parkland. Cattle can be seen grazing in the Waunita Valley, and the Continental Divide is a mere 10 miles from the ranch itself. Still, the ranch resides on a relatively flat plateau, meaning that you will find the terrain easy to navigate as you become acclimated to the thin air during your first few days in Colorado.

For anyone looking for an activity-filled vacation where they can soak away the day's muscular exertions in a warm-water hot springs pool, the Waunita will make you think you have found nirvana. The Pringle family's personal involvement and attention to friendly service keeps people coming back year after year.

---

## Waunita Hot Springs Ranch

80007 CR 887
Gunnison, CO 81230
Phone: (790) 641–1266
Fax: (970) 641–0650
E-mail: info@waunita.com
Web site: www.waunita.com

**Owner:** The Pringle Family

**Accommodations:** Guest capacity, 45; guests stay in one of the ranch lodges. Guest rooms have private baths, most with queen beds, bunkbeds, and double beds for kids. The Hillside Lodge, with 4 rooms on each side that can be combined to form suites, is ideal for families. The Main Lodge is the epicenter of ranch activities, providing easy access for those who lodge in its clean, comfortable rooms.

**Meals:** A high percentage of return guests attests to the quality of food served at the Waunita Hot Springs Ranch. Western home-style cooking best describes the kitchen fare, which includes oven-baked muffins, biscuits, rolls, cakes, and pies. Dinner typically includes the standard salad selections, vegetables and fruits, poultry, fish, pork, or beef dishes. Not fancy, but fulfilling. Weekly cookouts offer a nice change of pace. No alcohol served to preserve the family atmosphere.

**Activities:** This is a great place for families; kids, particularly, love the large hot springs pool and having their own horse for the week. Horseback riding, hayrides, backroads auto tours into the high country, hiking, fishing, and a white-water rafting or relaxing float trip are staples of the weeklong visit. There are lots of parlor and out-door games to be enjoyed. Inquire about off-site golfing and winter skiing opportunities at nearby resorts. Also offered are winter snowmobiling and cross-country skiing for groups only.

**Amenities:** Naturally heated hot springs pool is a unique amenity; masseuse available

**Special Programs:** No formal kids' program. Children are included in most activities at the ranch. Riding begins at 6 years of age, with special kids-only activities. Kids' counselors for times when parents need some "alone time."

**Rates:** $–$$ American plan. All-inclusive fee includes meals, lodging, and ranch activities.

**Credit Cards:** Visa, MasterCard. Cash and personal checks accepted.

**Season:** Summer, June through Septemⁿ. winter, December through March

**Getting There:** Guests fly into Gunnison. Free shuttle service to the ranch.

**What's Nearby:** Crested Butte, a former mining town and ranching community now best known for its world-class ski resort. Be sure to set aside half a day to make the trip to Crested Butte to enjoy its lovely Victorian-era homes and businesses, its quaint shops, and perhaps to enjoy a meal at any number of fine-dining and family dining establishments. Also nearby is Monarch Mountain, which offers a summer tram ride to the top of a nearby peak and unmatched vistas of the Continental Divide. A day trip can be made to the Black Canyon of the Gunnison, one of Colorado's most beloved geologic features.

# WIT'S END
# GUEST RANCH & RESORT
### Vellecito Lake, Colorado

A historic guest ranch, the Wit's End was established on the banks of Vallecito Lakes in 1858. Located in the heart of the Southern Colorado Rockies on what locals refer to as "the Western Slope," it is truly one of the most scenic and well-situated wilderness properties to be found in the lower 48. The ranch sits in a small valley, surrounded by soaring peaks that tickle the sky at elevations of between 12,000 and 14,000 feet. Breathtaking!

Horseback riding is among the specialties of the Wit's End Guest Ranch & Resort; with more than 500 acres of private land,

the trail system is extensive and varied in terrain. A herd of roughly one hundred horses is there to accommodate riders of all abilities, from beginner to advanced. There are even horses suitable to children. Guests can receive arena instruction, join guided trail rides, and participate in overnight pack trips, cowboy rides, and breakfast rides.

Perhaps equally important is the Wit's End fishing program. One of a handful of Orvis-certified lodges in North America, the Wit's End provides anglers with a wide variety of opportunities, from lake fish within hollering distance of the lodge to exclusive free-stone fly fishing on gold-medal streams and rivers. The nearby waters here have very little fishing pressure, owing to their private ownership. Those wishing for a true wilderness fishing experience can join in on backcountry pack trips into the San Juan National Forest and the Weminuche Wilderness. Here, one can cast to trophy-size cutthroat and rainbow trout or join in lake fishing expeditions to go after pike and smallmouth bass. For kids and novice anglers, there are even three stocked ponds on the ranch itself. An on-site fly-fishing lodge has everything you'll need for an ideal fishing experience.

One would describe the overall experience at the Wit's End as one of refined elegance. Adult evening entertainment begins with a cocktail hour, where guests get a chance to mingle and crow over the day's experiences, as well as sign up for the following day's activities. During and after the candlelit dinner, local and national-caliber entertainers provide a mix of country and popular music.

The Spa at Wit's End is one of the features that is particularly of interest to mothers who desire relaxation and rejuvenation (of course, men are welcome to join in, too). The facilities include four relaxing massage and treatment rooms, steam showers, a Swedish sauna, and hot tubs overlooking a small, peaceful, and relaxing pond. There is also a lounging deck and exercise room with the latest, most popular workout machines.

While you relax at the spa, you can be sure your kids are enjoying themselves. Wit's End Guest Ranch has one of the most comprehensive kids' programs to be found, with a wide variety of daily activities and trained counselors to help them choose from the assortment. Parents and kids come together for the weekly gymkhana, where they get to play arena games in a friendly competition that allows them to show off the riding skills learned during their stay.

## Wit's End Guest Ranch & Resort

254 County Road 500
Vallecito Lake, CO 81122
Phone: (800) 236–9483; (970) 884–4113
Fax: (970) 884–3261
E-mail: reservations@witsendranch.com
Web site: www.witsendranch.com

**Owners:** Jim and Karen Custer

**Accommodations:** Guest capacity, 120. Each of the 40 cabins is furnished and decorated with rustic French country period furniture. Queen-size beds and sofa beds complement all cabins, and twin beds are furnished in the larger units. Great views from any room or from a porch swing. Full kitchens, hand-painted fireplaces, and bathrooms featured in every log cabin. Daily maid service and nightly turndowns included.

**Meals:** 3 meals daily. Every meal is prepared in or around the ranch centerpiece, The Old Lodge at the Lake, a century-old barn built of rock and timber that has been renovated to serve as the main lodge. Homemade baked goods served at each meal. Typical dinner menu includes classic French country cuisine to Western barbecue meals. This is refined gourmet dining prepared by culinary-school chefs. Cocktails, wine, and beer. Full bar with crystal mirror circa 1836.

**Activities:** This resort offers an extremely wide choice of daily activities. A partial list: archery, hayrides, hiking, horseback riding, sailboating, skeet- and trap shooting, mountain biking, lake and stream fishing, local sightseeing, campouts, rafting, rock climbing, and water skiing. Off-site golf. Consult with the daily activities planner for a list of the day's activities and to plan your participation.

**Amenities:** General store, spa, swimming pool, youth entertainment area, tennis courts, shooting range, hot tubs, full-service spa, tennis courts, river on property. Confer-

Wit's End Guest Ranch & Resort, Colorado

© Christopher Marona

ence facilities to accommodate up to 300. Conference planning assistance available.

**Special Programs:** Well-structured children's program. Trained counselors are available to help with even finicky children. Activities include gold panning, swimming, nature hikes, outdoor crafts, water sports, fishing, arena riding, campouts, and scavenger hunts. Winter alpine skiing at Durango Mountain Resort. Also, winter cross-country skiing, snowmobiling, sleigh rides, ice skating, and snowshoeing.

**Rates:** $$–$$$$$ American plan. Also, European plan (cabin-only) rental at the sister steam-side lodge.

**Credit Cards:** Visa, MasterCard, American Express. Also, travelers' checks, personal checks, and cash accepted.

**Season:** Open year-round

**Getting There:** Nearest airport in Durango, Colorado (La Plata County Airport). Ranch is located 24 miles northeast of Durango, directly off County Road 500 and Highway 160. Rental car suggested.

**What's Nearby:** Durango, a Victorian-era frontier town with lovely shops, restaurants, and nightlife. Visit the Durango-Silverton Railroad for a scenic trip through the mountains. Other attractions include Mesa Verde, with its ancient Anasazi Indian cliff dwellings, and the Four Corners region, where four states touch corners. Day trips to Telluride, a Victorian mining town turned world-class winter resort and summer festival destination with excellent shopping, dining, and golf.

# THE LODGE AT MOLOKAI RANCH

### Maunaloa, Molokai, Hawaii

Cattle ranching? In Hawaii? Believe it. The "Aloha!" traditions of the *paniolos* (Hawaiian for "cowboy") live to this day at Molokai Ranch in a unique blend of cattle ranching, adventure travel, and pure resort luxury. If you are seeking something a little exotic in your western ranching adventure, this is the place. After all, it doesn't get much more western than Hawaii!

Just a short flight from Honolulu, Molokai Ranch Lodge is located on the Hawaiian island of Molokai. The 54,000-acre ranch was originally given to Princess Bernice Pauahi Bishop by King Kamehameha V. For a brief while, it was a sugar plantation, and it even served as an African wildlife preserve. But for more than a century, the Molokai has been a cattle ranch, one that has spawned generations of cowboys dressed in straw hats and floral-print shirts.

Molokai Ranch is a fabulous mix of white sand beaches, expansive green pastures, seaside cliffs, and lush tropical valleys. It encompasses most of the western half of the island and has remained unspoiled and undeveloped. Over the years, the resort portion of Molokai Ranch has evolved into a favorite base camp for a wide variety of outdoor adventure activities that

The Lodge at Molokai Ranch, Hawaii

© The Lodge & Beach Village at Molokai Ranch

include mountain biking, horseback riding, ocean kayaking, hiking, shoreline fishing, and more. You can even try the thrilling and traditional native sport of outrigger-canoe surfing.

Molokai Ranch is divided into separate "camps," each with its own distinct character. An hourly shuttle service whisks guests between the various lodging areas and activity sites.

Kaupoa Beach Village is located amid palm tree groves, where deluxe canvas bungalows on wood floors look out over a broad, white sand beach. Far from being simple camp tents, these rooms offer comfortable queen-size beds, solar-powered lights and ceiling fans, spacious lanai decks with deck furniture, outdoor dining areas, and private bathrooms.

Guests may also opt to stay at Molokai Ranch Lodge, a deluxe resort facility with twenty-two guest rooms, main lodge, and sleeping cottages. The feeling here is one of historic authenticity, with antique appointments from the 1920s and 1930s that give it an "old school" Hawaiian resort feel.

The horseback program offers a chance to ride amid some of the most overwhelming and beautiful scenery on earth. You may visit ancient archaeological sites while learning about the history of the *paniolos* and early Hawaiians, trek through Molokai's lush plains along the dramatic cliffs overlooking Kalaupapa, and visit historic sites whose stories are related by the ranch's native-born *paniolos*. Or head down to the arena for the "Paniolo Round-Up" to enjoy traditional rodeo events and to take part in relatively safe but challenging contests such as cattle penning and herding.

All in all, the Molokai is a refreshing alternative to most vacation destinations—a guest ranch with Hawaiian aloha spirit and an ingrained sense of adventure.

## The Lodge at Molokai Ranch

100 Maunaloa Highway
Maunaloa, HI 96770
Phone: (808) 660–2824
Reservations: (888) 627–8082
Web site: www.molokairanch.com

**Owner:** Molokai Properties Limited

**Accommodations:** 200+ capacity. The 40 deluxe canvas bungalows at Kaupoa Beach Village offer the perfect blend of luxury and adventure. You'll enjoy a queen-size bed, solar-powered lights and ceiling fan, spacious lanai with deck furniture, an outdoor eating area, private bathroom with hot-water shower and self-composting toilet, and daily maid service. The Hawaiian Lodge features 22 guest rooms, offering an eclectic combination of new and historic furniture (no 2 rooms are exactly alike). Located in the main building and in separate sleeping cottages, the rooms were designed to take advantage of unobstructed ocean views while offering privacy. All rooms include a wet bar, refrigerator, robes and slippers, cable television, and private lanai.

**Meals:** Meals are served in open-air pavilions and feature Hawaiian specialties as well as sumptuous American dishes. Breakfast, lunch, and dinner are prepared to order by on-staff chefs and feature such specialties as omelets, barbecued hamburgers, and grilled fish and steak. Boxed lunches available for daytime excursions.

**Activities:** Trail rides and activities for riders of all skill levels and abilities. Mountain biking with instruction for everyone from the novice to the expert cyclist. Guided ocean kayaking, shoreline fishing for Papio, Ulua, Ta'ape, Weke, and Uhu. Guided snorkeling and spearfishing. Sport shooting and archery range. Be sure to sign up for one of Molokai Ranch's cultural hikes. The *moolelo* (storytelling) integrated into these

The Lodge at Molokai Ranch, Hawaii

unique hikes brings West Molokai's cultural past alive.

**Amenities:** Exercise room, sauna, pool, shower and locker facilities, daily *New York Times,* dedicated Internet access, use of snorkels, fins, masks, Boogie Boards, beach toys, beach chairs, umbrellas, and fishing rods at Kaupoa Beach Village. Unlimited use of shuttles to and from lodging and activity sites. Concierge service, recreation areas and outdoor sports.

**Special Programs:** Activity programs for kids ages 5 to 12. Half-day and full-day Kamali'i EdVenture programs include tidepool explorations; the Creature Feature, in which they learn about bugs; and the Menehune Mele, in which they learn the hula, play Hawaiian musical instruments, take guided hikes, and sing popular island songs. Packaged activities allow guests to tailor their vacations to their interests.

**Rates:** $$$–$$$$ full American plan, including transportation to and from the airport at Molokai and transportation among the various sites. Prices vary widely by accommodations and selected activities. Discounted children's rates.

**Credit Cards:** Visa, MasterCard, American Express, Discover. Traveler's and personal checks accepted.

**Season:** Open year-round. High season, December through March.

**Getting There:** Direct flights from Honolulu, Oahu, and Maui. Shuttle service provided to the resort.

**What's Nearby:** The Molokai Ranch is a self-contained resort offering an all-inclusive vacation experience. Guests may wish to plan a few extra days to visit some of Hawaii's other beautiful islands.

# BAR H BAR RANCH
## Soda Springs, Idaho

Idaho's Bar H Bar Ranch is a working cattle ranch. Guests take part in actual cattle work right alongside the ranch's able cowboys. As owner McGee Harris likes to say, "When you are helping to do something at Bar H Bar, you're doing it because it needs to be done, not because you need something to do."

The Bar H Bar sprawls over 10,000 acres of forest and open pasture in the heart of the Bear Valley. The land is rimmed by snowcapped mountain peaks that provide the natural runoff supplying the Bear River, which runs through the property. McGee and his wife, Janet, limit the number of guests (generally four to six individuals) so that everybody who visits gets personal attention and a chance to really participate in meaningful ranch work. Although there are ample opportunities to "do your own thing," the real fun of a Bar H Bar vacation is the chance to work (and play) like a cowboy.

What exactly does a working cowboy do? Well, on the Bar H Bar, you may participate in everything from mending fences to herding cattle between pastures or riding out to replenish the salt-block supply. If a sick calf needs doctoring, you may be given the task of minding the rope horse, and if a cow is giving birth, you'll be there to witness the calf being born. It's an amazing and unforgettable vacation.

When the work is done (or if you simply decide to "take a day off"), you can angle for trout or take a nature hike on the ranch. Wildlife resides quite happily with the cow herd, and your explorations on horseback or on foot are likely to reveal elk, deer, and moose as well as a variety of small game and upland birds.

Guests lodge in traditional cowboy fashion, in a restored four-room "bunkhouse." The rooms are furnished with rustic lodgepole-pine furniture and antiques that reflect the ranch's pioneering heritage. Each room has an individual entrance and a comfortable porch where one can rest out of the summer sun. When it comes time to shower up for dinner, you may choose to do so in the clean, modernized facility, or get clean the cowboy way by taking a dip in Bear River, which runs through the property.

The Bar H Bar isn't for everyone. Small children are discouraged (the ranch recommends a minimum age of twelve), and even if you take teens, they might not be as enthralled with living the cowboy life as you are. Teens with a high degree of maturity, a good work ethic, and a desire to really dig in and experience alternative ways of life seem to be best suited to the Bar H Bar.

For vacationers who genuinely want to experience a fading way of American life, the Bar H Bar is ideal.

---

**Bar H Bar Ranch**
1501 Eight Mile Creek Road
Soda Springs, ID 83276
Phone: (800) 743–9505; (208) 547–3082
Fax: (208) 547–0203
E-mail: barhbar@aol.com
Web site: www.barhbar.com

**Owners/Managers:** McGee and Janet Harris

**Accommodations:** 4 rooms in a refurbished bunkhouse. Private entrances and porches. Queen-size or matched double-size beds. Decor is rustic, with lodgepole-pine furniture and western antiques. Capacity is 6.

**Meals:** Served ranch style; guests and ranch workers dine together at a common table. 3 hearty meals served daily. Home-baked bread, pies, rolls, and desserts.

**Activities:** The Bar H Bar program revolves around real cattle-ranch work. Guests participate in the daily ranching chores, which may include everything from gathering and moving cattle to preparing cattle for shipping. Guests may opt out of the daily routine to go fishing or to enjoy an afternoon of nature hiking.

**Amenities:** The authentic cattle ranch is clean and modern but relatively spartan. Guests who expect spas and pampering will be disappointed.

**Special Programs:** None. Children over the age of 12 are welcome, but be certain that working on a real cattle ranch is something they will not become bored with and that

they are self-motivated and able to entertain themselves among adults.

**Rates:** $$ full American plan. Family rates available.

**Credit Cards:** None. Cash and checks accepted.

**Season:** Summer: May through September

**Getting There:** Nearest airports include Pocatello, Idaho (60 miles); Jackson, Wyoming (100 miles); Idaho Falls (120 miles); and Salt Lake City (184 miles). Ranch is 60 miles east of Pocatello off Highway 30 to Soda Springs. Discuss ground transportation from Pocatello with the ranch owners.

**What's Nearby:** Lava Hot Springs (swimming and hot tubs), Minnetonka Cave, natural soda-water springs, Pickleville Playhouse (melodrama), historic Mormon Pioneer Tabernacle, golfing.

# BAR H RANCH
## Driggs, Idaho

Every guest ranch finds a marketing niche. Working ranches tout their authentic cowboy experience. Mountain ranches offer exquisite scenery. Some ranches offer five-star services and facilities; others emphasize adventure sports such as rock climbing and mountain biking. The Bar H Ranch is unique in that it caters only to women.

Ranch owner Edie Harrop is a third-generation Teton Valley cattle rancher who decided that she wanted to share her rural revelry with other women in a friendly and, we should add, supremely beautiful place. For close to two decades, the Bar H has

been a haven for mothers and daughters, friends and coworkers to literally let down their hair and be cowgirls. Guests may choose to trail ride from the ranch's main lodge or embark on adventuresome overnight and extended pack trips in the breathtaking Teton wilderness along the Idaho and Wyoming border. Either way, the scenery is postcard perfect.

Bar H Ranch's high-country trail guides have extensive experience with horses and clients that ensures that strong bonds will form, both with your assigned animal and with the other women who share in your odyssey.

But the adventure doesn't end with horse riding. The Teton Valley, nestled between the majestic and famous Grand Tetons and the Big Hole Mountain Range, offers a multitude of activities that include hiking, mountain biking, and fly fishing. In addition, guests are in close proximity to Yellowstone National Park, Grand Teton National Park, and the famous Jackson Hole, a western town that offers exceptional dining, shopping, and nightlife.

Bar H schedules a number of backcountry trips of varying difficulty. These special camps vary from challenging weeklong campouts in the high country to a luxurious stay at the AAA 4-Diamond Rio Rico Resort in Tucson, Arizona. Be sure to ask about these camps when making your trip plans!

For a less structured vacation, relax and enjoy a week at the ranch in a private and uniquely appointed loft. Enjoy the fully equipped kitchen, take in the sweeping mountain views from your deck, and delight in a soak in an old-time claw-foot tub. Highlight your trip with an optional trail ride in the Tetons, or ride the ranch to check cattle. If you wish, just relax, hike, fish, or sightsee.

---

**Bar H Ranch**
P.O. Box 297
Driggs, ID 83422
Phone: (888) 216–6025; (208) 354–2906
Fax: (208) 354–8804
E-mail: barh@tetonvalley.net
Web site: www.tetontrailrides.com

**Owner/Manager:** Edie Harrop

**Accommodations:** Backcountry guests stay in 4-person dome tents, with 2 guests per tent. Guest capacity varies according to trip length and participation. A small number of guests may be accommodated at the ranch itself.

**Meals:** Meals on the trail consist of basic but generous camp fare. 3 daily meals, including a trailside lunch. A camp chef prepares barbecue and Dutch-oven dinners featuring garden-fresh salads and homemade desserts in the chuckwagon kitchen.

**Activities:** Backcountry pack trips are the focus of the Bar H activities. These vary from mild to wild and include a special trip to Rio Rico Resort in Tucson, Arizona, a full-service spa and resort. Ranch guests may partake of numerous activities, including mountain biking, fishing, and day trips to Jackson Hole. Inquire of the host for tourism advice.

**Special Programs:** North Leigh Canyon Camp features daily high-country trail rides from a base camp in North Leigh Canyon; advanced riders may partake of the High Altitude Camp into the Jebediah Smith Wilderness; High Country Heaven is a less rigorous program that still takes riders to the heights of the Grand Tetons; the Rio Rico trip centers around a deluxe resort in the Arizona desert, complete with spa, Jacuzzi, sauna, and outstanding recreational opportunities.

**Rates:** $–$$$ Ranch stays are structured a la carte, with horseback riding and other activities charged additionally. Accommodations include a fully equipped kitchen and a dining area. Pack trips and stays at the Rio Rico Resort in Arizona are on the full American plan.

**Credit Cards:** None. Personal and traveler's checks preferred.

**Season:** May through October

**Getting There:** Most guests fly into Jackson, then rent a car to reach the ranch. Alternate airport destination is Idaho Falls, Idaho.

**What's Nearby:** Jackson, Wyoming; Yellowstone National Park; Grand Teton National Park; and the Idaho towns of Driggs and Tetonia

# DIAMOND D RANCH
## Stanley, Idaho

If you are looking for a down-home guest ranch that won't break the family budget, the Diamond D just might be the place. Located in the sparsely populated forests of central Idaho in the middle of the 2.3-million-acre Frank Church Wilderness, the Diamond D preserves a period in dude ranch history where families actually invited guests into their ranch homes to share in an authentic western lifestyle experience. Ranch owners the Demorest family have operated the ranch for more than half a century! A visit to the Diamond D can be characterized by lots of outdoor fun and activities, horseback riding, and simple but excellently prepared meals served in ample proportions.

That's what makes this a gem—a return to simplicity. The log cabin–style main lodge with its big green roof is among the more lovely buildings to be found in this book; its big stone fireplace is a welcoming gathering point where guests share their day's experiences. (If you are fond of an evening cocktail or glass of wine, you'll need to pack your own supply; the ranch doesn't feature its own bar). You'll truly feel like ranch owners Tom and Linda Demorest have welcomed you into their own home.

This is a ranch vacation for adventurers. The ranch resides amid the rugged, snow-capped mountains of the Salmon Range at the confluence of three flowing streams, with forests of pine and quaking aspen, blue lakes, and azure skies. Horseback riding and fly fishing are the main activities, but hiking, nature observation, informal games, and just fooling around the many lakes, streams, and scenic waterfalls in the area also command guests' attentions.

There's also plenty of time to commune with your fellow ranch guests and your children. Evening campfires, barbecues, card games in the lodge, and the simple cama- raderie of shared meals ensures that you'll enjoy the company and fellowship of a shared experience.

Horse enthusiasts will find themselves particularly at home at the Diamond D. The experienced ranch wranglers lead two daily rides as well as weekly lunch rides, ensur- ing that you will get plenty of saddle time. Those wishing for advanced instruction can take additional lessons upon request. Chil- dren as young as six can join in the trail rides; those younger can be led on horse- back in the ranch corral.

Those who want a true backcountry excursion can participate in custom pack trips. Because the ranch has extensive wilderness hunting experience, you can be assured of a memorable and comfortable pack trip. If your idea of a backcountry vacation includes small, cramped pup tents, wet sleeping bags, and freeze-dried food, you will be pleasantly surprised by how much more comfortable the trip can be when you have strong packhorses shoulder- ing the load!

One of the unique features of the ranch is a stone wedding chapel hand-built from river rock. The quaint and lovely chapel took eleven years to complete and offers a truly memorable and scenic setting for holding a wedding or renewing one's vows. Linda Demorest is a minister and this chapel was her dream. She will enthusias- tically preside over the ceremony, or you can bring along your own minister as a guest. Located along Loon Creek, it is hard to imagine a prettier or more romantic setting for a small wedding ceremony, and of course, the ranch makes the perfect place for a secluded honeymoon. The Demorests will be happy to cater your reception, too.

---

### Diamond D Ranch

P.O. Box 35
Stanley, ID 83278
Phone: (800) 222–1269; (208) 861–9206
E-mail: diadlld@aol.com
Web site: www.diamonddranch-idaho.com

**Owners:** Tom and Linda Demorest

**Accommodations:** Guest capacity, 40. Accommodations are basic but clean and attractive, in keeping with the economic value of this guest ranch. Two-bedroom cabins with room for 6, a 4-bedroom cabin that sleeps 10, and two lodge suites that house singles and couples, plus 5 lodge rooms.

**Meals:** 3 family-style meals are served daily. Expect standard, hearty American breakfasts of eggs, meats, fruits, and pancakes; lunches are often served on the trail. Dinner is a family affair in which all guests are seated together. Homemade pies and cakes are a specialty. If you have special dietary requirements, the ranch will meet them with adequate advance notice. For a change of pace, the ranch hosts twice-weekly outdoor barbecue dinners. Liquor, wine, and beer are not available, but guests are welcome to bring their own supplies.

**Activities:** Daily horseback rides vary in length and difficulty of terrain; daily morning and afternoon rides, plus 2 all-day lunch rides each week. Horses matched to rider skills; "Slow horses for slow riders, fast horses for fast riders, and for riders who don't like to ride, horses that don't like to

be ridden." Hiking on miles of trails, fly fishing in Mystery Lake and area streams, authentic gold panning, swimming, horseshoe tossing, volleyball, target shooting range. Inquire about pack-in fall hunting camps, spring bear hunts.

**Amenities:** Target range, conference room facilities for small corporate get-togethers, wedding chapel, "dry" bar for dancing and entertainment, game room, general store, saunas, hot tub, swimming pool

**Special Programs:** Children 6 and older take part in activities alongside their parents; younger children will be entertained with daily supervised games, swimming, arts and crafts, and horseback riding in the ranch corral. Babysitting for children under the age of 3 can be arranged.

**Rates:** $$ American plan. The Diamond D offers an affordable choice for families looking for a basic dude-ranch vacation with lots of time for horseback riding, hiking, fishing, and quality family time. It offers a handsome main lodge and a picturesque chapel ideal for small weddings.

**Credit Cards:** None. Payment by cash, money order, traveler's checks.

**Season:** June 1 to October 15

**Getting There:** Diamond D Ranch is located 40 miles north of Stanley, Idaho, on U.S. Highway 75. Most guests fly to Boise, then rent a car or charter a small plane. Air transportation is also available to Twin Falls, Idaho Falls, and Sun Valley. A local charter service can provide flights from the airports to the ranch. Anyone wishing to fly into the ranch should inquire first, as mountain flying requires experience and excellent skills.

**What's Nearby:** Sun Valley, although not close, offers a viable choice for an added day or two in Idaho.

# IDAHO ROCKY MOUNTAIN RANCH

Stanley, Idaho

Imagine being able to go back and see the West as the Corps of Discovery's Captains Lewis and Clark did two centuries ago. It's possible at the Idaho Rocky Mountain Ranch, a historic guest ranch located in the heart of the Sawtooth National Recreation Area, the largest wilderness area in the continental United States.

This is truly a special place, ideal for individuals looking for a relaxing scenic getaway or an outdoor adventure that is truly far from the trodden path. The ranch was created in 1930 as a private retreat, available only to club members and their invited guests. Carpenters handcrafted the lodge and adjacent buildings from native lodgepole pine. The buildings have aged beautifully and provide a pleasant rusticity to the property. Edmund and Ruth Bogert bought the ranch in 1951, and it has since passed into the capable hands of their daughter, Rozalys Smith. In 1995 the ranch was added to the National Register of Historic Places as a well-preserved example of the earliest guest ranches in the American West. A tradition of family owners continues with new owners Steve and Courtney Kapp and Diana Kapp and David Singer.

Guests take great pleasure in the original handcrafted furniture, furnishings such as mounted trophy animals and generations-old photographs, and decorative ironwork, while relaxing in the comfort of thoughtfully upgraded modern amenities.

Although most guest ranches can boast of beautiful scenery, this ranch is situated in one of the truly more outstanding natural areas in North America. The craggy and steep Sawtooth and White Cloud Mountain Ranges remain snow-covered throughout most of summer. The forests here are deep and lush with evergreens. And the entire area is crisscrossed with flowing streams, rivers, and lakes crowded with fat trout. The main lodge offers a panoramic view of the mighty Sawtooth Range, making it the favorite place for guests to congregate after an active day.

There are plenty of activities to keep you engaged here. The horse program is focused on wilderness exploration on well-established bridle paths. If you prefer, you can rent a mountain bike and explore under your own power. Individuals who want to get wet can take a thrilling raft ride on the Payette River or opt for a more leisurely float down the Salmon. Anglers will find excellent lake and river fishing, whereas shutterbugs can simply grab a camera and go "hunting" for the perfect shot—it won't be hard to find! After your exertions, you can relax in the ranch's large swimming pool, which is fed by local hot springs.

Large groups may wish to rent the meadow ranch site for a special occasion, such as a wedding. Located near Gold Creek, a five-minute walk from the main lodge, this site offers lovely views of the Sawtooth Range and provides rustic tables and benches in a covered pavilion ideal for the sumptuous Dutch-oven meals and grilled specialties served up by the ranch's head chef.

In addition, the ranch offers conference and large-group packages that allow you to essentially rent the ranch, custom-tailoring your activities and meals to your own program.

**Idaho Rocky Mountain Ranch**
HC 64, Box 9934
Stanley, ID 83278
Phone: (208) 774–3544
Fax: (208) 774–3477
E-mail: idrocky@ruralnetwork.net
Web site: www.idahorocky.com

**Managers:** Sandra Beckwith and Bill Leavell

**Accommodations:** 21 total units; maximum occupancy, 42. 16 duplex cabins include rock fireplaces and king-size beds. Some cabins have adjoining doors to accommodate families. Special Honeymoon Cabin also available. Additional lodging in 4 rooms in the main lodge. All rooms and cabins have private baths. No in-room phones, televisions, or radios, but a courtesy phone, pay phone, and office services are available to guests.

**Meals:** Guests dine in the historic lodge dining room, complete with central fireplace. 2 seated meals a day, with picnic lunches available at extra cost. Breakfast consists of a continental buffet and hot breakfast items, fresh fruits, and fresh-baked goods. Evening dining includes a 5-course meal of appetizers, soup, salad, choice of entrée, and desserts. Entrees include specialties such as mountain trout, lamb, paella, duck breast, prime rib. Thursday night barbecue, Monday night outdoor cookout with traditional Dutch-oven meal. Special diets accommodated with advance notice.

**Activities:** Guided horseback rides, hiking, nature walks, mountain biking, fly fishing, and lake fishing. Guests may arrange off-site river rafting, hikes in the Sawtooth National Recreation Area, canoeing, and kayaking. Anglers can request a horseback ride into secluded, high-alpine lakes. Species include rainbow, cutthroat, brook and bull trout.

**Amenities:** Hot-springs pool; library and board games; complimentary laundry facility; handcrafted furniture and original "pioneer" furnishing; cabins equipped with individual fireplaces

**Special Programs:** Children's play hour available 3 nights per week. Children's rates and meal plans also available.

**Rates:** $$ modified American plan. Guest price includes breakfast, dinner, lodging, and use of all ranch facilities. Additional prices charged for activities, including horseback riding, mountain-bike rental, off-site trips, etc. Inquire about activities and costs before committing to a reservation. Rates do not include 15 percent service charge/gratuity and state and local taxes.

**Credit Cards:** Visa, MasterCard. Personal checks, traveler's checks, money orders also accepted.

**Season:** Mid-June through mid-September

**Getting There:** The ranch is 9 miles south of Stanley, on Highway 75 between mile markers 180 and 181. Nearest airports are Boise (130 miles) and Sun Valley/Hailey (65 miles).

**What's Nearby:** Sun Valley, one of the loveliest all-season resort towns in the West; nearby ghost-town tours; Sawtooth National Recreation Area

# TETON RIDGE RANCH

### Tetonia, Idaho

When most people think of the Teton Range, they conjure images of the beautiful Jackson Hole valley and its famous resort town, Jackson, Wyoming. It's perhaps, then, a well-kept secret that the Idaho side of that same range is every bit as striking but quite a bit less crowded with showcase millionaires' ranches and SUVs. Think of it as Jackson Hole, circa 1940.

It's here that the luxurious Teton Ridge Ranch is located. Situated on 4,000 acres of private land bordered by the Targhee National Forest, the ranch offers close proximity to Yellowstone and Teton National Parks and is but an hour's drive from Jackson, with its world-renowned shopping, museums, and restaurants, not to mention two first-rate ski areas, Grand

Targhee and Jackson Hole. Winter or summer, this ranch offers all the scenic beauty of the mountain West along with the amenities and gracious living afforded by a first-rate resort hotel.

Teton Ridge Ranch boasts a 10,000-square-foot main lodge of modern log-cabin design, with huge windows that look out onto stunning views. The interior is simply outstanding, with warm knotty pine, cathedral ceilings, exposed beams, and stone fireplaces. The dining room is particularly elegant, with guests seated at candlelit tables and feasting on gourmet meals prepared by professional chefs.

With a mere seven suites (five in the lodge, two in the nearby cottage) to accommodate guests, the feeling here is one of intimacy. Each of the suites features its own private deck, woodstove, king-size bed, opulent bathroom, and even a Jacuzzi bath.

As befits such a top-shelf resort property, the menu of adventures is quite extensive. Shooting-sports enthusiasts and first-time shooters alike can hone their aim from the ranch's shooting towers or blast away on the challenging shooting clay course. In fall, guests may take part in pheasant or partridge hunting, ably assisted by trained English setters.

White-water rafting on the Snake River is another popular activity. Anglers can wet their lines in any number of rivers, including the Snake, Madison, and Teton. All are world-class fishing destinations, and expert guides will help you find the best waters. If hiking is your idea of a day well spent, the ranch offers 14 miles of marked trails.

In addition to these activities, the ranch hosts can arrange for off-site hot-air ballooning and guided mountain-bike rides;

## Grand Targhee Winter Resort

Skiing aficionados recognize Grand Targhee Winter Resort as one of the West's best-kept secrets. With more than 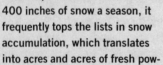 400 inches of snow a season, it frequently tops the lists in snow accumulation, which translates into acres and acres of fresh powder. To make things even better, Targhee offers unique Sno-Cat adventures that take advanced skiers into the backcountry, where face shots in untrammeled fields of powder are the norm.

And that's not all: Even in-bounds, the lifts are seldom crowded; the snow often remains pristine even days after a storm. Visitors can also visit the resort's ice skating rink or take a dogsled trip through stands of pine and fir trees.

Teton Ridge Ranch, Idaho

you can even try tandem hang gliding. Just about any outdoor adventure you can think of (with the exception of, say, surfing) can be arranged during your stay.

And of course, there's horseback riding. In addition to daytime rides from the ranch, guests may opt for overnight pack trips that take them high into the Teton mountains, where trappers and mountain men once flourished.

In winter the resort lends itself to a plethora of sports, including cross-country skiing, snowshoeing, horse-drawn sleigh rides, and even dogsledding.

---

**Teton Ridge Ranch**
200 Valley View Road
Tetonia, ID 83452
Phone: (208) 456–2650
Fax: (208) 456–2218
Web site: www.tetonridge.com

**Guest Services Manager:** Jan Betts

**Accommodations:** 7 total units; 14 guests. 32-day guest limit for conferences or family get-togethers. Suites include balconies, woodstoves, oversize bathrooms, mountain views, Jacuzzi hot-tub baths.

**Meals:** 3 meals served daily. Cuisine focuses on regional specialties, such as roast loin of elk, breast of duckling, fresh fish, and locally picked wild mushrooms. Dinners include 4 courses. A typical menu: French onion soup, medallions of salmon and beef tenderloin, buttered asparagus, saffron rice, walnut-pecan wheat bread, linzertorte, raspberry coulis. Special diets accommodated with advance notice. Beer and wine served with dinner.

**Activities:** Activities are tailored to guests' desires. Horseback riding, overnight pack trips (extra), hiking, stream and lake fishing, cross-country skiing, snowshoeing, shooting sports, sleigh rides, dogsledding. Additional activities, such as downhill skiing, mountain biking, ballooning, snowmobiling, and more can be arranged at extra cost. Fall upland bird hunting available.

**Amenities:** A small but luxurious guest ranch with the amenities one would expect in an expensive resort hotel. Guest rooms feature steam baths and Jacuzzi hot tubs, reading areas. In winter, cross-country skiers can schuss on 19 miles of groomed trails. On-site masseuse.

**Special Programs:** None. Well-mannered children over 6 welcomed. Guests arrange activities and schedules through the ranch's activities planner.

**Rates:** $$$$ full American plan. Reduced rates during the off-season and corporate rates; 1-week minimum stay in July and August (peak season).

**Credit Cards:** Visa, MasterCard. Personal checks and traveler's checks preferred.

**Season:** Summer, June through mid-October; winter, January through mid-March

**Getting There:** Closest airports are Jackson Hole, Wyoming, 45 miles; Idaho Falls, Idaho, 75 miles. Pickup or delivery to Jackson at $90 per vehicle, one way. Rental car recommended.

**What's Nearby:** Jackson Hole, Wyoming, Jackson Hole and Grand Targhee Winter Resorts, Yellowstone National Park, Teton National Park. Nearby town of Tetonia offers shopping, restaurants, services.

# TWIN PEAKS RANCH
### Salmon, Idaho

Twin Peaks Ranch is a place of great diversity, both in its natural setting and its activities. Truly, it is a place where one can live out one's adventure fantasies.

Homesteaded in 1924 as a working cattle ranch on the banks of the wild Salmon River, Twin Peaks has evolved into one of the premier guest ranches in a state rich with such destinations. The ranch also takes full advantage of its river setting, giving visitors the chance to raft some of the best rapids in the West; guests can also try their hands at running some milder rapids in a kayak. Sportsmen will love this setting, where one can fly fish on the banks or from the gunwales of an outboard boat. True nature lovers will want to thrill to the overnight backcountry pack trip through land teeming with elk, deer, moose, bighorn sheep, and even a few bears.

Twin Peaks encompasses several thousand acres of private land offering a parklike setting. Massive peaks rise several thousand feet above the principal ranch lands, adding an inspiring scenic backdrop to the ranch's open pastures and forested trails. Instead of one single ranch compound, Twin Peaks has several staffed outposts, each offering a unique experience. During your stay, you will move between the various camps, each offering different opportunities for entertainment, dining, and diversion.

You'll pack in to the North Basin, a high-mountain tent camp. The Williams Lake

Twin Peaks Ranch, Idaho

Lodge fishing camp gives anglers and would-be anglers the chance to lure trout in a subalpine lake.

All in all, Twin Peaks Ranch is an ideal place for singles, couples, and families in search of an unforgettable adventure. Your week will be crammed full of adventures as you ride the banks of the Salmon, climb to the 9,000-foot-high country camp at North Basin, fish in stocked ponds and flowing rivers, even take a few hours to learn archery and marksmanship at the archery and trap- and skeet-shooting range. Finally, your week will end in true cowboy fashion with a Western cattle drive and horseback games in the ranch's ample arena. All the while, you'll be entertained by cowboy singers, evenings of country dancing, and even a hayride on a wagon pulled by stout draft horses.

---

**Twin Peaks Ranch**
P.O. Box 774
Salmon, ID 83467
Phone: (800) 659–4899
Fax: (208) 894–2429
Web site: www.twinpeaksranch.com

**Owners:** Allen and Lenabelle Davis

**Accommodations:** Capacity, 55. 7 rustic cabins accommodate 2 to 4 persons each, with individual bathrooms. Deluxe cabins feature 2 bedrooms with whirlpool tubs. A 3-bedroom unit is also available, complete with full bath and game table. A suite is available at the Salmon Run Cabin.

**Meals:** Meals are served in the main lodge in a comfortable dining hall with excellent mountain views. Sojourners will enjoy trailside lunches and outdoor cookouts of barbecued steaks, corn on the cob, salad, baked beans, and cobbler. Similarly, hearty breakfasts are served out of the ~amp's cook tent. At the Ram's Head

Cafe, guests enjoy dinners based on the original menu. In short, the dining opportunities are as varied as the activities themselves.

**Activities:** Trail rides take in the scenic possibilities of the Salmon River to the high-alpine setting of the North Basin, destination of the overnight pack trip. River rafting on the Salmon with float trips and white-water rapids. Anglers can enjoy everything from stocked ponds to white-water pools, with fly-fishing instruction and outboard trolling available. Archery and shooting sports, cattle work, and an arena play-day.

**Special Programs:** A full program is available from mid-June through August for children age 6 and up. Meeting facilities and activities for up to 55 available.

**Amenities:** Singing cowboy musicians, a western dance band, western dance instruction, authentic Yellowstone open-topped tour bus, riding arena, fishing camps with tackle supplies, outdoor pool at Salmon run, hot-tub baths

**Rates:** $$$ American plan. Children's, group, off-season discounts available. Shortened stays (3 days) also available.

**Credit Cards:** Visa, MasterCard. Cash and cashier's and personal checks accepted.

**Season:** June through September

**Getting There:** Located 18 miles south of Salmon, 40 miles north of Challis, Idaho. Located off Highway 93. Commercial air transportation to Idaho Falls, Idaho, and Missoula, Montana. Local shuttle flights available to Salmon. Complimentary airport transportation to and from Missoula and Idaho Falls airports. Inquire about the shuttle schedule.

**What's Nearby:** Missoula, Montana, a delightful and historic college town three hours north, provides an interesting opportunity for dining, shopping, and cultural events.

# WAPITI MEADOW RANCH

Located in the heart of the largest wilderness in the continental United States, Wapiti Meadow Ranch is a place where avid anglers and horse enthusiasts can go to "get away from it all."

Owners and hosts Diana and Barry Bryant bought the historic guest ranch property from the Cox family, who had operated it as a guest ranch since the 1920s. The Bryants set about completely renovating the immense log-and-stone lodge and cabins to create what they call "a twenty-first-century experience in a nineteenth-century setting."

Diana, an east-coast transplant with a background in English riding and professional entertaining, brought a gracious sense of style to the renovation project. Barry, a westerner by birth and longtime backcountry traveler, helped to bring the ranch's fly-fishing and outdoors programs up to the highest possible standards. The result is a guest ranch that is tasteful, beautiful, secluded, and welcoming, where modern comfort and amenities fit snugly with old-fashioned frontier traditions of hospitality.

Fishing is of major importance to the Wapiti Meadow operation; it is one of only a handful of Orvis-endorsed lodges in the United States. Orvis, a fishing supply retailer and manufacturer, bases its endorsements not only on the high-quality amenities of its chosen properties but also on the quality of sport fishing available. With more than 50 miles of freestone streams in its program, Wapiti offers beginner and experienced fly-fishing enthusiasts the best in wade fishing. Guests and guides ply the headwaters of the Salmon River system, including the

Blue-Ribbon cutthroat waters of the mighty Middle Fork. There are also opportunities to fish high-alpine lakes, remote streams that have scarcely been touched by rods, and for beginning casters, a stocked pond on the ranch that is the ideal place to perfect one's rod-handling skills.

With an on-site Orvis shop, guests can purchase all of their "tip-end" supplies; there is also a selection of the finest rods and reels with which to experiment. Equipment is complimentary for guests who book any of the several fly-fishing packages. The guest-to-guide ratio on these trips is two-to-one, ensuring that you will get the most individualized instruction and advice possible.

Obviously, anyone booking a reservation should have a strong interest in fishing, but that is not the sole focus of Wapiti Meadow. The ranch also has an excellent horse riding program that allows guests to visit miles of trails surrounding the property. You'll be able to attain lofty summits that offer spectacular views of the Frank Church "River of No Return" Wilderness, the largest wilderness area in the continental United States.

The ranch also offers excellent opportunities for wildlife observation, offering occasional photography safaris. There is also mountain biking, hiking, and visits to Victorian-era mining towns, now abandoned.

At the heart of the operation is the log-and-stone lodge, which features a massive stone hearth surrounded by western artifacts. Diana's influence can be seen in the antiques that reflect her Virginia upbringing. Comfortable couches and easy chairs entice guests to curl up with a book from the ranch's substantial library or engage others in animated "fish stories" about the day's adventures. A large hot tub is strategically placed so that one has views of the grazing horse herd and an excellent place to watch the setting sun.

Attention to detail typifies the private guest cabins. Enjoy fresh-baked goods, a fruit basket, coffee service, and soft drinks any time. You can strike up a wood stove for atmosphere, but each cabin also has baseboard heat to ward off the chills. With modern baths, large living rooms, kitchenettes, plush sofas, and a host of amenities, you'll find these among the most comfortable guest rooms you've ever had the pleasure of experiencing.

Adult-oriented, Wapiti Meadow Ranch is perhaps not the ideal place far a family vacation unless you have mature children who can truly appreciate a remote wilderness experience based around outdoor activities.

---

**Wapiti Meadow Ranch**
1667 Johnson Creek Road
Cascade, ID 83611
Phone: (208) 633–3217
Fax: (208) 633–3219
E-mail: wapitimr@aol.com
Web site: www.wapitimeadowranch.com

**Owners:** Diana and Barry Bryant

**Accommodations:** Guest capacity, 15. 3 luxury suites in the lodge; 4 separate cabins with either 1 or 2 bedrooms. Rooms offer panoramic views of the surrounding mountains; each refurbished cabin features fresh flowers, snacks, a fridge with soft drinks, coffeemaker, fruit basket, modern bath, large living room, kitchenette, and daily maid service.

**Meals:** Dining room serves 18; service on fine china with silverware. Fine-dining ʾenus take advantage of painstakingly pre-

pared dishes that include seasonal vegetables and fruit plus products indigenous to the Rocky Mountain region. Low-carb menu also served upon request. Sample dinner entrees include prime rib, grilled salmon, Cornish game hen, selection of elk tenderloin, rack of lamb, muscovy duck breast, and stuffed pork tenderloin. A truly inspired dining experience at every meal under the direction of Diana, a former gourmet caterer.

**Activities:** One of a handful of Orvis-endorsed fly-fishing resorts, Wapiti Meadow prides itself on its excellence in fishing, with lake and stream fly fishing and instruction a specialty. Also, horseback riding with professional guides on mountain trails; wilderness pack trips; hiking amid pine forests and mountain meadows; leisure sports including basketball, volleyball, badminton, horseshoes and croquet; photography including planned camera "safaris"; 4x4 sightseeing; gold panning; mountain biking. Off-site golfing at Tamarack Resort (inquire about split-stay golfing/fly fishing packages). Winter snowmobiling, cross-country skiing.

**Amenities:** Group and family reunion meeting facilities for 16; hot tub; bait and tackle shop; gift shop; laundry service; spa; wedding facilities

**Special Programs:** No special kids' programs. Given its emphasis on fly-fishing instruction, gourmet dining, and intensive wilderness exploration, this ranch is best suited to adults and mature teens. Families with children, however, are not discouraged.

Special split-stay program with Tamarack Resort offers the chance to enjoy guided fishing and resort golf on a Robert Trent Jones–designed course. Visitors spend 3 days at fishing and riding at Wapiti Meadow, 3 days golfing with luxurious resort amenities at Tamarack.

**Rates:** $$–$$$$$ American plan. All-inclusive stays from 3 to 6 nights include lodging, meals, horseback instruction, guided fly fishing and equipment, and flight to and from the Middle Fork of the Salmon River; unguided guest stays considerably lower in cost.

**Credit Cards:** None. Cash, personal check, or traveler's checks.

**Season:** Summer, June 1 through October 31; winter, December 26 to March 7

**Getting There:** Most guests fly to Boise (approximately 80 miles) and rent a car. Air charter service available from Boise.

**What's Nearby:** Wapiti Meadow Ranch is located in the Frank Church Wilderness and surrounded by several million acres of undeveloped land; guests should expect to spend most of their vacation on the ranch, as there are very few attractions in this area of Idaho.

# WESTERN PLEASURE RANCH
## Sandpoint, Idaho

Although still a relatively young guest ranch, the Western Pleasure has a rich family history. The ranch was founded in 1940, when family patriarch Riley Wood pulled up stakes in Colorado and sought out a new beginning in the Idaho Panhandle. Since that time, the family has operated a working ranch here. In the 1990s the ranch acquired additional acreage, and the family began searching about for new things to do with their original ranch lands. They began offering day rides on horseback. The trips grew so popular that Riley's granddaughter, Janice, and her husband, Roley Schoonover, decided to build a guest-ranch facility to accommodate their burgeoning clientele.

The ranch lodge, completed in 1995, is truly a work of art. The entire building is made of locally cut timber in the traditional log-cabin style. Modern log cabins complement the lodge, giving the entire ranch a feeling of rusticity and continuity. Each cabin accommodates up to six people and is well apportioned with a bedroom, loft,

furnished kitchen, bathroom, and traditional woodstove. Additional guests stay in six separate rooms in the main lodge, whose amenities (recreation room, pool table, river-rock fireplace, and outdoor hot tub) make it a favorite gathering place for all.

Outdoors, the activity focuses on riding. The Western Pleasure horse program begins with a fun and informative riding lesson, including the careful selection of horses to match riders' abilities. Rides take full advantage of the family cattle tradition, with riders passing through pastures crowded with grazing cattle, or riders may head through the woods, where they may encounter a variety of wildlife in their native habitat. Beautiful views of the Selkirk and Cabinet Mountain Ranges and Lake Pend Oreille create lasting memories. Rides last from a moderate two hours to a full day, with lunch at a scenic waterfall.

The Schoonovers often include guests in the actual work of a family cattle ranch, and so you may get the chance to herd the eighty pairs of cows and their calves among the various pastures. "The guests' involvement depends on where we're moving cattle," Roley said. "Sometimes it involves opening a gate and letting them into a different pasture. If we're moving them to the neighbor's leased pasture, the guests get to drive them down the road." It's simple, but can be thrilling, particularly when one of the bulls decides that he wants to put up a fuss rather than cooperate. Fortunately, experienced hands are always available to keep the bovines in line!

Nearby Lake Pend Oreille offers the opportunity for water sports, including a kayaking adventure and a dinner cruise. In winter, guests can visit nearby Schweitzer Ski Area, one of the better ski resorts in the Pacific Northwest. In the evening, enjoy a ride in a sleigh pulled by two herculean Percheron draft horses. Be sure to visit the town of Sandpoint, a century-old former mining town on the shores of 41-mile-long Lake Pend Oreille.

---

## Western Pleasure Ranch

1413 Upper Gold Creek
Sandpoint, ID 83864
Phone: (208) 263–9066
Fax: (208) 265–0138
E-mail: info@westernpleasure.com
Web site: www.westernpleasureranch.com

**Owners/Managers:** Roley and Janice Schoonover

**Accommodations:** Capacity, 34. 3 cabins, 6 lodge rooms. Cabins accommodate from 2 to 8 individuals. Each cabin has a loft, bedroom, bathroom, and woodstove. Main lodge has 6 guest rooms with private baths.

**Meals:** Meals are served family style in the main lodge dining room. Western fare with ranch-raised beef (prime rib, steaks) are a specialty.

**Activities:** Horseback riding is the main activity. Guests are sometimes invited to participate in cattle work. Rides based on experience: slow, medium, and fast-paced rides. Arena instruction offered. Cross-country skiing and downhill skiing available in winter.

**Amenities:** Luxurious 10,000-square-foot main lodge made of hewn logs taken off the land; horse-drawn buggy rides; outdoor recreational game facilities, children's playground, rec room with video library

**Special Programs:** Children's program for ages 8–17. A summer-camp program for kids, Fiddler on the Hoof, is offered in July. The program teaches equitation and music instruction based on folk fiddling. Additional kids' camp programs also offered. Camps include wagon rides, barbecue dinner, western equitation, and a horse show put on by the kids.

**Rates:** $$–$$$ full American plan. Reduced rates for children 6–12. Ask about special rates for family reunions, weddings, and retreats.

**Credit Cards:** Visa, MasterCard

**Season:** Open year-round. Summer packages June 1 to September 30.

**Getting There:** Nearest commercial airport, Spokane, Washington (approximately 90 miles). Located 60 miles north of Coeur d'Alene, Idaho; 16 miles northeast of Sandpoint, Idaho.

**What's Nearby:** Sandpoint, a century-old mining and logging town; Schweitzer Winter Resort; Coeur d'Alene Lake Resort and the city of Coeur d'Alene

# TURKEY CREEK RANCH

Theodosia, Missouri

Missouri has been known as the Gateway to the West since the nineteenth century, and the Turkey Creek Ranch might officially be proclaimed the place where the West begins. Its owners, the Edwards family, have provided a warm, western welcome for more than four decades, and that hospitality now extends down through three generations.

Nestled in the Ozark Mountains on the shores of Bull Shoals Lake, Turkey Creek Ranch provides the best of two worlds: horseback riding and summer fun on the

water. The Edwardses like to refer to their retreat as "a lake resort with a dude-ranch flavor." It's appropriate that the ranch brand is a "swimming" T.

A 700-acre cattle ranch set amid rippling hills provides the perfect backdrop for exploration on horseback. The ranch maintains a solid string of western pleasure horses of various breeds, colors, and temperaments, and in a range suitable for the most inexperienced "greenhorn" to the trail-hardened horseman. For novices, the ranch wrangler will provide instruction on the art of horsemanship. Then, it's off to the bridle trails, lined with colorful trees and blooming wildflowers.

When the heat becomes searing, you can head for the lake, where pontoon boats, paddleboats, and canoes await. If waterskiing is your fancy, you can do that, too. There are also bass boats available for some serious lake-fishing action. There's even a dock where you can park your own watercraft.

For landlubbing recreationists, the ranch has a slew of amenities that include a putting green, an outdoor pool, whirlpool, and recreation rooms with pool tables, Ping-Pong tables, and video games.

When owners Dick and Elda Edwards first married, they bought this property with the idea of turning an old farm into an inviting guest resort. With the addition of cabins, casitas, and numerous renovations (along with the addition of five children of their own), they've achieved that and more. The Edwards family knows how to have fun, and their enthusiasm and experience makes it easy for their guests to enjoy themselves, too. Return guests are the norm here. As one guest said, "We have such a good time there, why go anywhere else?"

## Branson: Entertainment in a Southern Setting

Branson, Missouri, has a well-deserved reputation as the Entertainment Capital of the World. Beginning in the 1960s, 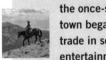 the once-small Ozark Mountain town began attracting a tourist trade in search of recreation and entertainment. Soon, recording stars such as Mel Tillis, Andy Williams, and Mickey Gilley discovered the charms of the town, purchased properties, and developed hotels and show clubs, where they frequently headlined. At present, the town's various music showcases (thirty theaters in all) draw music-lovers from throughout the United States and, indeed, the world. In addition to Branson, guests enjoy Silver Dollar City, a popular theme park that opened forty years ago. While in the area, catch a show on Country Music Boulevard, the heart of the Branson music scene.

**Turkey Creek Ranch**
HC 3, Box 3180
Theodosia, MO 65761
Phone: (417) 273–4362
Web site: www.turkeycreekranch.com

**Owners/Managers:** The Edwards Family

**Accommodations:** Capacity, 150. 24 total units; guests stay in cabins or casitas. Cabins, both deluxe and standard, have screened porches, full kitchens with microwave ovens, coffeemakers, air-conditioning, TV, full baths, separate bedrooms, picnic tables, and barbecue grills. Casitas are 1-room efficiencies with full kitchens, living room/dining room areas, AC, TV, and full baths. Cabins accommodate 4 to 10 people; casitas house 1 to 4 people.

**Meals:** Guests can prepare meals in their own cabins or visit any of several restaurants in the area. Catering for group functions available on request.

**Activities:** Daily guided horseback trips of 1-hour duration go out throughout the day; otherwise, no scheduled activities. Hiking on bridle paths. Most activities focus on water sports: paddleboating, canoeing, waterskiing. Riding and boat rentals at additional cost. Resort activities also include swimming in an indoor pool, a whirlpool, outdoor pool and children's pool, tennis, shuffleboard, volleyball, basketball, a putting green (golf courses nearby). Guests sometimes participate in cattle activities.

**Amenities:** Indoor and outdoor pools, whirlpool, piano and organ for entertainment, daily newspaper delivered to your cabin, a wide variety of watercraft for rent, dock, barbecue and picnic areas, recreation rooms, children's playground

**Special Programs:** No specific children's programs, although children are welcome, and there are plenty of activities they can participate in with their parents.

**Rates:** $–$$ Inquire for rates; prices vary by accommodations, length of stay. Activities such as horseback riding and boat rental are extra. Meals not included.

**Credit Cards:** Visa, MasterCard. Personal checks accepted.

**Season:** March through November

**Getting There:** Located 47 miles east of Branson, Missouri. Nearest airport in Springfield, about 85 miles.

**What's Nearby:** Branson, Missouri, approximately 45 miles. Theme parks, entertainment, musical performances, shopping, dining.

# AVERILL'S FLATHEAD LAKE LODGE
## Bigfork, Montana

For some people, the ideal vacation involves lounging on a beach; for others, there are simply not enough hours in a day to fit all ⁀e activities they want to do. Averill's Flat-

head Lake Lodge is the place for the latter type of vacationers.

Situated on the banks of Flathead Lake (the West's largest freshwater lake) in northwest Montana, Averill's sprawls over 2,000 acres of the northern Rocky Mountains. An ample beachfront on the east shore of the lake makes it an ideal spot for water sports. The ranch offers everything from sailing to sea kayaking, canoeing, and waterskiing. Guests looking for an adrenaline rush can river raft or take white-water kayak lessons, whereas guests looking for a slower-paced activity can try their hand at sailing. The ranch maintains everything from small dinghies to two magnificent 51-foot sloops, which transport guests on regular tours of the vast Flathead Lake. These two historic boats, the *Nor'Easter* and *Questa,* were built in the late 1920s as prototypes for America's Cup racing boats.

One favorite cruise takes wayfarers up Flathead River through a waterfowl preserve, where sightings of bald eagles are commonplace. Waterskiing originates at the boat dock, and even young kids can take part, riding atop the skiffing "boogie boards."

Horseback riding makes up the main component of the Flathead Lake Lodge experience. Trails take riders through the nearby mountains as well as the ranch's private game preserve, stocked with elk and American bison. Inexperienced riders can get saddle time in a riding arena under the watchful eye of skilled instructors. The confidence this instills in guests encourages them to explore this sizable property.

Children also ride, and the ranch has an excellent Junior Wranglers program in which they learn saddling, horse care, grooming, and barn duties. They get to tag along with real cowboys and cowgirls, learning the ins and outs of caring for the large herd of horses—valuable and character-enhancing experience.

Early risers can even head out on horseback for a pancake breakfast, the perfect way to start an active day. If you'd rather sleep in, you can saddle up for the evening barbecue ride, where you will be served out of an authentic western chuckwagon.

If you're saddle sore, you don't have to ride to eat. Guests dine together in the main lodge, where the meals are served family style and include homemade baked goods. A separate children's seating makes it easier for adults to simply relax and enjoy their meals, and it's a heck of a lot of fun for the kids, too.

Of course, everyone needs some time to just read and relax. For those quiet moments, you can visit the heated pool, or walk on the beach, or just kick back in the overstuffed buffalo-hide couches close by the massive river-rock fireplace in the main lodge. You'll sleep well at night in the cozy log-style cabins, all decorated with western style. Additional motel-like "family rooms" are available in the main lodge and are ideal for small families.

Averill's prides itself on having one of the biggest menus of activities of any guest ranch in the West, and with more than five decades of experience, the folks here know how to please. Bring lots of suntan lotion and be prepared to take plenty of long, soothing baths to relax your tired muscles. You're in for a whirlwind of exciting adventures.

---

**Averill's Flathead Lake Lodge**
P.O. Box 248
Bigfork, MT 59911
Phone: (406) 837–4391
Fax: (406) 837–6977
E-mail: flatheadlakelodge@centurytel.net
Web site: www.flatheadlakelodge.com

**Owners/Managers:** Doug and Maureen Averill

**Accommodations:** Guest capacity, 120. Total units, 31 including 13 private cabins, 15 rooms in the south lodge, another 3 sleeping rooms in the main lodge. Family rooms in the lodges provide private common areas for families; rooms have 1 queen-size bed, 2 sleeping beds in a loft area, and a private bath. Cottages have queen or twin beds in separate bedrooms, a living room, bathroom, and a porch overlooking the lake.

**Meals:** 3 adult sittings daily; separate kids' seating. A typical breakfast menu might include eggs Benedict, hash browns, breakfast meats, cereal bar with fresh fruits, cowboy coffee cake, and juices. Lunch: salad bar, roasted chicken and potatoes, fresh fruit and vegetables, chocolate cake. Dinner: Caesar salad, herb bread, whole roasted pig, roasted baron of buffalo, twice-baked potatoes, green beans almondine, chocolate mousse. Dinner, lunch, and breakfast rides.

**Activities:** Horseback riding, trail riding, arena competitions, sailing, waterskiing, kayaking, and canoeing, lake tours, fly fishing, lake fishing, boat fishing, rodeos, roping contests, mountain biking, rafting, golf at nearby resort, evening barn dances, more. Averill's prides itself on offering more activities than any other guest ranch—and they mean it!

**Amenities:** In-room coffeemaker, complimentary guest basket, daily newspapers in the main lodge, Saddle Sore Saloon, rec room, use of sailboats, fishing boats, waterskiing, tennis courts, beach fires

**Special Programs:** Children's Junior Wranglers program includes horseback riding, arts and crafts, fishing, games, and more. Children under 6 may ride in a supervised arena program. Child care available.

**Rates:** $$$–$$$$ full American plan. Children's rates, teen rates, infant rates. Most on-site activities are included in the price; a few activities are charged extra, especially off-site activities such as golf and river rafting.

**Credit Cards:** Visa, MasterCard, American Express. Personal checks accepted.

**Season:** May through October

**Getting There:** Nearest commercial airport in Kalispell, 17 miles. Contact the ranch in advance to arrange ground transportation.

**What's Nearby:** Glacier National Park, the National Bison Range

# BEAR CREEK LODGE
## Victor, Montana

The Bear Creek Lodge experience was well summed up in an article that appeared in *Condé Naste Traveler:* "Owner Roland Turney has elevated the notion of a log retreat into something of an art form: eight comfortable rooms overlooking the forest, exceptional gourmet meals, and an atmosphere of tranquil relaxation that lends itself to adventurous exploring or solitary exploration."

Turney, a former schoolteacher, has indeed stamped the ranch with his own

infectious personality, from the gracious log lodge built from timber rescued after the Yellowstone fire of 1988 to the portrait of his grandfather (in full Cossack uniform) that hangs above the lodge's river-stone fireplace.

Bear Creek Lodge is, indeed, a retreat. Guests come away feeling as though they visited an old friend—one who happens to have a stunning mountain home, gourmet chefs, and a staff that caters to one's every whim. Guests can take rejuvenating hikes along the timbered banks of Bear Creek, cross paths with white-tailed deer, elk, and moose. Many guests take advantage of the Blue Ribbon fishing waters made famous in the novel *A River Runs through It.* Mountain biking, canoeing, and whitewater rafting can all be arranged through the lodge, along with golf at an 18-hole championship course, tennis, or workouts at a top-drawer athletic club in nearby Hamilton.

Trail riding on horseback is, of course, a favorite activity. Guests can ride as much or as little as they like, from short one-hour jaunts to full-day trips into the Bitterroot Mountains. A local outfitter provides horses, tack, and guides. Those wishing to bring their own horses may stable them in a barn or on pasture. More than twenty-five Forest Service trails through the woods assure that you'll never trace the same steps or see the same scenery twice during your stay— unless, that is, you want to.

Although many guests feel so comfortable that the thought of leaving the ranch itself never crosses their minds, it should be noted that this area offers more than its share of interesting diversions, all within an hour's drive. To the north is the National Bison Range, home to one of the last remaining herds of wild American buffalo. Two different wildlife refuges will satisfy bird-watchers. The historically minded will want to visit St. Mary's Mission, home of the first permanent white settlement in Montana, and the Daly Mansion, the opulent home of an early copper baron. And the Big Hole Battlefield demarcated the site of an epic struggle between Nez Perce Indians and the U.S. Army in 1877.

Bear Creek is a small place with a maximum capacity of sixteen. The owners share meals and their time with guests, giving the ranch a very personal and intimate feeling. Although not "traditional" in the sense of many guest ranches, this retreat goes to the original intent that began the guest-ranch tradition: inviting travelers into one's home to share in the wonderful blessings of God's creation.

---

**Bear Creek Lodge**
1184 Bear Creek Trail
Victor, MT 59875
Phone: (406) 642–3750
Fax: (406) 642–6847
E-mail: info@bear-creek-lodge.com
Web site: www.bear-creek-lodge.com

**Owners/Managers:** Roland and Janet Turney

**Accommodations:** Capacity, 16; Total units, 8. Guests are lodged in a beautiful log lodge, completed in 1991. Guests share a common deck, library, game room, exercise room, and sauna. Rooms complete with private baths.

**Meals:** A flexible menu to accommodate guests' activities. Menu varies appreciably, but a typical evening menu gives a sense of the care in preparation: salad of greens, feta, and pine nuts dressed with a tart lemon vinaigrette; wine-marinated chicken breast with figs and olives; wildrice pilaf with lentils and barley; baby carrots with orange juice and cumin glaze; and pear frangipane tart with a delicate toasted-almond crust for dessert. Picnics available for daytime activities. Evening cocktail bar and wine served with hors d'oeuvres.

**Activities:** Horseback riding on wooded forest trails; fly fishing in several local rivers; hiking; mountain biking; bird-watching; backpacking; visits to nearby attractions, wildlife preserves, historic sites. The private trail system has been expanded to access

National Forest lands. One mile of private fishing on Bear Creek is available to guests.

**Amenities:** Robes, hair dryers, redwood hot tub, self-service fruit, baked goods, and beverages; satellite television

**Special Programs:** No formal children's program. Children 12 and over are always welcome; younger children welcome when the entire lodge is reserved.

**Rates:** $$$ full American plan. Guided service such as riding, fishing, etc., additional. 20 percent service charge and bed tax not included.

**Credit Cards:** Visa, MasterCard, Discover

**Season:** March through October

**Getting There:** Missoula, 45 miles north of Bear Creek Lodge, is the nearest commercial airport. Rental cars available at the airport. Hamilton airport serves general aviation with a 4,200-foot runway, 12 miles south of Bear Creek Lodge.

**What's Nearby:** 18-hole championship golf course, athletic club in Hamilton; National Bison Range; Lee Metcalf and Otto Teller Wildlife Refuges; Daly Mansion, St. Mary's Mission, Big Hole Battlefield

# THE COVERED WAGON RANCH

### Gallatin Gateway, Montana

Montana's Gallatin Canyon area boasts one of the most intense concentrations of guest ranches and outfitters in North America. The Covered Wagon is a stately elder citizen among that community, having opened way back in 1925. Throughout the years, it has earned a reputation as a traditional western dude escape with an authentic, rustic appeal, while constantly upgrading and modernizing to ensure that its guests remain comfortable.

The ranch is a mere 3 miles from Yellowstone National Park, amid the green mountains of the Gallatin. Wildlife thrives in this natural setting, and on any given day you are likely to spy deer, elk, moose, big-horn sheep, even a bear and the occasional mountain lion. Human activity won't impinge on the wildlife here. Guest capacity is just twenty-four individuals, which translates to privacy and a great deal of personal service. (Come

fall, the ranch serves as the perfect outpost for big-game hunters. Inquire if you are interested in a dream hunt in Big Sky country. The Covered Wagon offers an outfitting service to ensure a memorable hunt.)

The Covered Wagon Ranch treats every guest like cherished family. As one might expect at home, the pace here is set by the individual guests, who may partake of a short menu of on-ranch activities, from fly fishing (a Montana staple) to hiking and, of course, horseback riding.

More activities can be easily pursued nearby, such as mountain biking, golf, and tennis. Guided fly fishing on world-renowned Blue Ribbon waters will please both casual and avid anglers. The staff will be glad to help set you up with the appropriate local outfitter or make reservations for activities such as snow-coach trips through Yellowstone Park.

Evening activities are similarly casual. Guests and wranglers often gather around the campfire to share stories, sing, and listen to the baying of coyotes and, sometimes, wolves. A rec hall is especially popular with teens, but anyone who is game can participate in billiards, Ping-Pong, and foosball.

Guests gather in the recently built grand dining room, a beautiful example of log-cabin architecture that features huge log beams and plenty of windows looking out onto the forest and the mountains. Like all things at the ranch, dining is an informal activity, served family style. This is a teetotaling outfit: Those diners who like a beer or cocktail before or after dinner should bring their own.

Daily horseback trips take riders through the Gallatin and Madison Mountain ranges as well as Yellowstone Park. All-day rides are especially popular and include a midday break for a trailside lunch. After a full day in the saddle, you'll want to soak in the ranch hot tub to get your muscles good and relaxed for the next day's adventure. For the adventurous, the Covered Wagon offers overnight pack trips into Yellowstone National Park.

---

**The Covered Wagon Ranch**
34035 Gallatin Road
Gallatin Gateway, MT 59730
Phone: (800) 995–4237
E-mail: info@coveredwagonranch.com
Web site: www.coveredwagonranch.com

**Owners:** Jerry Taylor and Debra Naccarto

**Managers:** Kurt and Rebecca Puckett

**Accommodations:** Capacity, 24. 10 total units, consisting of rustic, original 1- and 2-bedroom cabins, each with log furniture, private bath, and covered porch.

**Meals:** Basic, hearty American ranch cuisine (think meats, vegetables simply prepared, potatoes), served family style in a spacious, modern log cabin–style lodge. BYOB in cabins only.

**Activities:** Fly fishing, horseback riding, mountain biking, hiking, and indoor recreational games. Off-site river rafting, tours of Yellowstone National Park, golf, and tennis.

**Amenities:** Spacious guest ranch features comfortable furniture and a modest reading library, recreation room, hot-tub.

**Special Programs:** No structured kids' programs, although children are welcome guests. Mature children may ride, with their parent's permission.

**Rates:** $$–$$$ full American plan, with or without horseback riding. Higher rates reflect in-season visits and full horse and wrangler service. Children's rates, off-season reduced rates.

**Credit Cards:** Visa, MasterCard. Personal checks preferred.

**Season:** Summer: May through October

**Getting There:** 54 miles south of Bozeman, 34 miles north of West Yellowstone on state Highway 191. Nearest commercial airports, Bozeman and West Yellowstone. Ranch shuttle available at either airport.

**What's Nearby:** Yellowstone National Park, Big Sky Winter Resort

# KLICK'S K
# BAR L RANCH
Augusta, Montana

Dick and Nancy Klick offer an old-school approach to guest ranching: Keep things simple, mind the little details, and let nature exert her own powerful force and beauty on the guests. It has been a winning formula at the K Bar L since 1925, when family patriarchs Emil and Sam Klick first settled in this still-unspoiled wilderness and began guiding hunters through the backcountry.

For generations, the Klicks have been the sole residents of the Sun River Game Preserve, and they have a profound respect for and enjoyment of their remote outpost. There's no easy road into the Klick's main ranch: Guests must either take a thrilling jet-boat ride across Gibson Lake or mount up and ride a saddle horse around the lake shore, their gear dutifully carried by pack mules. Clearly, your adventure begins even before you arrive at the spectacular ranch compound.

The K Bar L is surrounded by wilderness; not only is it part of the game preserve, the trails also dip into the mighty, million-acre Bob Marshall Wilderness, perhaps the least-trodden, wild, and wonderful wilderness area in Montana. "The Bob," as locals refer to it, is wilderness most people can only imagine: rugged peaks, alpine lakes, cascading waterfalls, grassy meadows embellished with shimmering streams, a towering coniferous forest, and big river valleys.

This region of Montana includes the North and South Forks of the Sun River and the Middle and South Forks of the Flathead River. It runs for 60 miles along the Continental Divide, with elevations ranging from 4,000 feet to more than 9,000 feet. A huge escarpment called the Chinese Wall, a part of the Divide, highlights The Bob's vast untrammeled beauty, with an average height of more than 1,000 feet and a length of 22 miles. Guests wishing to see this magnificent formation up-close can opt for an extended pack trip that departs from the Klick's ranch; those preferring a shorter trip may take two- or three-day "overnighters" during their weeklong stay, including a trip to the Prairie Reef Lookout, from which you can see the Chinese Wall.

But you don't have to spend days in the saddle to enjoy the Klick's outfit. Many guests prefer to simply stay "in camp," enjoying the spacious lodge, playing volleyball, throwing horseshoes, and swimming in the natural hot-springs pool, which maintains a year-round temperature of 86 degrees.

Schedules scarcely exist here: The Klicks work with guests, planning daily wilderness horseback rides and fishing trips according to their guests' own proclivities. Fishing is a major focus here: Beginners can learn a great deal, and the Klicks have an encyclopedic knowledge of what flies work best for the more seasoned anglers.

Fall is hunting season on the ranch, and you won't find better, more experienced guides. From deer and elk to big-horn sheep and black bear, you'll find an abundance of trophy animals in this awesome and remote wilderness. And if you don't desire to shoot them, the folks here will gladly help you preserve the animals—on photographic paper.

**Klick's K Bar L Ranch**
P.O. Box 287
Augusta, MT 59410
Phone: (406) 562–3589 (winter, spring);
(406) 562–3551 (summer, fall)
Web site: www.kbarl.com

**Owner/Manager:** The Klick Family

**Accommodations:** Guest capacity, 35. 1-,
2-, and 3-bedroom cabins with traditional
western ranch furniture, Indian and western
furnishings, heavy wool blankets. A hydro-
electric generator powers the ranch; water
comes from natural springs. Separate
shower house and modern toilet facilities.
This is a remote property, but comfortable.
Here, you'll "rough it" in relative comfort.

**Meals:** Meals served family style. Weekly
cookouts, trail-side pack-trip meals. BYOB.

**Activities:** The horse program is at the center of activities. Exceptional fishing as close
as the stream that runs in front of your
cabin door. Lake fishing, fly fishing, stream

fishing. Extended and overnight pack trips
into the Bob Marshall Wilderness (inquire
for details). Volleyball, horseshoes, sing-
alongs, and swimming.

**Amenities:** Natural hot-springs pool maintains a year-round temperature of 86
degrees.

**Special Programs:** Young children (under
age 6) not advised. Fall hunting programs,
guided fly fishing, backcountry pack trips.

**Rates:** $$–$$$ full American plan. Mini-
mum 5-night stay. Shorter stays available in
June, September.

**Credit Cards:** None. Personal or traveler's
checks accepted.

**Season:** June to mid-September; extended
hunting season

**Getting There:** Nearest airport, Great Falls.
Ground transport with prior arrangement
(additional cost). Ranch is 35 miles west of
Augusta, 75 miles west of Great Falls.

**What's Nearby:** Yellowstone National Park

# LONE MOUNTAIN RANCH
## Big Sky, Montana

If fine dining in a luxurious ranch setting
within hollering distance of Yellowstone
National Park is your idea of a perfect vacation, look no farther than Lone Mountain
Ranch. Guests and journalists alike rave
about the food, served in the spacious, gracious, and charming main lodge dining
room, a voluminous log building decorated
with elk-antler chandeliers, a massive stone
fireplace, and tasteful western decor.

Ranch chefs prepare health-conscious
adaptations of classic French cooking tech-

niques that feature the local organic bounty
of the Northern Rockies. Here's just a taste
of what you can expect (excerpted from the
evening dinner menu): crab and tuna cakes
served with baby greens and lemon-basil
vinaigrette and topped with mango coulis;
spinach salad with sautéed mushrooms,
bacon and tomatoes with a toasted almond
dressing and goat cheese; elk medallions
and braised elk osso bucco paired with
madeira mushrooms or caramelized shallot
butter.

## What Is a Geyser?

A geyser is a plume of superheated water that erupts from fissures in the earth's surface—and the Yellowstone National Park has more of them than anywhere else on earth. About half of the earth's 800 or so known geysers can be found there. Geysers form in areas where groundwater contacts volcanic magma near the earth's surface; the superheated water is "plumbed" through silica-rich rock formations that can withstand the awesome force of an eruption.

Renowned gourmet and travel publications, including *Town & Country, Travel & Leisure,* the *New York Times,* and the *Los Angeles Times,* have all heaped their acclaim on the Lone Mountain Ranch's dining. You may never want to leave the dining room!

But leave you must, and will, to partake of the equally enticing ranch activities. This is a top-shelf ranch vacation spot offering a multitude of must-do opportunities. Visit the Yellowstone Park and enjoy its natural wonders; take a hike with a llama, and learn about the native geology, history, and flora and fauna; take a canoe trip on a mountain river; and of course, spend lots of time getting acquainted with your equine buddy on dozens of forested trails. Winter guests have their pick of cross-country or downhill ski adventures, guided winter fly fishing, sleigh rides, and evening entertainment. And if you get sore from all the activities, you can schedule a session with a licensed massage therapist.

Winter or summer, guests not only get a lot of physical activity but an enjoyable educational experience, too. Lone Mountain is renowned for its naturalist program, and all of the staff are quite knowledgeable when it comes to identifying the species in this biologically diverse region of Montana and edifying people on the natural world surrounding the ranch.

The plethora of choices doesn't end with the outdoors, however. Even before you arrive, you can select from a variety of accommodations that range from rustic bungalows to family-size cabins. There are also six private couples' rooms in the Ridgetop Lodge, a great place to meet other sojourners or to hold a conference event. But don't dawdle—it's not unusual for spaces to be booked up as much as a year in advance.

Lone Mountain Ranch is one of the premier family-owned and -operated guest ranches in North America and well deserving of its many accolades earned in more than half a dozen national magazines and periodicals. It comes highly recommended.

---

**Lone Mountain Ranch**
Box 160069
Big Sky, MT 59716
Phone (800) 514–4644
Fax: (406) 995–4670
E-mail: lmr@lmranch.com
Web site: www.lmranch.com

**Manager:** Ennica Williams

**Accommodations:** Capacity, 70. 30 total units. 21 1- and 2-bedroom log cabins accommodate from 2 to 9 guests each; 6 additional rooms in the Ridgetop Lodge. Rooms and cabins include bathrooms with full baths, rock fireplaces or woodstoves. Cabins are located near a burbling brook and feature front porches.

**Meals:** Breakfast and lunch served buffet style. Dinner menu includes a choice of numerous entrees, which vary daily. Special diets accommodated. Full-service bar. As noted, Lone Mountain serves some of the finest dining available in the guest-ranch business.

**Activities:** Fly fishing year-round; horseback riding and equitation instruction; off-site tennis, swimming, white-water rafting. Rock climbing lessons on the ranch's own climbing wall, plus a challenging skills course and high/low ropes course designed to develop physical confidence. Extensive naturalist program and tours of Yellowstone National Park. Extensive winter activities menu includes fly fishing, snowshoeing, sleigh-ride dinners, and more. This ranch was featured as one of the best cross-country ski destinations in North America; alpine skiing also available at nearby Big Sky Winter Resort.

**Amenities:** Video services for guests, hot tub, masseuse; conference facilities, outdoor specialty equipment shop

**Special Programs:** Well-designed and supervised program for children ages 4 to 12; kids take part in a wide variety of activities ranging from naturalist hikes to rock climb-

ing to horse and pony rides. Fly fishermen can participate in special fishing packages, including a 2-week fly-fishing marathon that includes Montana's top spots. Inquire if you love to fish! Winter includes several adventure packages centered on alpine or cross-country skiing.

**Rates:** $$$–$$$$ full American plan. Reduced children's rates, off-season rates, and winter rates. Special package rates; special nanny rates. Guided fly-fishing trips and instruction, massage therapy, photo clinics, and tours (on space-available basis), additional cost.

**Credit Cards:** Visa, MasterCard, Discover

**Season:** Summer: mid-June to mid-September; winter: early December to mid-March

**Getting There:** Located 40 miles south of Bozeman on Highway 191; shuttle service available for guests staying 4 days or longer. Nearest commercial airport: Bozeman.

**What's Nearby:** Yellowstone National Park, Big Sky Winter Resort

# MOUNTAIN SKY GUEST RANCH
## Bozeman, Montana

An upscale guest ranch with a friendly, informal ambience best describes Mountain Sky. Set in the aptly named Paradise Valley, just south of Bozeman and a short distance from the north entrance of Yellowstone National Park, Mountain Sky has a long and storied history in the western guest-ranch business. One of the oldest guest ranches in the state (it opened its doors to dudes

back in 1929), Mountain Sky was known as the Ox Yoke. Now, under the capable management of owner Shirley Arsenault, the ranch has a new name and a new face. An extensive renovation has helped to elevate this property to one of the most comfortable and modern in the guest-ranch industry.

Despite the modernization, the ranch retains the very things that made this historic guest ranch inviting: Its rustic original cabins retain their charm, the horse program remains outstanding, and warm and friendly service continues to attract guests from throughout the world. Simple but elegant touches, such as fresh-fruit baskets delivered to guest rooms each day and lovely flower baskets decorating cabin porches, add a touch of distinctive graciousness and beauty to each new day.

Activities at Mountain Sky cover the usual menu of most guest-ranch vacations. Horseback riding, fly fishing and pond fishing, nature hikes, and river rafting trips make up the backbone of the daily activity list. Great care is taken to ensure that guests are entirely comfortable and engaged in the day's activities; for example, those who embark on the all-day trail ride are treated to a fabulous picnic spread and wonderful vistas of the Paradise Valley.

In the evening you won't want for things to do, either. Each night, guests are entertained with western dances, cowboy and folk sing-alongs, special gourmet sit-down dinners, dinner barbecue ride, hayrides, and campfire storytelling sessions.

During the summer months, the ranch is very family oriented, with an outstanding kids' program that includes riding, arts and crafts, cookouts, hiking, swimming, and fishing. During spring and fall, however, the mood turns romantic as the ranch welcomes couples and singles looking for a tranquil escape and adventure in the company of other adults.

Individuals who are interested in improving their horsemanship won't be disappointed. The ranch divides its rides based on experience, and riding groups seldom exceed eight, giving guests and wranglers a great opportunity to work together. A variety of rides go out each day, including an early-morning breakfast ride featuring a campfire breakfast complete with fabled "cowboy" coffee. Those guests who request additional riding instruction can take part in informal classes in the arena headed by Mountain Sky's expert horse hands.

---

**Mountain Sky Guest Ranch**
P.O. Box 1219
Emigrant, MT 59027
Phone: (800) 548–3392; (406) 333–4911
Fax: (406) 333–4537
E-mail: Use Web site
Web site: www.mtnsky.com

**Owner/Manager:** Shirley Arsenault

**Accommodations:** Capacity, 85. 30 total units composed of guest cabins suitable for 2 to 7 guests. Older cabins completely renovated with full-size bathrooms; newer cabins feature large-view windows, full baths, and sitting rooms. All cabins have front porches with deck furniture.

**Meals:** Twice-weekly, 5-course gourmet meals featuring inventive continental and American cuisine; evening barbecue cookouts, buffet-style breakfasts and lunches with homemade breads and breakfast pastries, breakfast trail rides. Special diets accommodated. Sample dinner menu: duck confit appetizer with balsamic glazed apples served with warm polenta; nectarine and roasted pepper salad served with mixed greens; smoked loin of lamb and stewed summer vegetable entree; warm Valrohna cake served with homemade huckleberry ice cream and fresh huckleberries.

**Activities:** Broad horse program featuring daily trail rides, half-day and full-day rides, breakfast rides, arena instruction; fly fishing and pond fishing; swimming in an outdoor heated pool; nature hikes; tennis. Evening western dances, sing-alongs, Saturday Showdeo performance and riding games. Guided fishing trips on Blue Ribbon waters arranged at guests' request.

**Amenities:** 1 all-weather tennis court, hot tub and sauna, full bar and wine service, comfortable main lodge with library and a grand piano

**Special Programs:** Daily children's program includes riding, cookouts, arts and crafts, hiking, swimming, fishing. Babysitting service. Spring and fall adults-only programs.

**Rates:** $$$–$$$$ full American plan. ~dren's rates, off-season rates available; inquire.

**Credit Cards:** Visa, MasterCard. Personal checks accepted.

**Season:** Mid-May to mid-October

**Getting There:** Located 60 miles southeast of Bozeman, 30 miles south of Livingston. Nearest commercial airport: Bozeman.

**What's Nearby:** Yellowstone National Park (30 miles)

# THE RESORT AT PAWS UP
## Greenough, Montana

Among the premier guest ranches in this book, if not *the* premier guest ranch, is The Resort at Paws Up. This is the place for individuals, couples, and families seeking a vast array of active outdoor activities, fine dining in a variety of settings, deluxe accommodations, and personal service that rivals that of the finest hotels in the country.

Opened in 2005, the resort has already gained distinction as a member of Small Luxury Hotels of the World, a collection of independently owned, exclusive resort hotels in more than fifty countries. It is the only Montana property recognized among the organization's more than 300 luxury hotels. It was also featured in the upscale lifestyle magazine *The Robb Report.*

As one might expect, this is an opulent place that pampers its guests. One of the most intriguing features is its "Spa Town," a group of tents on a meadow that offer a wide selection of spa services in a natural, relaxing setting. Another unique feature is "Tent City," a group of wall-tent accommo-

dations in which guests "rough it" with all the luxuries one is accustomed to at a fine resort hotel—only this one is surrounded by wilderness.

More conventional guest accommodations can be found in the resort's luxurious cabins and vacation homes. Widely varied in size, each of these unique accommodations includes high-end conveniences such as hot tubs, big-screen televisions, Internet access, and luxuries such as feather beds, fine linens, and contemporary western furnishings. Guests are further pampered by such things as in-room spa services and room service—a very rare treat not common to the guest ranch experience!

While guests have any number of reasons to stay in bed, there are as many more to get out and explore. The menu of activities at The Resort at Paws Up is truly staggering, from ATVs to well-bred quarter horses, water sports on Seeley Lake to guided wilderness exploration. With nearly 37,000 acres of wilderness to explore, guests can easily fill

The Resort at Paws Up, Montana

their days without visiting the same place twice. For those who desire a return to civility, an off-site golf trip at the Double Arrow Golf Course can be arranged; for those who want an even deeper wilderness experience, there are backcountry pack trips, guided fly-fishing journeys on Blue Ribbon waters, and big-game hunting in season.

Needless to say, a resort of this caliber also features fine dining to match the best restaurants you'll likely encounter this side of Manhattan. Culinary-trained chefs design the daily menus, which range from four-course gourmet meals to casual outdoor barbecues and cookouts.

Drawing from the agricultural wealth of Montana and the West, the chefs at Paws Up create world-class cuisine using fresh meats, produce, and ingredients. Envision freshly picked huckleberries served with a breakfast of french toast and handmade sausage, or a dinner of Rocky Mountain trout sauteed with herbs and served with a Napa Valley chardonnay. Or a lavish barbecue of steaks served with a vintage pinot noir. Dining is an adventure itself!

Clearly, The Resort at Paws Up is one of the finest guest ranch resorts to be found anywhere. If you are looking for a very satisfying vacation in a beautiful Rocky Mountain setting, with the luxurious touches one might expect in a first-class resort, this is undoubtedly one of your best bets.

## The Resort At Paws Up

40060 Paws Up Road
Highway 200, Mile Marker 25
Greenough, MT 59823-9210
Phone: (800) 473–0601; (406) 244–5200
Fax: (406) 244–5242
E-mail: theresort@pawsup.com
Web site: www.pawsup.com

**Owners:** Dave and Nadine Lipson

**Manager:** Bryan Kindred

**Accommodations:** Guest capacity, 86. A contrast of rustic elegance and luxury refinement, The Resort at Paws Up offers a wide variety of accommodations, from the intimate 2-bedroom Meadow Homes to the family-friendly 3-bedroom Ponderosa Pine Cabins, whose 2,300 square feet of space suit up to 8 guests. Each cabin features a loft, spacious great room, hot tubs on the back deck, flat-screen televisions with satellite channels, DSL Internet connections, and cordless telephones.

For those seeking togetherness amid authentic ranch trappings, The Bunkhouse is a traditional barn converted to a living area for 6. It is ideal for buddy trips, bachelorette parties, or other group get-togethers.

Finally, for those who want the ultimate camping experience, the resort offers "Tent City," spacious, well-appointed wall tents whose interiors are reminiscent of luxury resort hotel rooms. The tents (and we are reluctant to call them that) feature real beds, fine linens, art on the walls, and, yes, electricity. Truly a unique way to spend a vacation!

**Meals:** Guests enjoy a wide variety of dining experiences, from gourmet four-course meals to outdoor cookouts. An on-site restaurant, Pomp, is open nightly and offers guests one of the finest culinary experiences in Montana. The Tank & Trough, which serves breakfast and lunch, features casual dining. Guests staying in the Tent City dine at the Tent City Dining Pavilion. The resort will accommodate any dietary requirements you may have with advance notice.

**Activities:** Paws Up offers a strikingly broad variety of activities, from the expected fly fishing and horseback riding to lake water sports (waterskiing, wake boarding, personal watercraft), white-water rafting, kayaking and canoeing, mountain biking, shooting sports including sporting clays, upland bird hunting, ATV excursions, and off-site golf. Inquire about guided wilderness adventures for big-game hunting, fly fishing, pack trips, photography, and natural history tours.

In winter the resort offers snowmobiling, snowshoeing, ice skating, sleigh rides, ATV adventures, horseback riding, ice climbing, and more.

**Amenities:** "Spa Town," 11 oversize tents offering massage and spa treatments; event and wedding planning service; big-screen televisions with satellite reception, DSL Internet in cabins; helicopter service; in-room washer/dryer and kitchens in some accommodations; room service

Conference room for 300 and break-out facilities, business center, all with AV support; river-side picnic area for large groups

**Special Programs:** Children's program welcomes kids ages 5 and over. "Family-friendly" daily activities allow everyone over age 7 to participate together. (Nanny service for kids under 5). "Kids Corps of Discovery" program for children ages 5 to 12 offers activities tailored to children; kids learn about horses and other ranch animals, hike, cook, make crafts, fish, play games and sports, swim, and more.

Resort vacation planners can help with conferences, weddings, reunions, and other special events. Hunting trips, fishing on

Blue Ribbon waters, and backcountry pack trips available through Paws Up outfitters program.

**Rates:** $$$$$ Substantial off-season and late-season discounts. Nightly rates include airport transfers, on-site transportation, with meal plan and most activities charged separately.

**Credit Cards:** Visa, MasterCard, American Expresss, Discover. Cash, personal checks, certified checks, and wire transfers accepted.

**Season:** Open year-round

**Getting There:** Located 35 miles northeast of Missoula, in the Blackfoot Valley. Guests fly into Missoula airport, which is served by seven commercial airlines and also offers private jet service.

**What's Nearby:** Glacier National Park (about 3 hours), Yellowstone National Park (5 hours), and the college town of Missoula with its pedestrian-friendly downtown, shops, restaurants, and outdoor-oriented populace.

© The Resort at Paws Up

The Resort at Paws Up, Montana

# 63 RANCH

## Livingston, Montana

In case you're wondering, the 63 Ranch brand was established in 1863, hence, its name. As one might expect of a historic dude ranch, the 63 is as authentic as they come. A working cattle ranch situated amid the breathtaking mountain scenery of Big Sky Country, the 63 was the first dude ranch in the state to earn designation as a National Historic Site.

Paul and Jinnie Christensen welcomed their first guests in 1929. Their daughter, Sandra, and Sandra's husband, Bud Cahill, have continued the family tradition on into the twenty-first century. It would be hard to imagine a more idyllic setting for a western ranch: Bordered by the Gallatin National Forest, the ranch straddles Mission Creek Canyon and extends to the foothills of the Absaroka Mountain Range. The grassy hills are ideal for livestock, the ridges are sharp and scenic, and the ranch is situated not far from the banks of the Yellowstone River. Yellowstone National Park is a mere 50 miles to the south, so plan on including that in your travel plans as well.

A true working cattle ranch, the 63 invites guests to join in gathering and moving cattle, and learning to rope, too. Horses outnumber guests two to one, so you'll never exhaust the supply of fresh mounts. These horses are in top condition and of excellent quality, and guests are not limited to a pokey walk along a bridle trail. If cantering through the woods or across an open pasture is your desire, the folks at the 63 will be glad to oblige you. And for guests who appreciate a more leisurely ride, nobody will complain if you choose instead a contemplative ride through the woods. There are even gentle "kids' horses" for children as young as six years of age.

Day rides take guests into the Absaroka-Beartooth Wilderness, an especially wild and beautiful backcountry.

Although riding is the focus here, there are numerous other diversions as well. You won't be held to a rigorous schedule. If you want to sleep in, you can do so. If you're up at the crack of dawn, you can watch the cowboys as they bring in the remuda. Anglers enjoy Mission Creek's banks, where trout jump in the pools. Please, put them back, though. The ranch adheres to a catch-and-release ethic. Kids can fish in a stocked pond, which is also an ideal place to practice fly casting. Avid anglers can explore several nearby rivers with Blue Ribbon sections.

Photographers will be able to gather an album full of memories: beautiful sunsets over the mountains, cowboys and cattle, wildflowers and wildlife. The possibilities are as varied and endless as your imagination. Be sure to spend some time in Livingston, a picturesque ranch town with a restored historic district, restaurants, saloons, museums, and shopping.

There are dozens of other recreational activities available at the 63, from volleyball and horseshoe tossing to parlor games, billiards, and square dances. Off-site activities include white-water rafting, visits to the Lewis and Clark Caverns, the Custer Battlefield, and historic Virginia City.

**63 Ranch**
P.O. Box 979
Livingston, MT 59047
Phone: (406) 222–0570
E-mail: 63ranch@starband.net
Web site: www.sixtythree.com

**Owners/Managers:** Sandra and Bud Cahill and son Jeff Cahill

**Accommodations:** Capacity, 30. Guests stay in 10 individual cabins ranging from 1 to 4 bedrooms. Each has log furniture, fresh seasonal wildflowers upon arrival, baths and showers, and twin or double beds.

**Meals:** Wholesome meals, served family style, draw raves from guests. The menu operates on a 21-day cycle, ensuring that no two meals will be the same. Lean grass-fed beef from the 63 Ranch herd served along with pork, poultry, and fish; fresh fruits, vegetables, and baked breads. Sunday-night buffet. Steak barbecue on Mission Creek on Saturday evening. Special diets (low cholesterol, high fiber, vegetarian, pork-free, or food allergies) accommodated with advance notice.

**Activities:** Horseback riding is the central focus of daytime activities. Western riding instruction available, in addition to trail rides. Fishing is a favorite pastime; guests may fish on Blue Ribbon tributaries of the Yellowstone, in Mission Creek, or in "secret" spots, by special arrangement. Request a fishing brochure. Stocked ranch pond for kids. Pond swimming, hiking, nature walks, local history lesson, parlor games, recreation room. White-water rafting off-premises. Evening entertainment includes sing-alongs, square dancing, and entertainment in the ranch pavilion. Local rodeos (ask for a schedule).

**Amenities:** Ranch "newspaper." Pay telephone, soda machine, wireless Internet. Think simple, rather than opulent.

**Special Programs:** No formal children's programs. Babysitter available. Kids as young as 6 are allowed to ride. 4- and 5-year-olds led at the barn.

**Rates:** $$ Rates are based on a 7-day stay and are not discounted or reduced for persons staying less than 1 week. Reduced rates for children to age 11.

**Credit Cards:** None. Personal checks, traveler's checks accepted.

**Season:** Mid-June to mid-September

**Getting There:** Nearest commercial airport, Bozeman (50 miles). Shuttle by prior arrangement, at additional charge. Car rentals available at the Bozeman airport. City-county airport with landing strip in Livingston; no charge for pickup.

**What's Nearby:** Livingston, a charming ranching town with a lively historic district. Also, Yellowstone National Park, Lewis & Clark Caverns, Nevada City (a restored mining town), Custer Battlefield, scenic Beartooth Highway. Fourth of July Rodeo, annual county fair.

# 320 GUEST RANCH

### Gallatin Gateway, Montana

A famous historic ranch, the 320 Guest Ranch is celebrating a full century of welcoming guests from all over the globe. It's not hard to understand why this pioneering guest ranch has remained in business for so long. First, its location in the Gallatin Canyon places it just minutes from Yellowstone National Park, Big Sky Winter Resort, and the million-acre Gallatin National Forest. Second, the ranch is bisected by 2

## Doctor McGill and the
## 320 Ranch Legacy

Caroline McGill was a forward-thinking woman with a love of the outdoors. Montana's first woman physician and its first pathologist, Dr. McGill purchased the 320 in 1936, hoping to create a place for her patients to convalesce, and as a healthful place for friends and patients to recreate. Years before Montana received electricity, Dr. McGill installed a gas generator (made from an old Cadillac engine), which powered the ranch for more than a decade. In 1940 she built a lovely gambrel-roofed barn whose picture has appeared in publications and advertisements throughout the world.

Dr. McGill was loved throughout the region, and her staff eventually expressed their affection by building a custom home for her, with each individual marking their contribution with a small note and their name. The house, which was finished in 1955 on Christmas Day, became known as the Christmas Cabin. When McGill passed away in 1959, her extensive collection of antiques was used to create the Museum of the Rockies and to help restore the famous historic mining towns of Virginia and Nevada Cities.

miles of the Gallatin River, which provides access to Montana's famed fly-fishing habitat. And finally, the ranch offers high-level service and upscale accommodations, making it one of the most acclaimed resort properties in the West.

In fall the ranch lends itself to big-game and bird hunting; in winter it's the perfect locale for snowmobiling, skiing, dogsled trips, and snowshoeing. In spring the pastures come alive with wildflowers, and in summer the high country opens itself up to horseback riding on miles of well-established trails.

Overall, the appearance of the ranch is classic, with chinked-log cabins, lodges, and lodge buildings. More than simply a guest ranch, the 320 is a full-blown western resort complete with a popular steakhouse and convenience center. Its size gives the ranch a flexibility not often found in the guest-ranch business. The 320 accommodates about 200 people—perfect for weddings and meetings.

Visitors are welcome to stay a day, a week, or a month! The flexibility extends to the types of guests the ranch attracts, everyone from Yellowstone visitors just passing through to international visitors enchanted with the idea of staying at a true western cattle ranch, to adventurers eager to do some backcountry snowmobiling, to soon-to-be newlyweds looking for the ideal romantic wedding site. And, of course, there are the traditional guest-ranch vacationers who are looking for an all-inclusive package that includes dining, activities, and lodging. Such guests can choose between deluxe four-day or seven-day packages, as well as "basic" packages that include lodging only.

During the busy summer season, the action centers around horseback riding and fly fishing. An indoor arena affords riders the chance to improve their skills and is also the site for rodeo performances and ropings. Anglers can take advantage of an on-site outfitter whose professional guides can help to provide the perfect fishing excursion (and guide you through a fully stocked fly-fishing shop). Guests may also take part in guided rafting trips on the Yellowstone and day trips to famed Yellowstone Park.

## 320 Guest Ranch

205 Buffalo Horn Creek
Gallatin Gateway, MT 59730
Phone: (800) 243–0320; (406) 995–4283
Fax: (406) 995–4694
E-mail: info@320ranch.com
Web site: www.320ranch.com

**Owner:** David Brask

**Accommodations:** Capacity, 200. Accommodations are upscale and vary from single cabins to 3-bedroom log homes. Some cabins include kitchenettes and fireplaces. All have telephones and cable TV. Daily maid service.

**Meals:** Guests dine in the full-service restaurant, which serves breakfast, lunch, and dinner. Restaurant is open to the public. A full-service bar is also available.

**Activities:** Horseback riding and fly fishing are the backbone of the summer activities program. 6 rides go out daily, giving riders the choice of long or short excursions. On-site fishing-guide service can treat guests to fishing in several local rivers. River rafting through local guide service. In winter, guests may take part in snowmobile tours in Yellowstone Park (ask about snowmobiling packages), alpine skiing at Big Sky Resort, and cross-country skiing or snowshoeing on the ranch. Also available: dogsledding and sleigh rides. Fall hunting trips available.

Inquire for additional hunting info and requirements.

**Amenities:** A full-service ranch, the 320 includes a renowned steakhouse and saloon. Weekly "cowboy" entertainment, dances, rodeos during summer. Wedding facilities and conference facilities available year-round.

**Special Programs:** No children's program, but babysitting is available. Kids 6 and older may participate in activities with their parents.

**Rates:** $$–$$$ full American plan. Prices vary widely based on lodging, length of stay, activity level, time of year. Single rooms as low as $90. Winter snowmobiling packages available. Check "special deals" on the ranch Web site, www.320ranch.com. Children's discounts.

**Credit Cards:** Visa, MasterCard

**Season:** Summer: late May to early October; winter: mid-November to mid-April

**Getting There:** Nearest commercial airport, Bozeman, 50 miles. Regional airport at West Yellowstone, 34 miles. Ranch is 12 miles south of Big Sky, 36 miles north of West Yellowstone on Highway 191, mile marker 36.

**What's Nearby:** Yellowstone National Park, Big Sky Resort

# TRIPLE CREEK RANCH

## Darby, Montana

Triple Creek is an adults-only luxury-resort property, with all the amenities one might expect to find in a Club Med. If you want to work on your forehand lob or practice your putting stroke, there is a tennis court and a putting green. Or is a mountain bike more your speed? You pick. You can even work out in the weight and fitness center, or just laze around in a hammock beneath the pines. Whatever your heart desires, chances are the staff will be able to accommodate your every whim.

Situated at the foot of Trapper Peak, the ranch takes full advantage of its secluded mountain setting. This region is resplendent in native wildlife such as moose, elk, and white-tailed deer, any of which you are likely to see during daily trail rides and cattle drives experienced on the back of your own horse. While you are out on the trail, you'll be able to stop for a picnic lunch at a stunning overview that looks out on the French Basin and the Anaconda-Pintler Wilderness.

You're welcome to go off the ranch as well and visit the nearby art galleries and specialty shops of the Bitterroot Valley, a favorite haunt of Hollywood stars who maintain vacation homes in the area. Adventurers can opt for a white-water river-rafting

© Triple Creek Ranch

Triple Creek Ranch, Montana

© Kelly Gorham

Triple Creek Ranch, Montana

excursion, whereas serious anglers can partake of the Blue Ribbon trout streams of the Bitterroot River.

Amenities abound here: Guest cabins feature wood-burning fireplaces, hot tubs, stocked wet bar, a refrigerator, satellite television with DVD/VHS players, air-conditioning, and room service. A variety of accommodations is available to suit different budgets.

As one might expect, guests dine in a superb setting with gourmet meals prepared by master chefs. There's a complimentary wine service and a fully stocked top-shelf bar to help you ease into happy hour.

Come winter, guests may enjoy numerous sports adventures including snowshoeing, downhill skiing, and cross-country skiing on groomed trails. Christmas comes alive with the spirit of the season: Guests can enjoy hot cocoa by the fireplace. If you want to experience the bracing cold and the clear azure of the Big Sky state in winter, a horse and guide will be at the ready down at the corral, anxious to take riders past snow-laden meadows in search of a spectacular overview.

Triple Creek is truly a unique and inspired property, one that will create memories to last a lifetime. For vacationers looking for the ultimate in a pampered ranch getaway, this just might be your place.

**Triple Creek Ranch**
5551 West Fork Road
Darby, MT 59829
Phone: (406) 821–4600
Fax: (406) 821–4666
E-mail: tcr@bitterroot.net
Web site: www.triplecreekranch.com

**Managers:** Wayne and Judy Kilpatrick

**Accommodations:** Capacity, 48; 20 total units plus lodge suites; accommodations vary from the modest Cedar cabins to the opulent Sapphire and Stage Stop mountain cabins. All cabins and suites, however, afford guests a high level of luxury amenities such as king-size beds, fireplaces, fully stocked bar, satellite television and DVD player, and daily housekeeping. Luxury cabins feature king-size log-post beds, steam showers, and private hot tubs.

**Meals:** Rates include 3 sumptuous daily meals and picnic lunches at guests' request. The menu varies weekly, but suffice it to say it is always adventurous. A sample menu might include breakfast selections of strawberry french toast, Florentine Eggs Benedict, and chocolate chip pancakes. The lunch menu might feature pan-seared Idaho trout with almonds, sage, and saffron sauce; mandarin orange salad with mixed greens; and barbecued lobster sandwich. And for dinner, herb and tomato soup and Flathead Lake whitefish cakes for starters, an heirloom summer bean salad, and for entrees, seafood risotto, cocoa nib–raised Oregon rabbit, and dry aged beef tenderloin. Their dessert menu is equally sumptuous. Amazing!

**Activities:** A truly unbelievable array of choices: horseback trail rides and arena lessons, swimming in a heated pool, hiking, photography, fly-fishing lessons, tennis, white-water rafting, mountain biking, ATV riding, cattle drives. Winter downhill and cross-country skiing, snowshoeing, snowmobiling.

**Amenities:** Outdoor heated pool, tennis court and exercise facility, individual hot tubs in select cabins and a hot tub near the remaining cabins, putting green, helicopter pad, mountain-bike rentals, complimentary cocktails and house wines, room service, wood-burning fireplaces; some cabins with kitchens or kitchenettes

**Special Programs:** Children under 16 are allowed only if the entire ranch is rented; otherwise, this is an adults-only facility. Vintners Series, a culinary and wine-tasting extravaganza combining the exceptional talents of the Triple Creek chefs with visiting Vintners staff. Wine seminars, DVD player, wine pairing and food seminar, 4-course dinners with matched wine selections, and farewell reception. Inquire for rates and dates.

**Rates:** $$–$$$$$ full American plan. Rates include all meals, snacks, cocktail and wine service, use of facilities, fly-casting lessons, horseback riding, tennis, putting green, and much more. Some activities, such as ATV rides, snowmobiling, white-water rafting, and scenic river floats, available at additional expense.

**Credit Cards:** Visa, MasterCard, American Express, Discover

**Season:** Closed November, March, and April

**Getting There:** Nearest commercial airport, Missoula. Highway 93 to Darby to Highway 473; ranch is located just off the highway. Airport transportation to the ranch available.

**What's Nearby:** The Bitterroot Valley area offers many museums, restaurants, and specialty shops and is well worth the visit.

# WHITE TAIL RANCH

Ovando, Montana

The White Tail Ranch lies on the border of the Bob Marshall Wilderness area of western Montana. Though not as famous as the Yellowstone National Park, "The Bob," as it is known throughout the state, is regarded by many as a true jewel of the Rockies. If a place far away from the crowds that flock to Yellowstone in the summer is something you desire, you will find peace, tranquility, and an abundance of untrammeled nature here at the White Tail.

Managers Bob and Carol Blanchard are native Montana ranchers, raised in the traditions of western hospitality. Working with recent new owners Joel and Sandy Jewett, the couple has maintained the attention to detail and friendliness that has characterized the White Tail Ranch for decades. They are here to serve you in a gracious and friendly fashion befitting this historic and lovely property.

White Tail Ranch began as an outfitting business, eventually expanding to encompass the variety of experiences and options of a full-fledged guest ranch. The overall feel is of simplicity and rusticity, but with carefully chosen appointments that make even the most persnickety city folk feel comfortable and at ease. The guest cabins are cozy structures arrayed along the banks of the trout stream that cuts through the property. They afford guests lovely views of the surrounding mountains as well as a sense of privacy. The beds have Pendleton Wool covers, and the bedside tables are fashioned from pack boxes, giving the rooms just the right feeling of authenticity and Old West style.

The century-old main lodge houses the dining room and common areas, where guests congregate and socialize. An old-fashioned dinner bell calls the guests to meals, but guests also have the option of dining family style in the privacy of their own cabins. The simple, home-cooked meals are steeped in western culinary traditions and are complemented by home-baked breads and desserts.

Guest activities are organized in an informal fashion. If horseback riding is your desire, you can explore to your heart's content on all-day rides or ease into the rigors of the trail with shorter loop trips. Hiking, bird-watching, and mountain-bike touring are other favorite activities. Guests who are looking for exhilaration can take a white-water rafting trip; those who prefer more solitude can dip a line in Salmon Creek, which runs through the property, or try the challenging eddies of the famed Blackfoot River.

Winter visitors can choose from dogsledding, cross-country skiing, snowshoeing, and snowmobiling. Spring and fall offer particularly fine wildlife viewing and a chance to see Montana's lovely wilderness unfold in fields of wildflower or fantastic autumn displays. This part of Montana abounds with white-tailed deer, red fox, and bald eagles, so keep your eyes open and your binoculars close at hand.

In the evening, guests can settle in and relax amid a delightful array of parlor games, an extensive library, or join a sing-along at the piano. Enjoy a campfire with your family or just stare up at the huge sky filled with twinkling stars—more, perhaps, than you've ever seen in your life. For a special treat, inquire about visiting a Native American pow-wow meeting.

**White Tail Ranch**
82 White Tail Ranch Road
Ovando, MT 59854
Phone: (888) 987–2624
Fax: (406) 793–5672
E-mail: info@whitetail.com
Web site: www.whitetailranch.com

**Owners:** Joel and Sandy Jewett

**Accommodations:** Capacity, 50. 11 total units. Guests stay in comfortable cabins along the banks of Salmon Creek. All rooms feature private baths. All have electric heat.

**Meals:** 3 daily seatings served family style or buffet style. Vegetarian and special diets accommodated on request.

**Activities:** Complete horse program with daily trail riding and arena instruction. Trails meander through gentle meadows and steep mountain trails with striking views. Mountain biking, hiking, bird-watching, fly fishing on the Blackfoot River, float trips. Anglers may inquire about guided trips on pristine trout waters. Additional activities at nearby Cooper Lake. Winter season includes cross-country skiing, snowshoeing, and guided or unguided snowmobiling. Dogsledding and sleigh rides, too.

**Amenities:** Hot tub, outdoor recreational facilities (badminton, croquet, volleyball, arena roping), library, parlor games, sitting room in main lodge

**Special Programs:** Children's program offered during the day; kids take part in hikes, arts and crafts, games, swimming, and trail rides. Babysitting available with advance notice.

**Rates:** $$–$$$ full American plan. Reduced off-season rates, reduced children's rates for ages 6–14. Minimum 3-night stay.

**Credit Cards:** Visa, MasterCard, American Express, Discover. Personal checks and traveler's checks accepted.

**Season:** Closed March through April

**Getting There:** Nearest commercial airport, Missoula (60 miles west) or Helena (75 miles southeast). Airport transfer available at additional cost.

**What's Nearby:** Missoula, 1 hour's drive west, is a charming college town with art galleries, restaurants, and shopping.

# 71 RANCH

Elko, Nevada

For those who grew up dreaming of riding the range with Gene Autry—or, for that matter, Jack Palance—the 71 Ranch is your kinda place. An authentic working ranch for more than a century and one of the most historic ranches in all of Nevada, the 71 is the perfect place to be transformed from a "city slicker" into a fledgling cowpoke.

Founded in 1879, the 71 derived its name from one of the owner's original brands. By 1900 the ranch was among the biggest outfits in Nevada. It became well-known throughout the region for the quality of its purebred Hereford cattle and its imported stock of Shire draft horses. Year after year, the 71 has weathered the

71 Ranch, Nevada

vagaries of climate and of roller-coaster cattle markets, staying true to its original purpose: the raising of quality beef cattle.

As a guest, you get to take part in that mission as a bonafide ranch hand. You will ride alongside real cowboys, doing chores such as moving cattle through pastures, doctoring, vaccinating, sorting, gathering, and branding. You may be called on to ride for hours hunting down strays and bringing them back to the herd. This is real cowboy work, done on real ranch horses, with a genuine purpose in ensuring the welfare of the 71 Ranch herd.

Horses are assigned according to the rider's skills, and you may ride several horses during your stay, depending on activities. Safety, of course, is a concern: Guests are led through the basics of staying safe on horseback and go through a training program that amounts to Cowboy 101; courses offered daily. Nothing is staged for

the benefit of guests, so the day's activities relate directly to the actual operation of the ranch.

But don't expect your vacation to be all work and no play. The pace here is relaxed, with time set aside for recreational activities such as barn dances, barbecues, and, if the guests elect, honing one's cowboy credentials in the practice pen. Other recreational pursuits such as fishing, clay pigeon and target shooting, and trips to a variety of historic sites or to Elko, the epicenter of cowboy poetry, allow you to take a day off.

The Ellison family has a real affinity for the cowboy and ranching lifestyle, and they make it their goal to share in their passion with guests. The folks here are genuine and warm, the cowboys well-mannered and interested in imparting their hard-earned know-how to visitors. Spring is a particularly good time for those wanting to share in the ranch work; the cows are calving and the cowboys are busy sorting, gathering, doctoring cows, and moving pairs to summer pastures. Short cattle drives of a day or less are common, and every day offers new adventures.

Summers are a little less hectic, as the cows have now settled into fresh pastures and the calves are growing more independent. This is an ideal time for families looking for a more leisurely ranch experience. By fall, things once again grow busy as the cattle drives commence once again, cattle are sorted for market, and the laying in of hay and feed for winter occupy the days.

If you are looking for a real adventure and want to satisfy your dreams of living life like a real cowboy, the 71 Ranch is a great place to spend a vacation. Unfortunately, unlike a real cowboy, you won't be able to draw your wages at week's end. However, what you will gain in experience and lifelong memories will far outspend the money you put forth to become a part of this great Western ranching tradition.

---

### 71 Ranch
HC 64 Box 6
State Road 229
Deeth, NV 89823
Phone: (866) 717-7171; (775) 753-6745
Fax: (775) 738-3320
E-mail: cowboys@71-ranch.com
Web site: www.71-ranch.com

**Owner:** The Ellison Family

**Accommodations:** Guest capacity, 12. Bunk in the recently remodeled 100-year-old ranch headquarters lodge or stay in privacy in the adjacent 2-room "Buckakroo" cabin. Private rooms sleep from 2 to 4 persons. Ranch rooms are simply furnished, with knotty-pine wall paneling and simple furniture of a distinctively western style. It's not the Hilton but still quite comfortable, especially after a long day's ride!

**Meals:** "Ranch cooking with gourmet flair" is how the ranch literature describes meals at the 71. Down-home ranch cooking might be more accurate, but the simple meals are prepared with care, from the homemade baked pastries served at breakfast to the barbecued ribs served for supper. Breakfast rides and dinner rides are a regular part of the festivities at the 71; those with special dietary requests can be accommodated with advance notice.

The ranch doesn't hold a Nevada liquor license; guests may bring their own beverages for personal use.

**Activities:** The 71 is a genuine Nevada cattle operation and one of the most historic ranches in all of Nevada. Ranch work, done the traditional way on horseback, is a big reason people come here from all over the United States, and the world. Horseback riding and cattle work, both in the arena and out in the pasture, are the main activities. Guests join in work such as moving, sorting, doctoring, gathering, branding, and just about any other tasks performed on a real ranch. You can also learn cowboy skills, such as roping and team penning, the latter involving separating cattle from a herd and moving them down the arena into a pen.

In the evenings the ranch holds social events such as barn dances, and there is often downtime to play ranch games such as pitching horseshoes, games on horseback, hay-wagon rides, clay pigeon and target shooting, volleyball, and yard games. Guests can also take a day off and make a trip to historic and scenic sites in the area, and there is a planned evening trip to the casinos of Elko.

Nearby Elko offers a variety of off-site activities, from hiking, biking, fishing, boating, cross-country and downhill skiing in winter, to gaming and cultural events. Ask for help in planning an extra day or two of vacation time off the ranch.

**Amenities:** The 71 is a true working cattle ranch; do not expect the kinds of resort amenities featured in other properties in this book. That said, the ranch does have computer services and e-mail services available to guests; it also has basic conference facilities for small corporate get-togethers.

**Special Programs:** As a true working ranch, the 71 restricts guests to children over the age of 8; there are no provisions for younger children. Special "family" weeks, with less taxing activities, are held for guests with young children; others weeks are best suited to older children, teens, and adults. No structured children's program.

**Rates:** $–$$ American plan. Guests stay for a full week (6 nights).

**Credit Cards:** Visa, MasterCard, Discover. Checks and cash also accepted.

**Season:** Open year-round

**Getting There:** Located 27 miles east of Elko, Nevada. Most guests fly to Elko, with free shuttle service provided to the ranch. Salt Lake City and Boise, Idaho, are both 250 miles, with rental cars available.

**What's Nearby:** Elko, home to the annual winter Cowboy Poetry Gathering, one of the most interesting and fun cultural events in the West. Enjoy real cowboys and wannabe cowboy poets reciting their works, performing in skits, selling authentic cowboy and western crafts, and performing traditional western music (inquire for dates).

# THE BISHOP'S LODGE RANCH RESORT & SPA

## Santa Fe, New Mexico

New Mexico has an entirely different feel and appeal compared to its neighboring western states. The influence of Hispanic and Native American culture stretching back over centuries is strong here and reflected in everything from the apparel to architecture to art. Even the food is distinctively different than one is likely to encounter in, say, Montana or Colorado, with green chile, posole, and tortillas being standard fare at tables and restaurants across the state.

So it is no surprise that the Bishop's Lodge Ranch Resort & Spa has a decidedly different feel and flare than most of the other guest ranches in this book. Once

the private retreat of Bishop Jean Baptiste Lamy, the Bishop's Lodge was solely owned and operated by the family of James R. Thorpe from 1918 to 1998. Since its sale, it has been under corporate management, and many feel that the standards of service and quality have slipped. Still, it is hard to beat the intrinsic charm of the historic adobe buildings so characteristic of Santa Fe, its beautiful natural setting amid 450 acres of pinon and juniper woodlands, its proximity to the shops, museums, restaurants, and galleries of Santa Fe, and the allure of its wonderful spa. One only hopes that the new owners will restore the traditions of gracious service that helped make this one of New Mexico's most highly regarded resorts.

If one gets past the sometimes indifferent service, however, one is sure to enjoy this remarkable property. ShaNah, the resort's spa, offers a full array of spa amenities, including six indoor treatment rooms, two outdoor private massage gardens, an outdoor Japanese Watsu pool, whirlpool, fitness center, and hair salon. Guests can indulge themselves in such services as facials, waxing and shaping, body treatments, and Ayurvedic treatments, or get active with yoga, Pilates, and aerobics classes. For those who consider spa treatments to be an important part of their vacation, you'll find few places with finer facilities. By the way, ShaNah means "vitality and energy" in Navajo—another nod to the region's culture and heritage.

More a resort than a guest ranch, Bishop's Lodge nevertheless offers a number of activities traditionally associated with a ranch visit: There are miles of hiking and horseback riding trails to be explored, for instance. Nearby excursions such as hot-air ballooning (a staple in New Mexico, which hosts the largest ballooning festival in the country), golf, and winter cross-country and alpine skiing can all be arranged. Other off-site activities include Jeep tours, fly fishing, motorcycle rentals, and visits to the many cultural attractions found in Santa Fe.

Back at the lodge, guests can enjoy outdoor barbecue cookouts at scenic Vista Point, test their aim at the skeet- and trap-shooting range, or simply lounge by the lovely outdoor pool, which offers spectacular views of the lushly landscaped grounds and the nearby Sangre de Cristo Mountain Range. For active tennis players, the facility offers tennis courts,

instruction, and a pro shop. Parents in need of a little quiet time can take advantage of a babysitting service and a seasonal children's program.

Once the family reconvenes, there are a number of shared activities to be enjoyed, too, such as lawn games, evening movies, arts and crafts, and of course, meal times. As one might expect, the dining experience relies heavily upon New Mexican cuisine, but with innovative "nouveau Mexican" twists. Fine dining is enjoyed in the Fuentes (Spanish for "fountains)" Restaurant and Bar, which is richly decorated in Southwestern-style pine furniture and artifacts and features Navajo rugs and cozy fireplaces. An outdoor terrace offers views of the mountains and the Tusuque Valley. One can also enjoy poolside service from the Oasis Bar & Grille, open during the summer and fall months.

Listed on the National Register of Historic Places, the Bishop's Ranch Resort & Spa is a fine way to become acquainted with Santa Fe, one of the most culturally wealthy cities in the United States. It is particularly well-suited as a romantic getaway for couples, a honeymoon hot spot, and a place for families comfortable with setting their own schedules and exploring both within the confines of the resort and arranging self-initiated excursions throughout this delightful Southwestern city.

---

**Bishop's Lodge Ranch Resort & Spa**
P.O. Box 2367, Bishop's Lodge Road
Santa Fe, NM 87501
Phone: (800) 419–0492; (505) 983–6377
Web site: www.bishopslodge.com

**Owner:** Interstate Hotels & Resorts

**Accommodations:** Guest capacity, approximately 250. Guests stay either in the historic Central Lodge or in one of a dozen

The Bishop's Lodge Ranch Resort & Spa, New Mexico

newer lodges of various ages on the property. Many guests seem to enjoy the guest rooms of the Central Lodge particularly, due to the historic nature of the building and its authentic architecture. If one of the traditional rooms or suites in the Central Lodge doesn't fit your space requirements, there are a number of larger, more modern rooms, suites, and villas available, including the regal and roomy "Presidential Suite," with 2,000 square feet of space, 3 bathrooms, 3 fireplaces, and Jacuzzi tub in the master bedroom. For a more modest but still homelike atmosphere, inquire about the 1-, 2- and 3-bedroom vil-

las, which offer spacious vacation home–style layouts and modern appliances and amenities.

All rooms feature Southwestern-style furnishings; some have balconies and fireplaces.

**Meals:** Meals are billed separately from lodging. Dine in simple elegance at the Las Fuentes Restaurant and Bar, whose menu features "Nouveau Mexico" cuisine, a fusion of traditional New Mexican cuisine and culinary school–inspired innovation, along with a number of dishes one would simply categorize as "gourmet." A sample dinner menu might include roasted red pepper soup, goat cheese phyllo parcels, and snow crab cakes, for starters. Entrees such as Montana Elk Strip loin, pepper-encrusted filet mignon, Maine sea scallops, and pan-seared halibut are characteristic.

Those visiting Santa Fe will wish to sample some of the area restaurants, especially for lunch or dinner. You may also dine at the informal Oasis Cafe during the summer and fall months. Also offered are cowboy breakfast rides and outdoor barbecues.

**Activities:** Swimming in the resort pool; tennis, with clinics and private instruction; guided horseback riding for adults, teens, and older kids; pony rides for children; exercise classes; lawn games; arts and crafts for families; spa services. Off-site activities from golf to ballooning to Jeep tours and other sightseeing excursions.

**Amenities:** Full-service spa offers a variety of services, from yoga and Pilates to massage, facials, hairstyling, manicures, etc. Regular daily shuttle service to Santa Fe's historic Main Plaza. Modern conference facilities for meetings, corporate retreats, and special occasions.

**Special Programs:** Comprehensive and reasonably priced children's program for kids ages 4 to 11 (and younger, with a parent or babysitter). Includes hiking, playground time, and swimming. Evening sessions sometimes feature campfires and storytelling.

**Rates:** $$–$$$$ Activities and meals are charged to the final bill. Daily, per-person resort fee covers scheduled activities such as yoga, Pilates, tai chi, and any compli-

mentary family programs. Also included is unlimited access to the fitness center, swimming pool, Jacuzzi, tennis courts, hiking trails, and business center. This fee also includes parking, unlimited local phone calls, in-room high-speed Internet access, in-room coffee service, bottled water each day, in-room chips and salsa on your day of arrival, daily newspaper delivery, and scheduled shuttle service to and from the Santa Fe Plaza.

A number of package vacations are offered, allowing guests to couple their visits with off-site recreational and cultural activities. The golf package, for instance, allows one to enjoy a daily round at the Marty Sanchez Golf Links; the Georgia O'Keeffe New Mexico Vacation Package includes two tickets to the Georgia O'Keeffe Museum, as well as complimentary breakfasts each morning and free shuttle service to the Santa Fe Plaza. Also popular are Spa Discovery Packages, which include credits to be used at the famous ShaNah Spa.

**Credit Cards:** Visa, MasterCard, American Express, Discover

**Season:** Open year-round

**Getting There:** The Bishop's Lodge is 10 minutes from historic downtown Santa Fe; most guests fly into Sante Fe, but it is also within a reasonable driving distance of Albuquerque. Rental car not necessary, as hourly shuttles are provided to Santa Fe; those wishing, however, to explore the surrounding area or ski may wish to rent a vehicle.

**What's Nearby:** Santa Fe, with its galleries, shops, restaurants, museums, and frequent cultural events

# THE LODGE AT CHAMA

## Chama, New Mexico

A sportsman's paradise best describes the Lodge at Chama. Imagine befriending a wealthy billionaire and being invited to his private fishing and hunting lodge. Upon your arrival, he treats you and your partner to cocktails at a privately stocked bar. Afterward, you settle in for a gourmet meal. You're shown to your private room. The bed is luxurious, with wonderful high-count sheets and big, plush pillows. The bathroom is huge and luxurious, with thick terry robes for your comfort. In the morning you eat a sumptuous breakfast. Your host greets you, and you are introduced to his personal fishing guide. For the next three days, you are schooled in the intricacies of fly selection, insect recognition, trout habitat, and casting technique. One afternoon, you spend time on the shooting range blasting clay pigeons to dust while your spouse takes spa treatments in an intimate salon; the next, you go horseback riding in a seemingly endless wilderness.

Minus the billionaire host, that about encapsulates the Lodge at Chama experience. This is a premier resort property located on 36,000 acres of Jicarilla-Apache–owned land in the San Juan Range of Northern New Mexico. This state's motto is "the Land of Enchantment," and you'll certainly feel as though you've been transported to a fairy-tale land of outdoor recreation and the ultimate in personal care and attention during your stay at the Lodge.

Considered to be one of the world's finest outdoor-sporting retreats, the Lodge at Chama hosts impressive hunting get-togethers in season. Guests hunt both upland birds (including wild turkey) and big-game animals including deer, elk, bear, and even buffalo.

If hunting isn't your thing, however, there are ample chunks of the year when you can simply watch and observe the native wildlife in a truly secluded wilderness setting. The 27,000-square-foot lodge building is spectacular: The exterior is a mix of smooth pine logs and impressive stone masonry; inside, the two magnificent Great Rooms feature 36-foot-tall cathedral ceilings and soaring view windows; in the evening you'll relax in front of a 20-foot-wide see-through fireplace. All the furnishings are luxurious and inviting.

The huge rooms are appointed with plush lounging chairs and ample private decks where you can enjoy cocktails or private get-togethers. Two new suites feature see-through fireplaces, satellite TV, and French doors that open onto outstanding vistas.

Brandy and Belgian chocolates will await you at bedside after a long and luxurious bath in the huge whirlpool and sauna. If you didn't get the workout you anticipated during the day, you can also visit a full-scale health spa with the latest in exercise equipment.

Winter guests are every bit as pampered. Those who visit during the cold months can expect a wide variety of daily diversions, from cross-country skiing and snowshoeing to ice fishing and snowmobiling. The winter offers an especially good time to elk-watch, as the animals have moved down from the high country to inhabit the lowland pastures of the ranch.

**The Lodge at Chama**
P.O. Box 127
Chama, NM 87520
Phone: (505) 756–2133
Fax: (505) 756–2519
E-mail: reservations@lodgeatchama.com
Web site: www.thelodgeatchama.com

**Manager:** Frank Simms

**Accommodations:** Capacity, 40. 22 total units. Guests rooms and suites located in the architecturally wonderful lodge. Oversize rooms feature private baths, satellite TV, posh linens and towels, complimentary brandy and chocolates, guest robes, and private decks. Four new luxury suites include see-through stone fireplaces and large sitting rooms.

**Meals:** True gourmet meals served in the lodge dining room. Breakfast buffet includes fresh-baked pastries, muffins, and coffee cakes; breakfast meats, eggs, French toast, and more. Gourmet picnic lunches provided for your daytime adventure. In the evening, guests are welcome to the fully stocked bar and select dinner wines from an extensive wine list. The evening dinner menu varies daily, based on the availability of seasonal and fresh ingredients and the whims of the lodge's executive chef.

**Activities:** Guided day-fishing trips; fly-fishing school (additional cost); full use of the Lodge facilities, including spa facility; sporting clay shooting, hiking, ranch tours, wildlife viewing, photography, horseback riding. Wintertime snowshoe-ing, cross-country skiing, snowmobiling, ice fishing, wildlife observation. All activities are guided and most are charged separately.

**Amenities:** Complimentary bar, full-service spa, exercise room, satellite TV, huge sitting rooms with overstuffed chairs

**Special Programs:** Bear-, elk-, deer-, and bird-hunting in season. Children must be at least 12 years of age, except by special arrangement.

**Rates:** $$$$$ American plan option, with activities included. Meals, complimentary bar, use of spa and conference facilities included in basic rate. Activities package includes the above, plus fishing, sporting clays, hiking tours, ranch tours, wildlife viewing and photography excursions.

**Credit Cards:** Visa, MasterCard. Personal and corporate checks accepted.

**Season:** Open year-round

**Getting There:** Nearest commercial airports: Colorado Springs, Durango, and Albuquerque. Ranch airstrip accommodates private aircraft. The Lodge is located 100 miles north of Santa Fe, 90 miles west of Taos. Inquire for specific directions.

**What's Nearby:** Taos, with its famed native arts and fine arts community, approximately 1½-hour drive. Durango, a vibrant western town located in the southwest corner of Colorado, offers excellent winter skiing at Durango Winter Resort. Summer guests, ask about the Cumbres and Toltec Railroad, which departs from Chama and winds through the mountains of southern Colorado.

# LOS PINOS GUEST RANCH

### Cowles, New Mexico

Simplicity and intimacy characterize Los Pinos Guest Ranch, a historic property set in the natural and beautiful Sangre de Cristo Range of the southern Rocky Mountains. If you're looking for a great escape from the pressures, schedules, and deadlines of modern living, this is the place.

Situated at an elevation of 8,500 feet, Los Pinos commands wonderful views of the surrounding peaks that are among the West's better-kept secrets. Its subalpine elevation means warm summer days of idyllic 70-degree weather and cool nights, when the thermometer often drops into the 40s—so pack plenty of sweaters! You'll definitely want them when you stray away from the lodge to gaze at the stars in one of the clearest skies you'll ever experience.

Los Pinos first began catering to adventurers in the 1920s. Throughout its ninety years of operation, the ranch has remained delightfully small, accommodating up to twelve guests. Imagine having your own summer retreat in the Rockies; that's the atmosphere you'll find at Los Pinos.

Guests stay in any one of four modest log cabins, each equipped with antique claw-foot tubs (perfect for soaking), front porches, and wood-burning stoves. The rooms are absent of phones and televisions, adding to the blissful serenity of the experience. You won't miss them, as there are many pleasant diversions to occupy your time. The sparkling waters of the upper Pecos River and the Mora River teem with trout and offer excellent opportunities for fly fishing. You can arrange guided half-day trips on the rivers, or you can take a rod along on a high-country horse ride that takes you to lovely high-alpine lakes.

The motto at Los Pinos is, "Where the road ends and the trails begin." A fitting expression, as trail riding and nature hikes constitute the main organized activities here. Guests take part in half- and full-day trail rides through the forests and alpine meadows of the Santa Fe National Forest. In early spring the lower elevations unfold in carpets of wildflowers, and the profusion of color continues through the summer as the growing season works its way up to the higher elevations. Wildlife abounds in this setting: On any given day, you may encounter deer, elk, coyotes, and rabbits; you may even see a furry marmot whistling at you from his perch in the upper-alpine tundra. Bird enthusiasts will be pleased with the variety of species to be found at the ranch or viewed from mountain trails.

Guests can stretch their legs on any number of excellent trails accessible from the ranch. Several choice alpine lakes can be reached on Forest Service trails. Or you may laze on the wide porch of the main lodge with a good book plucked from the McSweeney family library.

Dining is informal, but the service is superb. A full breakfast and four-course dinner (by candlelight) are served in the main dining room. Day hikers and riders can request packed sack lunches for the trail. If you wish to have an evening cocktail or glass of wine with your meal, you are welcome to bring your own.

There are any number of special places described in this book, all with special attributes that set them apart. At Los Pinos, those attributes can best be described as simplicity and gracious service in an outstanding and serene setting.

**Los Pinos Ranch**
Route 3, P.O. Box 8
Terrero, NM 87573
Phone: (505) 757–6213
(winter address, October–May)
P.O. Box 24
Glorieta, NM 87535
Phone: (505) 757–6213
Web site: www.lospinosranch.com

**Owner:** The McSweeney Family

**Accommodations:** Capacity, 12; 4 total units. Guests stay in 4 aspen-log cabins, each equipped with a front porch, private bath, and woodstove. The main lodge, built in 1912, is the central gathering spot. A large screened porch with rustic furniture provides the perfect setting for relaxation and socializing.

**Meals:** Simple, healthful foods characterize meals at Los Pinos; fresh-baked breads, soups, and homemade desserts accompany the evening meal, with sack lunches provided for daytime activities.

**Activities:** Horseback riding, hiking, birdwatching, and fly fishing are the main activities here; guests take great pleasure in nature observation and simple relaxation in this amazingly breathtaking mountain setting.

**Amenities:** Ranch library, with an emphasis on nature books and local history; piano in the main lodge. The ranch emphasizes serenity over luxury.

**Special Programs:** Children over 6 years of age are welcome; no formal children's programs. Parents are responsible for their kids' entertainment and activities, but most kids gladly take part in the informal ranch activities at Los Pinos, enjoying the pleasures of experiencing and exploring nature.

**Rates:** $$ Lodging and dining included in basic costs; horseback riding and guided fishing charged additionally. 2-night minimum stay. Children's rate. Discounts for full-week stays.

**Credit Cards:** None accepted. Cash or check, please.

**Season:** June through September

**Getting There:** Nearest airport, Albuquerque. Map and directions available.

**What's Nearby:** Santa Fe, with its fabulous art galleries, museums, restaurants, and native craft shops; nearby towns of Chimayo, Las Vegas (New Mexico), and Taos; all merit day trips. Also, the Pecos Historic Park.

# 1000 ACRES RANCH RESORT
## Stony Creek, New York

Long rides on horseback with panoramic views. The excitement of a professional rodeo. A good-old, down-home barbecue. Wyoming? Montana? Try the Adirondacks. That's the home of 1000 Acres Ranch Resort, a classic guest ranch

located in the "Old East." This historic upstate New York vacation getaway opened in 1942. Founders Jack and Esther Arehart envisioned a guest ranch vacation on the Hudson River that would rival anything available out West. Their son, Jack, still maintains the 1000 Acres Ranch Resort in that original spirit.

Over the years, the ranch has expanded greatly. The original lodge has been augmented with guest cabins, motel units, and a second ranch house to offer a more complete experience. But the same spirit that motivated the Areharts lives on, bold as ever.

As with most guest ranches, the emphasis here is on a horseback vacation. Each day, guests enjoy trail rides through some of the finest scenic riding trails that can be found in this beautiful area of the country. Beginning riders have nothing to fear: the expert ranch hands at 1000 Acres are used to "tenderfoots" and will go out of their way to make you feel comfortable. Even children can get in on the fun with carefully supervised pony rides back at the corral.

Among the high points of any 1000 Acres Ranch stay is the weekly rodeo, complete with standard events like calf roping, team roping, and barrel racing. Over Labor Day weekend, cowboys from throughout the region turn out to perform in a professional-caliber contest. If one doubts that true cowboys reside in upstate New York, one need only know that many-time world champion bull rider Harry Tompkins got his start in these parts, working as a dude ranch wrangler; now he is in the Pro Rodeo Hall of Fame.

Of course, horses and rodeos are only part of the action here. Golfers can tee off on the nine-hole course on the property, located right on the banks of the Hudson River. Guests can take a boat trip on the Hudson or paddle their own kayaks down this gentle stretch of the river. Anglers can fish for trout and small-mouth bass—the fishing is some of the best to be found in these parts. And if that's not enough, you

can play tennis, basketball, volleyball, or just lounge around one of three heated swimming pools.

Adults can enjoy socializing at nightly cocktail parties, then join in the fun learning country, swing, and line dances to the sounds of country and western bands. The ranch even has a regular singing cowboy.

Supper time is the part of the day when families reconvene to review the day's activities. As one would expect, the menu tends to feature hearty western fare, from barbecued St. Louis–style ribs and grilled chicken to an outdoor cookout with steaks and grilled catfish.

Holidays are special occasions: There is no end of reasons for the staff here to create special events. Memorial Day, Labor Day, Columbus Day, fall foliage, Thanksgiving. Some families come back year after year to make 1000 Acres Ranch part of their holiday tradition. Most of these special-event weekends feature horse-drawn carriage rides, country line dance lessons, wine and cheese parties, pizza parties, and more.

Fall is an especially beautiful time at 1000 Acres and offers something you won't see farther west—the lovely changing of the fall leaves that cover the hills in the full palette of reds, oranges, yellows, and greens. It is truly spectacular and well worth gambling your vacation time to try to view the deciduous trees at the peak of their fall vibrance. After a leisurely four-hour horseback ride, guests are greeted by a special event: a real chuckwagon cookout on the trail.

If you happen to live on the East Coast and want a convenient destination with all the hospitality of a western dude ranch, only closer to home, 1000 Acres has everything you're looking for—and then some.

## 1000 Acres Ranch Resort

465 Warrensburg Road
Stony Creek, NY 12878
Phone: (800) 458–7311; (518) 696–2444
E-mail: info@1000acres.com
Web site: www.1000acres.com

**Owner:** The Arehart Family

**Accommodations:** Guests either stay in private cabins or motel-like lodge rooms. Cabins overlook the Hudson River, or request adjoining rooms for extended families when staying in the Sequoia lodge. Duplex cabins for large families also available. Deluxe-view accommodations in the Buena Vista cabin, which overlooks the entire property from atop a high hill.

Most cabins have double or queen-size beds, some with single beds as well. Accommodations tend toward the inexpensive, not the luxurious, but feature private baths, phones, and wall-to-wall carpeting, refrigerators, and air-conditioning.

**Meals:** Three meals served daily in the spacious dining room or the pool-side pavilion. Meals are hearty, with typically western fare such as grilled steaks, grilled chicken, and seafood as the main dinner entrees, and a luncheon buffet and breakfast bar with egg dishes cooked to order. Far from gourmet, but very satisfying, particularly for families with young children who balk at the unfamiliar.

**Activities:** Amateur rodeo, boating, kayaking, dancing, golfing, horseback riding, river rafting (off-site), supervised kids' pony rides, volleyball, basketball, weekly amateur rodeo, nature hikes, arts and crafts for kids and teens, and more

**Amenities:** Golf course, indoor pool, two outdoor pools, hot tub, nightly entertainment, tennis courts, youth playground, conference meeting facilities

**Special Programs:** Supervised kids' program with regularly scheduled activities and dedicated counselors. Special "family bonus week" and "back to school week" offer reduced rates and special activities; holiday celebration events.

**Rates:** $–$$ American plan. Rates vary according to accommodations. A very affordable guest ranch vacation, especially considering the number of amenities and activities offered.

**Credit Cards:** Visa, MasterCard. Personal checks accepted.

**Season:** May through October.

**Getting There:** Stony Brook is located in Adirondack Park, east of Interstate 87 in upstate New York. It is within an easy half-day drive of New York City, Boston, Montreal, Canada, and a number of major eastern cities.

**What's Nearby:** Located in the Adirondack Mountains of upstate New York

# PINEGROVE RANCH
# AND FAMILY RESORT

Kerhonkson, New York

New York's Catskill Mountains have been a favorite vacation destination for nearly a century, making the Pinegrove Ranch a relative newcomer to the neighborhood. The ranch was opened in the early 1970s by owners Dick and Debbie Tarantino, who made this place one of the finest resort destinations in the region. Over the years, the ranch has earned numerous awards as an outstanding travel destination, including a "Ranch of the Year" award from *Family Circle* magazine.

Located in the ruggedly beautiful Sawangunk Mountains, Pinegrove abounds with wild animals, including migratory waterfowl, fox, raccoon, quail, pheasant, and a variety of songbirds. You'll definitely want to spend some quiet time exploring the ranch's 600 acres of rural countryside via the trails that intertwine across the rural landscape.

Pinegrove maintains a great string of well-trained and gentle horses, including a number of pure-bred quarter horses and Appaloosas. Rides depart hourly on ample trails offering outstanding mountain views. If you've always wanted to play cowboy, ask about participating in an authentic cattle drive on the ranch. Kids can take part in a Junior Wrangler program, as well as in daily supervised activities for children of all ages.

Pinegrove is a large resort, accommodating as many as 350 guests. As one might expect, the menu of daily activities is extensive, and the facilities offer a variety of choices to round out your vacation experience. Guests can enjoy lake and river fishing, paddleboating, rock-climbing practice on the ranch climbing wall, tennis, swimming, and more. Golf at preferred rates is available at a nearby course. Evening entertainment includes a cocktail lounge with live music, square dances and line dancing, a western saloon, a pool bar, a nightclub with an evening show, and hayrides. Kids will especially enjoy the indoor and outdoor waterslides!

It is nearly impossible to list all the activities offered at Pinegrove. Suffice it to say, you will always find something fun and entertaining to do here.

If you are interested in a winter getaway, Pinegrove accommodates guests who come to ski, ice skate, and enjoy snowtubing. With two slopes, it is the ideal place for neverevers to get their "ski legs" without the crowds and the hustle-bustle of expensive winter-resort destinations. Be sure to ask about the learn-to-ski package. Alpine and cross-country ski equipment is available, so all you have to bring is your mittens!

Pinegrove is as much a full-service resort as a guest ranch, and even people who are a little horse-phobic will find plenty to do here. This is an ideal location for families who have a diversity of interests and who want to spend time together—and time apart.

---

**Pinegrove Ranch and Family Resort**
P.O. Box 209
Kerhonkson, NY 12446
Phone: (800) 346–4626
Fax: (914) 626–7365
E-mail: info@pinegroveranch.com
Web site: www.pinegroveranch.com

**Owners/Managers:** David O'Halloran and family

**Accommodations:** Capacity, 350. Guest rooms in the motel-style main lodge are large, comfortable, and modern. Sizes vary from small rooms, with double beds suitable for couples with small children, to large suites featuring king and double beds, ideal for larger families. Rooms include TVs, phones, air-conditioning, and private baths.

**Meals:** 3 sit-down meals daily, extensive menu at each meal; twice-weekly barbecue lunch in summer. Complimentary snack bar serving fries, franks, burgers, and such until midnight.

**Activities:** Daily trail rides depart on the hour; riding instruction and evening riding seminars with video review; young children can take pony rides in the riding arena. Weekly cattle drive—inquire, as spaces may be limited. Fishing in a stocked pond. Boating on the ranch's lake. Other outdoor activities include tennis, swimming in a heated pool, archery, basketball, volleyball, miniature golf and boccie ball, and shuffleboard. Indoor recreation room. Evening entertainment and activities include nightclub show, country dancing, disco dancing, pool bar, live entertainment, and music. Winter activities include skiing, ice skating, sledding and tubing, sleigh rides, with equipment and ski lessons available.

**Amenities:** Game room, kids' playground, nursery, cocktail lounges and bars with live entertainment or deejays, sporting equipment, complimentary snack bar, indoor and outdoor pools with waterslides, day camp for kids, and plenty of planned activities

**Special Programs:** Kids' Junior Wrangler riding program, nursery, kids' activities, and teen programs

**Rates:** $$–$$$ full American plan. All-inclusive package includes accommodations, meals, free snack bar privileges, cocktail parties, horseback riding, Junior Wrangler program, and use of all facilities. Reduced rates for 1-week stays; reduced kids rates depending on ages; reduced off-season rates; group and senior discounts.

**Credit Cards:** Visa, MasterCard, American Express, Discover

**Season:** Open year-round

**Getting There:** Nearest airports in New York (Kennedy) and Newark, N.J. Located 100 miles north of New York City, 1 mile west of Kerhonkson off Route 209. Nearest train: Poughkeepsie, 25 miles.

**What's Nearby:** Guests may wish to explore the lovely towns of the Catskill Mountains, with numerous restaurants, stores, and antiques shops.

# RIDIN-HY RANCH RESORT
## Warrensburg, New York

When the Second World War ended, Americans released their pent-up desires to travel by heading West. Postwar Americans identified with the Hollywood cowboys, who personified strength and independence and freedom. If a family couldn't find the means to head out West, they slipped out of the Bronx or Queens or New Jersey and headed for the next best thing: Ridin-Hy Ranch Resort, as western a guest ranch as you'll find out East.

Currently, Ridin-Hy remains much as it did during its heyday back in the 1950s. A year-round family resort, Ridin-Hy is owned and operated by Andy and Susan Beadnell (Susan's father started the resort in 1940). It has grown over the years but still maintains the optimistic spirit and family-friendly fun that made it a success half a century ago.

Ridin-Hy is situated in the lush forest lands of the Adirondack State Park on the shores of Sherman Lake. From the lake, one can enjoy lovely views of the Adirondacks, which rise amid one of the largest public parks in the continental United States—more than six million acres!

Most of the guests here are repeat customers. Some have even created their own Web sites documenting their annual visits. It's not unusual to meet fellow guests who have been coming here since they were children and now bring their own kids and even grandkids.

What is it about Ridin-Hy that inspires such loyalty? First off, a staff that strives to make everyone comfortable and has loads of fun doing their jobs. The activities list is extensive: horseback riding, pony rides for young kids, a weekly professional rodeo and weekday guest "showdeos," fishing in either of two lakes and a rushing stream, and your choice of water activities on Sherman Lake. Enjoy a paddleboat or rowboat ride, swim in the lake or heated outdoor pool, go waterskiing or wakeboarding, or simply lounge around before taking a trip to the spa. There are also dozens of summertime games, including volleyball, softball, horseshoes, archery, or tennis on either of two private courts. As one visitor commented, "There are way more activities than anyone needs to be doing on vacation."

Even in winter the ranch bustles with activity. Favorite pastimes include cross-country skiing, sleigh rides, ice-skating, snowmobiling, alpine skiing, snowtubing, and horseback riding.

This is a large place, capable of hosting 195 guests. With more than 800 acres of private land, however, it's not difficult to find a serene place to spread out a picnic lunch and enjoy a relaxing afternoon with loved ones. When you decide it's time to socialize, there are square dances, barbecues, hayrides, and other evening activities.

This is a family-run and family-friendly ranch resort with high standards of professionalism honed over decades spent in the guest ranch business. If you live back East and want a taste of the West without the hassle of long-distance travel, you may find that you need go no farther than Ridin-Hy.

---

**Ridin-Hy Ranch Resort**
P.O. Box 369
Sherman Lake
Warrensburg, NY 12885
Phone: (518) 494–2742
Fax: (518) 494–7181
Web site: www.ridinhy.com

**Owners/Managers:** Susan and Andy Beadnell

**Accommodations:** Guest capacity, 195. Rooms vary from motel-like lodges to chalet-style pinewood cottages that can accommodate anywhere from 1 to 3 families. All have full bathrooms. The main lodge, which provides a focal point for most indoor activities, features a large stone fireplace in the lounge and a central dining room with outstanding views of the lake and the Adirondack Mountains.

**Meals:** 3 meals served daily. Families dine together in the main dining room. Menu selections are ample and varied. Nightly snacks include pizza parties, hot-dog roasts, and sundae parties. Weekly smorgasbord dinner with sliced ham and turkey.

**Activities:** Horseback riding includes arena instruction and mountain-trail rides, with slow, moderate, and fast-paced groups. Pony rides for children also available. Weekly professional rodeo and midweek guest "showdeos." Lake fishing and river fishing, waterskiing, rowboats, paddleboats, and swimming in the lake and in a heated indoor pool. Evening planned activities including dances, games, theme dinner, and outdoor sports. Nearby golf and alpine skiing in winter. Additional winter activities: snowmobiling, cross-country skiing, sleigh rides, and ice-skating, snowtubing, and horseback riding.

**Amenities:** Guest spa, whirlpool bath, cocktail lounge, game room, water sports supplies, and boats

**Special Programs:** Organized children's program with children's activity director. Babysitting available. Supervised pony rides for kids ages 7 and under.

**Rates:** $–$$ full American plan, with or without horseback riding. 2-night minimum stay. Off-season discounts and children's rates, by age.

**Credit Cards:** Visa, MasterCard, American Express, Discover. Personal checks accepted.

**Season:** Open year-round

**Getting There:** 65 miles north of Albany, 15 miles north of Lake George off Route 87

**What's Nearby:** Lake George, Stone Bridge Caves, Fort William Henry, and Lake Placid

# ROARING BROOK RANCH AND TENNIS RESORT

Lake George, New York

Although the emphasis of this book is family vacations, we realize that some readers may be looking for a place to hold a conference. Although the Roaring Brook Ranch and Tennis Resort certainly will appeal to family vacationers, it is also one of the largest guest-ranch resorts in the country and an exceptional place to hold a conference, especially if you are looking for plenty of recreational activities and a western flavor.

This ranch can accommodate 300 overnight guests and as many as 1,000 conference attendees. With more than 17,000 square feet of seminar and exhibit space, Roaring Brook has hosted corporate groups ranging from the General Electric Corporation to Chevrolet to Lincoln Logs, Inc. These groups, and many more, have found Roaring Brook Ranch to be an ideal location for a memorable and productive getaway.

That said, let's talk about family vacations. Roaring Brook has long been a favorite destination for New Yorkers and New Englanders who appreciate its picturesque locale on beautiful Lake George, a particularly scenic lake that has been a favorite vacation destination for more than a century. One reason for its popularity is the plethora of off-site attractions, including Fort Ticonderoga, the racetrack at Saratoga,

Howe Caverns, and "the Million Dollar Mile," a popular shopping mall.

The ranch has more than adequate facilities to please the most pampered guests, including a workout room, five tennis courts (two lighted), an indoor pool and sauna, two outdoor pools, and an extensive children's program. The horse program is particularly appealing; the ranch recruits actual cowboys from out West to serve as wranglers.

Each evening features entertainment and musical performances, often including national television and recording artists. There are two cocktail lounges, where guests mingle with one another and enjoy the live entertainment.

There are a number of recreational activities, too. You can shoot billiards, play table tennis, badminton, archery, horseshoes, or take part in a spirited game of beach volleyball.

Besides the usual ranch activities, this ranch also has an excellent tennis program. Players of all levels can improve their game with the help of the resident pro, and there are always plenty of guests ready and willing to toe up at the service line and test your ground stroke.

With close to 500 acres of property, the ranch is also a good place to take a contemplative walk and do some bird-watching. This is a full-service resort, one that you will likely want to return to over and over again.

---

**Roaring Brook Ranch and Tennis Resort**
Route 9N South
Lake George, NY 12845
Phone: (800) 882–7665; (518) 668–5767
Fax: (518) 668–4019
E-mail: mail@roaringbrookranch.com
Web site: www.roaringbrookranch.com

**Manager:** George Greene

**Accommodations:** Capacity, 300. The ranch features 140 rooms in 9 motel-like buildings. Rooms include private baths, heat and air-conditioning, TVs, and phones. Many have decks. Suites also available on a limited basis.

**Meals:** Meals are served in a commodious dining room. Expect a varied menu. Guests may also dine in the coffee shop.

**Activities:** 4 scheduled horseback rides depart daily in groups of 25 to 30; riders are grouped by experience. For new riders, group lessons are available. Tennis is probably the single most popular pastime here, and there are 5 courts, which are always in use. Other activities include swimming, recreational sports, and a popular shoreline cruise on Lake George.

**Amenities:** Workout facilities, 5 tennis courts, nightly live entertainment, indoor pool and sauna, direct-dial telephones, color cable TV in each room, nearby golf, activities director and children's counselors, many nearby attractions and tours

**Special Programs:** Modest children's program in summer accommodates kids of all ages but is not formalized. Activities include arts and crafts, pony rides, and games. Most kids take part in activities side by side with their parents. Nursery available by arrangement.

**Rates:** $–$$ modified American plan, including breakfast and dinner. European plan also available (no meals). Activities such as horseback riding, lake tours, and others charged additionally.

**Credit Cards:** Visa, MasterCard

**Season:** Mid-May to mid-October. Conferences scheduled year-round.

**Getting There:** Nearest commercial airport, Albany. Most guests arrive in private cars. Ranch is located 2 miles south of Lake George, off I–87, about 200 miles north of New York City.

# ROCKING HORSE RANCH

## Highland, New York

There's something irrepressibly fun about this ranch, and it begins with the name. As one might expect from a place called Rocking Horse Ranch, this upstate mountain resort is a kid's paradise. But adults love it too, as there are few resorts, much less guest ranches, that offer as many things to entertain you and occupy your day as are available here.

One writer from the New York Post aptly described it as "the Club Med of Ranch Resorts." Here's just a sampling of the many activities you can choose from: Ride the giant waterslide, ride a horse, pilot a paddleboat, water-ski, shoot an arrow on the archery range, play a round of miniature golf, play a game of beach volleyball, play tennis, take an aerobics class. Oh, and then at night, you can country dance, disco dance, see a comedian or magic show, take a hayride, watch movies on the big-screen TV, sing karaoke, or play parlor games in the game room.

Whew! Tired already? The Rocking Horse is also a great place to relax and do nothing at all. With 500 acres, it's relatively easy to find a quiet place to just stretch out and take a nap. There are two gigantic outdoor pools with waterslides for kids and adults, a wading pool for small children, and plenty of lounge furniture to kick back on. There's also lakefront property, great for watching your family learn to water-ski, and if the weather should turn cloudy, you can lounge beside the indoor pool.

Despite its playful name, the Rocking Horse takes its equine program quite seriously. There are more than one hundred horses on the ranch, giving a ratio of one horse to every four guests. Riding instruction is available. Riders are tested for ability and divided into groups of like aptitude. One-hour rides depart from the stable throughout the day. Small children can enjoy supervised pony rides in the arena.

Return guests know that losing weight is a difficult, if not impossible, proposition, as the meals are sumptuous and all-you-can-eat. The chefs update the menu regularly to ensure that you won't be selecting from the same items with each visit, but you can always count on fresh fruit and vegetables and high-quality breads and desserts.

The high standards set by the Rocking Horse have earned it numerous awards, including the AAA 3-Diamond Award and the Mobil 3-Star Award, both reflective of a high level of service.

If you take the best of western hospitality and mix it with the most efficient and attentive New York savoir faire, the result is the Rocking Horse Ranch, one of the premier resort properties in North America. If you are like most guests, you'll want to come back again and again and again.

**e Ranch**
**12528**
**691–2927**
Fax: (845) 691–6434
E-mail: info@RHRanch.com
Web site: www.RHRanch.com

**Owner:** The Turk Family

**Accommodations:** Guest capacity, 400. 120 units divided between two motel-style buildings, the Oklahoma and the Main Lodge. Rooms sleep up to 6 people and include TVs, air-conditioning, private baths, direct-dial telephones, and daily maid service. Deluxe rooms available with king-size bed, sofa bed, minifridge, and coffeemaker.

**Meals:** Menu varies on a regular basis but always includes hearty American staples. Huge breakfast buffet, ice-cream socials, 24-hour coffee-and-sandwich shop, cocktail parties in licensed bar.

**Activities:** Horseback riding, tennis, water-skiing, paddleboating, beach and water volleyball, court sports (basketball, handball, boccie, etc.), softball games, miniature golf, rifle and archery shooting, nature hikes, evening entertainment, and much more. Extensive winter activities include on-site skiing, giant tube run, ice skating, and horse-drawn sleigh rides.

**Amenities:** 2 outdoor pools, wading pool, water slides, court sports facilities, private lake, shooting gallery, archery range, video arcade, children's playground, parlor games, fitness room, sauna rooms, nightclub. Handicap accessible with special needs accommodated. Indoor/outdoor climbing wall and kids' "Fun Barn."

**Special Programs:** Supervised kids' programs and activities. Day-camp program for children 4 to 12 includes sports, hikes, games, swimming, crafts, treasure hunts, and more. Children's nursery and babysitting available.

**Rates:** $$–$$$ full American plan. Reduced prices for kids ages 4–15, no charge for children under age 4. Special preseason summer rates; off-season rates.

**Credit Cards:** Visa, MasterCard, Discover, American Express

**Season:** Open year-round

**Getting There:** Located in the mid-Hudson Valley off New York Thruway (I–87), 1½ hours north of New York City. Nearest commercial airport: Stewart International, Newburg, N.Y., about 20 miles from the ranch.

**What's Nearby:** West Point Military Academy; Roosevelt's Hyde Park Mansion

# CATALOOCHEE RANCH
## Maggie Valley, North Carolina

North Carolina's Great Smoky Mountains are one of the most beautiful and serene places in all of North America, a fact not lost on the original founder of the Cataloochee Ranch, Tom Alexander and his wife, Judy. Tom was a timber cruiser who appraised timberlands in the Great Smoky range. When the company he worked for went bankrupt during the Great Depression, Tom negotiated some land in exchange for back pay and opened a fishing camp.

The young couple opened the original Cataloochee Ranch in the newly created Great Smoky Mountains National Park, then relocated to the current site near Burnsville. They converted a sturdy stone-and-log cattle barn into the main ranch house and went about making improvements that included the first ski area south of Virginia. At present, this graceful North Carolina landmark ranch remains a sparkling jewel overlooking the rolling hills of Maggie Valley. With an elevation of 5,000 feet, it provides Southerners and other sojourners with a cool, pleasant place to while away their summer vacations. The ranch is still owned and operated by the family, principally Tom Alexander Jr., daughters Alice Aumen and Judy Coker, and their husbands, Tom Aumen and Rick Coker.

The ranch has 1,000 mountaintop acres that adjoin the Great Smoky National Park, giving guests unlimited opportunities to hike and explore. Outdoor recreation is a big industry in this part of North Carolina, particularly fishing, golfing, and river rafting. Golf fiends can tee up at any of six nearby courses, offering them a full week of golf, if that is their desire. If casino gaming is your desire, you can visit Harrah's Casino on the nearby Cherokee Indian Reservation. But be sure to give yourself plenty of time for on-site activities, especially horseback riding. It is still the ideal way to experience the lovely Smoky Mountains.

The Cataloochee is a pleasant mixture of western and southern hospitality and culture. A favorite entertainment is watching traditional mountain-clogging demonstrations or taking in a performance by local mountain musicians singing traditional and new folk songs.

In the evening you can join in the singing around the campfire, take a pleasant ride in the hay wagon, or take a sunset dip in the heated outdoor pool. The ambience here is informal, so guests can take things at their own pace. You can cram a full day of activities into your schedule or settle in with a good novel under a shade tree and work through it undisturbed.

The Cataloochee is a modest-size place as far as guest ranches go. With a maximum of sixty-five guests, the ranch allows for lots of personal attention. The Alexander family has close to three-quarters of a century of experience taking care of vacationers, and they do it with consummate grace and southern charm. You'll look hard to find a guest ranch that comes this close to perfection.

---

**Cataloochee Ranch**
119 Ranch Drive
Maggie Valley, NC 28751
Phone: (800) 868–1401; (828) 926–1401
Fax: (828) 926–9249
E-mail: info@cataloocheeranch.com
Web site: www.cataloocheeranch.com

**Owners/Managers:** Tom Alexander Jr., Alice and Tom Aumen, Judy and Rick Coker

**Accommodations:** Capacity, 65. 19 total units. Guests stay in well-appointed log cabins, some with kitchenettes, or in guest rooms in the original main ranch house. All cabins have fireplaces, refrigerators, coffeemakers, radios, and private bathrooms. The lodge is the main gathering spot here; the interior features antique furniture, a huge stone fireplace, and rustic chandeliers fashioned from oxen yokes. Conference facilities for 40 available.

**Meals:** Although some ranches claim to offer homemade foods, this one really delivers. Fresh local trout, Virginia ham, ranch-raised garden vegetables, and beef fill out the dinner menu; even the breads and desserts are homemade. Guests enjoy weekly outdoor barbecues, and the ranch hosts an annual fall wild-game feast featuring venison and elk.

**Activities:** Daily horseback rides on the ranch and in the Great Smoky National Park; creek and river fishing, pack trips, recreational games, swimming, hiking, tennis. Float trips and white-water rafting trips on nearby rivers and golfing at 6 local courses. Winter sports at nearby Cataloochee Ski Area.

**Amenities:** Conference facilities, children's playground, heated swimming pool

**Special Programs:** No formal children's programs, but kids are welcome. Children must be at least 6 years of age to ride horses.

**Rates:** $$–$$$ modified American plan. Meals and accommodations included;

horseback riding at additional cost.

**Credit Cards:** Visa, MasterCard, American Express. Personal checks accepted.

**Season:** April to November, late December to March

**Getting There:** Located 35 miles west of Asheville off I–40 and U.S. Highway 19. Nearest commercial airport in Asheville, N.C.

**What's Nearby:** White-water rafting, craft shops, golf courses, and recreational and historical sites, including the Appalachian Trail, Biltmore Estate, Blowing Rock, Blue Ridge Parkway, Cherokee Indian Reservation with Harrah's Casino, Chimney Rock Park, Ghost Town in the Sky, Grandfather Mountain, Linville Caverns, Mountain Heritage Center, Tweetsie Railroad, and the Cataloochee Ski Area.

# CLEAR CREEK RANCH
## Burnsville, North Carolina

Word has gotten out about North Carolina's western mountains and the fantastic vacation opportunities they provide. If you're considering a vacation in the Tarheel State, we might suggest the Clear Creek Ranch, nestled in the peaceful Blue Ridge Mountains.

Owned and operated by Rex Frederick and his wife, Aileen, Clear Creek was the realization of the couple's dream of opening a western–style guest ranch in this most southern of states. That they did in 1995, and Clear Creek has been gaining in stature as a guest-ranch destination ever since. Part of the allure is its location on

the edge of the Pisgah National Forest, which offers more than 80,000 acres of forested trails, streams, and mountain vistas. Adding to that is the Fredericks—as warm and inviting a couple as you are likely to find.

Clear Creek offers the usual menu of guest-ranch activities and then some. Horseback riding, of course, is a mainstay at the ranch. Guests can ride morning and afternoon, and those who stay all week can enjoy an all-day picnic ride on the Buncombe Horse Trail. The ranch also has a heated pool and hot tub with fabulous views of the Blue Ridge Mountains. Fishing is available in their stocked trout pond, or "real pros" can wet their line in the South Toe Ridge, where you match wits with rainbow and brown trout.

Golfers will appreciate the opportunity to tee it up on one of the finest mountain golf courses anywhere, just a three-minute drive from the ranch. Thrill seekers can indulge in white-water rafting offered twice weekly, or "tube" down the South Toe, which is done almost daily. Craft tours to local artists are offered, and children just love the weekly gem-mine trip.

In addition, Linville Falls, Grandfather Mountain, and Mt. Mitchell are all just a short drive from the ranch, and the magnificent Biltmore Estate in Asheville is about an hour's drive away.

Situated at an elevation of 3,200 feet, the Clear Creek Ranch is refreshingly cool in summer, and in springtime it is a showcase of spectacular flowers: dogwood, forsythia, tulips, daffodils, and magnificent weeping cherry trees. Fall brings a brilliant wonderland of color. Special rates are available in spring and fall, and senior citizens enjoy extra discounts on weekdays.

Evenings offer a variety of activities including karaoke singing, line dancing, a marshmallow roast, a special "Margarita" night, or a hayride and steak cookout down on the river. An end-of-the-week highlight is the Saturday rodeo and chicken-and-ribs cookout, as well as a hootenanny put on by the staff.

The overall ambience of the ranch is one of casual fun and down-home friendliness. For families or singles, it's a perfect escape, with exceptional facilities in a beautiful setting and a friendly staff eager to do all they can to make your vacation a memorable one. A return rate nearing 50 percent tells us that they have been successful!

## Clear Creek Ranch
100 Clear Creek Drive
Burnsville, NC 28714
Phone: (800) 651–4510; (828) 675–4510
E-mail: CCRDUDE@prodigy.net
Web site: www.clearcreekranch.com

**Owners/Managers:** Rex and Aileen Frederick

**Accommodations:** Guests stay in one of 3 buildings adjacent to the main lodge. The structures are all new, carpeted, air-conditioned, and heated, but have a rustic charm. All buildings have covered porches with rocking chairs and offer spectacular views of the mountains. The lodge is comfortably furnished with a massive stone fireplace and a fine library of the latest books, which are available to guests.

**Meals:** All meals are served family style with the exception of cookouts and picnics on the trail. Expect homemade soups, fresh-baked breads, pastries, and well-prepared main courses. Beer, wine, and mixed drinks are available to guests in the old-fashioned "cantina."

**Activities:** Horseback riding, hiking, fishing, tubing, and swimming, plus the fun of the weekend rodeo. Nearby golf and white-water rafting are available but do cost extra.

**Amenities:** Hot tub, heated pool, game room with pool tables and Ping-Pong, conference center for business meetings

**Special Programs:** During summer, special activities are offered for children 5 years and older.

**Rates:** $$–$$$ American plan. Rates include lodging and all meals and activities except those noted. Reduced rates are offered for children and seniors. Rates lower in November.

**Credit Cards:** Visa, MasterCard. Personal checks preferred.

**Season:** April 1 through the end of November; children's programs June through August

**Getting There:** Located 45 miles north of Asheville, North Carolina, which is also the site of the nearest airport. Pickup is available at a small additional cost.

**What's Nearby:** Biltmore Estate, Grandfather Mountain, Linville Falls and Caverns, and a wide variety of local artists. Rafting and golf available at additional cost.

# EARTHSHINE MOUNTAIN LODGE

## Lake Toxaway, North Carolina

Earthshine Mountain Lodge suffers from a bit of an identity crisis: Is it a country inn, a bed-and-breakfast, a guest ranch, or a family resort? Regardless of what it may be called, it is a wonderful departure from the conventional vacation destination.

Surrounded by the rolling hills of western North Carolina's Blue Ridge Mountains, Earthshine is indeed a picturesque place. Imagine a natural-wood lodge set in a broad, open pasture and surrounded by lovely forests that show their bold colors from spring until late fall. That pretty much summarizes the eye appeal. But there's more to Earthshine than meets the eye.

Hosts Marion Boatwright and Kim Heinitsh liken a visit to Earthshine to a fairy-tale trip to Grandmother's farm. The seventy-acre property abuts the Pisgah National Forest, providing endless miles of trails to explore. Two favorite hikes take walkers to the scenic French Broad River and the delightful King's Falls.

Just like at Grandma's farm, guests are welcome to help with feeding the animals and are encouraged to learn traditional farm crafts such as cider pressing, wool spinning, blacksmithing, and more.

Earthshine also offers more contemporary skills development, offering physical challenges that will excite young and old. One unique activity is the Flight through the Tree Tops Zip Course, an obstacle course in the treetops that tests one's nerve and agility—in a relatively safe setting, of course. There's also a climbing wall and a ropes course.

Earthshine is not, strictly speaking, a ranch. It is more akin to a farm. While it once offered a horse program, that activity has been discontinued (you can, however, take part in nearby off-site horseback riding). In its place, the Earthshine has increased its experiential programs, which include the Pioneer Heritage Festival, in which guests become apprentices in frontier crafts such as blacksmithing, yarn making, gem mining, apple cider pressing, and more. There's also the "Cherokee Times," where guests travel back in time to a secret encampment to learn traditional Native American basketry, grind corn, and even master the art of tomahawk throwing. There are also activities based around the abundance of natural waterways here.

The lodge is a handsome hand-constructed cedar-log building with magnificent views of the surrounding mountains. Visitors stay in tastefully decorated guest rooms that reflect the regional country charm of the Appalachian Mountains. You'll really enjoy the patchwork quilts, log beds, and comfy rockers that adorn these family-friendly lodgings.

In the evening the entire family will enjoy sing-alongs, mountain dances, Native American ceremonies, storytelling, and lots of fun games. For those who simply can't stay put, the folks at Earthshine can help guide you to exceptional whitewater rafting, tennis, fly fishing, golf, and mountain biking. Don't forget to allow enough time to take a scenic drive through the Blue Ridge Parkway, one of America's most scenic roads.

---

**Earthshine Mountain Lodge**
1600 Golden Road
Lake Toxaway, NC 28747
Phone: (828) 862–4207
E-mail: earthshine@citcom.net
Web site: www.earthshinemtnlodge.com

**Owners/Managers:** Marion Boatwright and Kim Heinitsh

**Accommodations:** Capacity, 41. 13 total units. Guests stay in the main lodge, which has private rooms, each with bathrooms, private balconies, quilts, and log furniture, or in the Sunrise Cottage, which has 3 family suites. 8 guest rooms have Little House on the Prairie sleeping lofts, a great place for kids. Kids may also stay a night in the barn loft, an experience they won't soon forget.

**Meals:** The Earthshine offers an all-inclusive stay including 3 daily meals.

Fruit and beverages included throughout the day. Emphasis is on fresh, healthful foods (vegetarians gladly accommodated). Fresh local trout is a specialty. Sunday brunch.

**Activities:** Barnyard tours, cookouts, nature hikes, unique and challenging ropes course and climbing wall. Off-site tennis, golf, river rafting, mountain biking, sightseeing.

**Amenities:** Large, shaded porch with "hidden hammocks" for relaxing, catfish pond for fishing, rock fireplaces, gift shop, conference center. Wheelchair accessible.

**Special Programs:** Earthshine goes out of its way to entertain and teach young children as well as curious adults. As an environmental-education center, the facility hosts upward of 2,000 school-age kids each year, providing programs focused on earth science and history. Destination: 1840 is a living-history experience that puts kids in touch with early pioneer life; the Success program teaches self-accomplishment and team interaction through the High Ropes Course; Earth Explorers is a science program that capitalizes on a mystical trip in which children encounter odd mythical creatures. If interested, be sure to ask more about these fascinating educational programs. Babysitting available for young children.

**Rates:** $$ full American plan. Reduced rates for kids and toddlers. Some activities are charged additionally.

**Credit Cards:** Visa, MasterCard, Discover

**Season:** Open year-round

**Getting There:** Nearest airport, Asheville (35 miles). Lodge is located in Transylvania County off Highway 64, 11 miles west of Brevard.

**What's Nearby:** River rafting, golf, Pisgah National Forest

# ASPEN RIDGE RESORT

Bly, Oregon

Aspen Ridge Resort offers vacationers the chance to visit and participate in a real working ranch while enjoying the refined creature comforts of a genuine resort.

Located in the mountains of central Oregon, the ranch began life in the 1850s. In 1992 plans to create a resort destination in which well-heeled visitors could take an active hand in daily ranch work came to fruition. Currently, hosts Steve and Karen Simmons welcome guests from throughout the world who are drawn to this unique and wondrous place.

Aspen Ridge Resort boasts 14,000 acres of broad pastures and thick stands of evergreen trees surrounded by the Fremont National Forest. It is an ideal place to raise cattle, and the ranch maintains a full-scale cow/calf operation with close to 1,000 head of commercial cattle. Activities tend to follow the ebb and flow of the ranching seasons; spring is particularly busy as cattle are shipped from the range in California and calving season begins. Guests may ride herd on the new arrivals, scattering cattle across meadows and occasionally doctoring cattle. Fences are mended, and the ranch is put back into tip-top operational shape.

Summer work often involves moving cattle to new pastures, weaning calves, and overseeing newborns, which begin arriving in August and continue to hit the ground through October. Guests are assured of plenty of opportunities to ride.

Fall is a good time to take in the Annual Lake County Fair and Rodeo, view the fall colors, and do some trout fishing. You may also be called on to help with gathering, separating, and shipping the cattle as the yearlings are prepared for market. In November the final gather takes place, and the cattle return to winter pasture in California.

Don't think, however, that it is all work and no play at Aspen Ridge. If playing cowboy loses its romance, you can break out your racquet and play tennis. Mountain biking is another favorite pastime as is wilderness hiking. Guests who like to fish can choose from many excellent and unspoiled fishing holes and streams.

Come winter, the cattle work is done. Guests strap on cross-country skis and explore thousands of acres in silent reverie. Those up for more raucous fun can head out on snowmobiles. Holidays are special times at the ranch, redolent of the spirit of the season.

Evening entertainment is homespun: Listen to the coyotes sing, watch the stars, or settle in with a good book. Occasionally, the ranch hosts a cowboy poet or balladeer, and guests are always welcome to demonstrate their own unique talents.

If you've always wanted to play at being a cowboy but are a little reticent about the primitive conditions that tend to characterize working ranches, you no longer have an excuse not to pull on your boots, pull down your hat, and saddle up your horse. This is the genuine item, but one with the genteel appointments that make it a great place to break in a "gunsel" used to the more urbane comforts of life in the big city.

**Aspen Ridge Resort**
P.O. Box 2
Bly, OR 97622
Phone: (800) 393–3323; (541) 884–8685
Fax: (541) 884–8685

E-mail: aspenridge@starband.net
Web site: www.aspenrr.com

**Owners/Managers:** Steve and Karen Simmons

**Accommodations:** Capacity, 40. An elegant log lodge with modern appointments and 4 commodious guest rooms form the centerpiece of the resort. Guests may also choose from 5 luxurious 1,200-square-foot cabins that house up to 6 people. Cabins include large kitchens, woodstoves, and bathrooms.

**Meals:** 3 meals are served daily in the ranch-house restaurant. Guests choose from a varied menu. Enjoy hearty country breakfasts, sandwiches, and salads. Dinners are the pride of the ranch—the boss barbecues choice beef, ribs, and chicken over mesquite coals on the back deck grill. Fresh-made desserts and baked breads. Cocktails and appetizers served in the Buffalo Saloon, open daily. Just passing through? The restaurant is also open to the general public.

**Activities:** Cattle work and horseback riding are the central activities here; take part in the actual workings of a true western cattle operation. Tennis, hiking, mountain biking, fishing, swimming. In winter, cross-country skiing and snowmobiling.

**Amenities:** Tennis courts, elegant lodge with antique furnishings, expansive guest quarters and cabins, cocktail lounge, swimming lake. A very civilized approach to a working-ranch vacation.

**Special Programs:** Ask about the fall rodeo in Lake County and special holiday celebrations on Thanksgiving, Christmas, and New Year's.

**Rates:** $$–$$$ European plan. Riding, dining, and fishing charged separately.

**Credit Cards:** None. Personal checks accepted.

**Season:** May through December

**Getting There:** Aspen Ridge Resort is located 18 miles southeast of Bly, off Highway 140.

**What's Nearby:** This is a secluded mountain property.

# BAR M RANCH AT BINGHAM HOT SPRINGS

## Adams, Oregon

Although most people think of the Pacific Northwest as a rainy land of thick evergreen forests, the eastern portions of Oregon and Washington are actually high-desert regions, with wide-open spaces and well-spaced stands of ponderosa pine peppering the rolling hills. It's in this environ that you'll encounter the Bar M Ranch at Bingham Springs, located in the Blue Mountains of eastern Oregon. The Bar M comprises 2,500 acres bisected by the Umatilla River, named for the local Native Americans who populate the region to this day.

Large grassland pastures provide perfect grazing for horses, and the Bar M takes great pride in their fat but fit riding string. Guests are encouraged to "partner up" with

Bar M Ranch at Bingham Hot Springs, Oregon

their horses, which are assigned for the week. Learn the basics of grooming and saddling; then head out on the trail with your new best friend!

The Bar M was first settled around the time of the American Civil War, and the original ranch house (built in 1864) provides the perfect testament to this ranch's long history. Updated to comfortably accommodate guests, the ranch house serves as the main dining area and is the place where guests tend to congregate and share laughter and good times after a day on the trail. A huge front porch and an indoor stone fireplace invite guests to kick back and relax.

For more than a century, folks have come to Bingham Hot Springs to soak in the mineral springs. You'll get to enjoy this spa-style luxury in the ranch's 40-by-60 foot pool, a great way to sooth sore muscles after a day of strenuous activity.

A favorite side trip is to visit the frontier town of Pendleton, home of the famous Pendleton Round Up and the Pendleton Woolen Mills. While there, be sure to take the underground tour, an adventure that will take you through nearly a half-mile of underground tunnels that facilitated commerce among the local businesses and also served as home to thousands of Chinese immigrants in the early days of settlement.

Back at the ranch, there are plenty of activities. Informal recreational games—including schoolyard favorites such as tetherball and volleyball, along with staples such as horseshoes, croquet, and badminton—invite spirited competition. You can also fish for trout in the Umatilla, participate in arena games on horseback, or go for a peaceful hike in the woods.

For guests who prefer leisurely fun to rigid schedules, the Bar M Ranch is a great choice.

---

**Bar M Ranch at Bingham Hot Springs**
58840 Bar M Lane
Adams, OR 97810
Phone: (888) 824–3381; (541) 566–3381
Fax: (541) 566–0100
E-mail: barmranch@eoni.com
Web site: www.virtualcities.com/ons/or/u/oruc501.htm

**Accommodations:** Capacity, 45. Accommodations vary from 8 guest rooms with shared baths in the Main Ranch House to 2 private cabins suitable for families. Homestead Lodge has 2-room suites, with a queen-size bed in the master bedroom and twin beds in the second sleeping room; also, a 3-room unit with queen, two twins, and a double bed and private bath. Brookside Cabin has 3 rooms, a queen bed and 3 twin beds, bathroom, and small refrigerator.

**Meals:** Country cooking emphasizes home-cooked ranch staples (beef, chicken, etc.), the occasional Mexican meal, fresh-baked breads and jams, fresh garden vegetables, and desserts. Weekly outdoor barbecue cookouts. BYOB.

**Activities:** Horseback riding is the main formal activity. The ranch has 45 saddle horses, ensuring that each guest has his or her own mount for the week. Overnight campout and lunch rides available. Riding instruction in the arena. Bingham Hot Springs is a favorite place to soak and relax. Fishing in the Umatilla River (equipment available). Private stocked fishing pond for kids. Dozens of recreational games such as Ping-Pong, tetherball, volleyball, basketball. Excursions to nearby Pendleton. Self-propelled boating on ranch pond. Evening campfires, sing-alongs, storytelling, barbecues, and barn dances in a real log barn.

**Amenities:** Hot-springs pool; main lodge with comfortable lounging furniture; coin-op laundry, ice machine, room refrigerators. No daily maid service.

**Special Programs:** Prefer children 6 and older; no formal children's program. Kids participate alongside their parents.

**Rates:** $$ full American plan

**Credit Cards:** Visa, MasterCard. Traveler's and personal checks accepted.

**Season:** Open year-round

---

## Pendleton Round Up

One of the most famous rodeos in America, the Pendleton Round Up began as an informal riding contest on the streets of town. Businessmen quickly realized that a festival would provide a great tourist draw, and the Round Up was born. Folks traveled from as far as Chicago and Seattle to see the earliest shows, which drew upward of 30,000 visitors.

At present, the Round Up continues to pull visitors from throughout the country and, indeed, the world. Held on a huge grass field on the Round Up grounds, the rodeo is as wild as the Old West ever was. In keeping with the heritage of the region, Native Americans from various tribes come to town to perform dances and ceremonies; many pitch tepees in the Indian Village. The event features daily parades, colorful costumes, a carnival midway, and non-stop entertainment.

**Getting There:** Bar M Ranch is 31 miles east of Pendleton, Oregon, and 45 miles south of Walla Walla, Washington. Horizon Airlines serves Kennewick/Tri-Cities, Pendleton, and Walla Walla Airports. Round-trip ground transportation from Pendleton airport available.

**What's Nearby:** Pendleton, home of the Pendleton Woolen Mills and the famous Pendleton Round Up Rodeo. Be sure to take the fun and fascinating Pendleton Underground Tour.

# ROCK SPRINGS GUEST RANCH

## Bend, Oregon

Rock Springs Guest Ranch was the dream of retired schoolteacher Donna Gill, who wanted to provide an outdoor classroom, of a sort, where parents and their children could share in a healthy, active, outdoor vacation. An extraordinary woman and world traveler, Gill owned and operated two other ranch properties, a girls' camp and the Indian Ford, before discovering her own Eden in the mountains of central Oregon.

Bend was a natural choice, given its outstanding scenery, fresh mountain air, and proximity to Oregon's main population center, Portland, a city renowned for its active and environmentally conscious citizenry.

Currently, Donna's nephew John and his wife, Eva, continue the Rock Springs Ranch tradition. One of the best features of Rock Springs is its children's program, which accommodates kids from ages four to twelve. An outgrowth of Donna Gill's years of work with children, the program utilizes full-time youth counselors to oversee the kids. Counselors participate alongside the children in activities ranging from horseback riding, swimming, team sports, and nature walks to arts and crafts and storytelling. A talent show put on by the kids for

the adults is one of the highlights of the week, along with a kid's campout and a Mexican piñata party. Hourly babysitting is available for children younger than four. As the ranch owners like to say, at Rock Springs, kids are guests, not merely the children of guests. Undoubtedly, this will be one of the most remembered vacations of your young children's lives.

While your kids are having a blast, you can find dozens of things to stimulate mind and body. Horseback riding, of course, is a summertime specialty. Trail rides offer scenic vistas of the giant volcanoes of the Cascade Range, some of the most spectacular peaks in the Lower 48. Small groups of six riders ensure the flexibility to stop and take lots of pictures.

The ranch also offers somewhat genteel suburban sports such as tennis (on two courts) or a round of golf with John Gill, who welcomes the opportunity to tee it up with guests at the Awbrey Glen Golf and Country Club, a private championship course and one of Oregon's premier golf-resort destinations.

The nearby Metolius and Deschutes Rivers provide anglers with world-class fly-fishing waters, or you can opt for the more serene shores of several large and well-stocked lakes. A local guide service can be employed to help you scout out the best waters and the proper lures and flies for the predominant species and the time of season.

After a day of activities, relax with a massage by a licensed massage therapist and get ready for a gourmet dinner featuring wild game. While the kids take part in evening activities with the counselors, adults get a chance to gather round the campfire to share stories, roast marshmallows, and relax tired bones.

In keeping with Donna Gill's educational intents, guests are invited to take nature hikes with a naturalist guide who will elucidate the native flora and fauna of Oregon's mountain region. Learn about the lives of Native Americans, whose culture was shaped by the verdant landscape, and the abundant wildlife of this particularly bountiful region of North America.

---

**Rock Springs Guest Ranch**
64201 Tyler Road
Bend, OR 97701
Phone: (800) 225–3833; (541) 382–1957
E-mail: info@rocksprings.com
Web site: www.rocksprings.com

**Owners/Managers:** John and Eva Gill

**Accommodations:** Capacity, 50. Cabins and condo suites with 2 and 3 bedrooms. Cabins include private entrance, sundeck, and bathroom adjoining each bedroom. The Owl's Nest and Killdeer Cabins, originally living quarters in old logging camps, were renovated for guests' comfort. Most cabins feature fireplaces, refrigerators, and wet bars.

Rock Springs Guest Ranch, Oregon

© Rock Springs Guest Ranch

**Meals:** Meals are served buffet style; a wide range of selections at each meal guarantees you won't tire of the offerings. Typically, guests may choose from select beef such as prime rib, native seafood specialties such as Pacific salmon, along with vegetarian entrees. Special diets accommodated. Fresh fruit, cookies, and lemonade always available in the main lodge to tide guests over between meals. Beer and wine service.

**Activities:** Guests can take advantage of dozens of lakes and streams near Bend, a popular fly-fishing destination. Be sure to bring a pole and tackle box. Horseback riding is done in small groups, assuring personal instruction and lots of flexibility. You'll enjoy excellent views of the Cascade Mountains. Weekly luncheon rides are also scheduled.

Hiking with a naturalist guide, tennis on the ranch's courts, guided canoeing trips. Nearby golf and white-water rafting. Be sure to go spelunking in the Central Oregon Lava Tubes and make time to visit the High Desert Museum, where Native American culture is mixed with natural history and animal exhibits—a truly inspired museum!

**Amenities:** Whirlpool, swimming pond, swimming pool, game room, licensed massage therapist, on-site photographer, conference facilities, tennis courts, half basketball court

**Special Programs:** Exceptional kids' program for children ages 4 to 12

**Rates:** $$$–$$$$ full American plan. Reduced children's and infants' rates. Off-season discounts.

**Credit Cards:** Visa, MasterCard, Diners Club, Discover, American Express

**Season:** Late June through August, Thanksgiving. Corporate retreats, conferences, and retreats scheduled throughout the off-season.

**Getting There:** Located 9 miles east of Bend, Oregon, approximately 3 hours' drive from Portland

**What's Nearby:** Golf on 30+ championship courses in and around Bend; High Desert Museum, a nationally acclaimed natural-history museum; the town of Bend, with shopping and dining; Oregon Lava Tubes, a fascinating set of volcanic blow holes that can be explored with a local tour company

# TRIPLE R RANCH
## Keystone, South Dakota

As a young man, Theodore Roosevelt left New York to go west, living a vigorous outdoor life on a family ranch in the Dakotas. The experience, which transformed him from a sickly city boy to a robust man, shaped the course of his life and his advocacy for "wild places."

Fortunately, South Dakota maintains those same restorative charms to this day.

The Triple R Ranch is located within the 27,766-acre Norbeck Wildlife Preserve and just a mile from the expansive Black Elk Wilderness Area, giving guests the chance to experience wilderness in its pristine majesty. Guests spend most days much as Roosevelt did, in the saddle, pursuing wild game (with a camera) and fishing in local waterways. And, of course, guests are always delighted to see Teddy himself at the national treasure, Mt. Rushmore, as well as to check on the progress of the huge sculpture of Crazy Horse that is being carved nearby. Plan as well on a visit to Custer State Park, home to large herds of native bison (the preferred name for buffalo).

Summers are comfortably cool and relaxed, thanks to the ranch's mile-high elevation. The air here is marvelously clean, with a hint of pine scent from the abundant forests that populate the land here.

Daily rides will take you to abandoned mining towns, interesting and odd geological sites (including the famed Outlaw Cave), and scenic overviews. Breakfast rides are a favorite way to get acquainted before hitting the trail; in the evening you'll thrill to the sight of the clear night sky, where you'll see more stars than you ever thought possible.

If you enjoyed the Kevin Costner film *Dances with Wolves,* you might like to know that many scenes from the film were made not far from the Triple R. You may tag along on an excursion to one of these sites.

Uniquely, the ranch owners, Jack and Cherrylee Bradt, have gone out of their way to make their property wheelchair accessible, truly making this a place that the entire family can enjoy. Guests with special needs are happily accommodated at the Triple R.

Visits include an evening "cowboy dinner," where you'll enjoy homespun meals much like those enjoyed by the cowboys who moved cattle into these parts a century and a half ago. The cowboy supper is followed by a rousing show and singing.

If your vacation designs include taking in the fabulous monuments of the Black Hills area, the wonderful wildlife of this truly wild state, and plenty of time in the saddle, the Triple R is your place. It's hard to imagine a place with so many fascinating things to see and do.

## Triple R Ranch

P.O. Box 124
Keystone, SD 57751-0124
Phone: (888) RRRANCH (777–2624);
(605) 666–4605
E-mail: rrrranch@sd.value.net
Web site: www.rrrranch.com

**Owners/Managers:** Jack and Cherrylee Bradt

**Accommodations:** Capacity, 18. Guests stay in cabins, each with private bath.

**Meals:** Home cooking based on robust ranch meals. Typical evening fare includes beefsteaks, barbecued ribs, and chicken. Meals served family style. BYOB.

**Activities:** Horseback riding and more horseback riding. Breakfast rides, barbecues, and lots of excursions, including all-day riding trips to Spokane Ghost Town, visits to the bison herds at Custer State Park, the Crazy Horse Memorial Monument, and an evening trip to see the lighting of Mt. Rushmore. Evening parties, cowboy talent shows.

**Amenities:** Simplicity characterizes the ranch. Rooms are simple but adequate and comfortable.

**Special Programs:** No kids' programs. The ranch is best enjoyed by mature children age 7 and up.

**Rates:** $$ full American plan. Nonrider rates, daily rates available.

**Credit Cards:** Visa, MasterCard. Personal checks accepted.

**Season:** May through October

**Getting There:** Triple R Ranch is located 25 miles from Rapid City off Highway 16A. Closest airport in Rapid City, 30 miles.

**What's Nearby:** Custer State Park, Mt. Rushmore, Crazy Horse Monument, gaming in Deadwood

# FRENCH BROAD
# OUTPOST RANCH
## Del Rio, Tennessee

If you live in Dixie, it may not be convenient to head for the mountains of Wyoming or Montana to enjoy a guest ranch vacation. If you'd rather stay closer to home, the Great Smoky Mountains of Tennessee offer a worthwhile alternative. Though the hills may not be as high and the trails as steep, the Great Smoky Mountains are, nonetheless, very picturesque and satisfying.

French Broad Outpost Ranch claims to be the only true dude ranch in the Great Smoky range. The origins of the ranch began with the current owners, the Gannon family. Desiring to live in the country and raise Arabian horses, the family purchased land along the French Broad River and began populating it with horses. Their original plan to sell the offspring proved a non-starter, as each horse born was precious to the family. So they decided that the best thing to do was invite guests to share in their equestrian love affair.

Naturally, the Gannons have both an affinity for the Old West and the Old South. The ranch is a synergy of both; the architecture of the lodge, for instance, borrows both from iconic western lodge design and the rural traditions of the southern hills that surround it. Recently, the family completed work on a western town complete with a saloon where guests can have libations and learn the latest country dance steps and traditional country square dances.

The lodge also has guest rooms where families can enjoy the atmosphere of the Old West. As the Gannons like to say, you'll feel like you've stepped onto the set of a John Wayne western! There are also private cabins offering seclusion and extra room for larger families to spread out without bumping into one another.

One of the nicest benefits of staying at the French Broad Outpost is that all activities and expenses, with a few small exceptions, are included in the weekly price. This includes horseback riding and two river-rafting excursions during your stay.

As one would expect from ardent horse fanciers, the Gannons have a horse program that may be among the best anywhere. Using the techniques of "natural horsemanship," a program that emphasizes understanding without coercion, the Gannons have trained their Arabians to be responsive and yet forgiving to guests. You will marvel at how these techniques work in practice and may get to see an exhibition of the marvelous training in the corral. Guests get to take part in the grooming and care of their horses—don't worry if you've never been around these big animals; the Gannons will teach you how to do things properly and safely. You will leave the ranch a more experienced rider, with a good basis for developing further skills if that is your desire.

Evenings include a variety of entertainment, including dances and bluegrass bands performing southern "mountain music." Downtime on the ranch can be spent relaxing on the big porch or taking part in athletic field games that may remind you of your old primary school days. When was the last time you competed in a good ol' three-legged race? Or an egg toss? Well, it's time for a little nostalgia and to show kids what young 'uns did before the advent of video games and skateboards.

For those who can't make it all the way to the West, you won't feel shortchanged by a stay at the French Broad Outpost Ranch. The scenery here is some of the best to be found in the South, the horses and cattle are just as real as they are in Montana, the food is excellent, and the memories will be just as vivid and heart-warming as they would if they were formed in Colorado. Plus, with the money you save on airfare, you might just be able to come back again next year!

---

**French Broad Outpost Ranch**
461 Old River Road
Del Rio, TN 37727
Phone: (800) 995–7678; (423) 487–3147
Fax: (423) 487–5224
E-mail: info@frenchbroadriver.com
Web site: wwwfrenchbroadriver.com

**Owner:** The Gannon Family

**Accommodations:** Guest capacity, 40. Ranch offers lodge rooms in its newly built "Wild West Town," each with a capacity of 4. Also, 4 private 1- and 2-story cabins with king- or queen-size beds, double beds or bunk beds for children, bathrooms, and kitchens. Cabins sleep 2 to 8 guests each. All rooms have air-conditioning and heaters.

**Meals:** Three daily meals served family-style; emphasis is on southern regional cooking, such as southern fried chicken, grilled steaks, and outdoor barbecues.

**Activities:** Summer activities include horseback trail rides, cattle drive, team penning competitions, white-water rafting (included in price), guided river fishing, guided hiking, and overnight pack trips. Nearby golf and hot-springs resort. Winter activities are limited but include downhill skiing and ice skating.

**Amenities:** One of the most intriguing features of the ranch is an "Old West" town that has been constructed on-site. It features a saloon, dance hall, and rooms for guests; room service, heated swimming pool, laundry service, corporate/small group facilities.

**Special Programs:** Children's program for kids ages 5 to 12. Children participate in a variety of structured activities and free play time; those over age 7 may accompany parents on trail rides and river rafting. Special children's rodeo on Friday.

**Rates:** $$–$$$ American plan

**Credit Cards:** Visa, MasterCard, American Express, Discover. Money order, personal check, travelers' checks accepted.

**Season:** Open year-round

**Getting There:** Nearest international airports in Atlanta; Nashville, Tennessee; and Charlotte, North Carolina (all about 4 hours by car). Regional air service to Knoxville, Tennessee, about 70 miles. Shuttle service available from Knoxville airport, at additional charge. Most guests arrive in private vehicles or rental cars.

**What's Nearby:** A variety of historic sites, including the Huff Cave, where original settlers lived before establishing a town site; old forts used in the defense of the region from Indian attacks during the French and Indian Wars; and the "Christy Mission," where a teenage woman from Asheville, Tennessee, established a school to help educate underprivileged mountain children

# CIBOLO CREEK RANCH

## Marfa, Texas

If you want to travel back to the Old West, this is the place. Cibolo Creek Ranch is a fascinating historical monument, an actual time machine back to the way the West was more that 150 years ago. Painstakingly restored in the late1980s to its original splendor (right down to the square-headed nails) by owner John Poindexter, Cibolo Creek began receiving guests in 1993.

Cibolo Creek is so wonderfully authentic that it has been a favorite location for fashion photographers. On any given day, you may find yourself sharing the porch with a vacationing Hollywood star or an in-demand supermodel. Just don't gawk; Cibolo Creek endeavors to cloak guests in comfortable serenity and relative obscurity, which is achievable in this remote area of west Texas, where neighbors often drive an hour or more just to visit.

The Cibolo Creek Ranch is not, strictly speaking, a dude ranch, but rather a working cattle ranch that raises registered Texas longhorn cattle for rodeos and "collectors." Cattle work isn't typically part of the guest experience. Groups of ten or more can arrange a special overnight chuckwagon camping trip, a special occasion you'll remember for the rest of your life.

Located 20 miles north of the Mexico border, Cibolo Creek is heavily influenced by the fluid border culture that has existed since before Texas was even admitted into the Union. Much of the architecture and furnishings borrow generously from Mexico. Rooms are furnished with authentic Mexican and Spanish antiques. You'll feel as though you've been transported to a foreign land and culture, while still maintaining a comfortable toehold in the United States.

As a world-class resort, Cibolo Creek pampers its guests. In addition to a standard list of activities (horseback riding, spa services, hiking, fishing, etc.), the ranch will also customize your vacation to meet your unique desires. If you want to make an extended trip into the rugged and little-explored backcountry of the 300,000-acre Big Bend Park, that can be arranged. Interested in a historical tour of Fort Davis or Fort Leaton? A tour of the Big Bend Region's colorful towns? Or a trip to the

## Cibolo Creek and the Fascinating History of West Texas

Milton Faver is known as the Mystery Man of the Big Bend. Local lore holds that Faver fled to this little-populated land after fighting a duel in which he killed his opponent. Faver married a Mexican woman and initiated a cross-border trading business, which prospered hugely, thanks to trade contracts with nearby Fort Davis.

Faver built el Fortin del Cibolo (the Fort of the Buffalo) as a personal estate, later adding two more fortresslike homes on his vast property. His fortresses withstood the attacks of native Comanches and Apaches and helped to protect his loyal employees during dangerous times. An early pioneer of the Texas cattle drives, Faver was a broad-shouldered and important figure in the early history of the Big Bend region of Texas.

Cibolo Creek Ranch, Texas

famous Chinati Hot Springs? Perhaps a rafting trip on the Rio Grande? Whatever your desire, the staff will work hard to fulfill it.

Cibolo Creek is first-class in every sense of the word. You'll revel in the Old West while enjoying all the privileges and perquisites of a wealthy cattle baron. If luxurious relaxation coupled with challenging activities and exceptional fine dining in a fascinating and authentic historical setting fires your imagination, you won't find a better place anywhere.

**Cibolo Creek Ranch**
HCR 67 Box 44
Marfa, TX 79843
Phone: (432) 229–3737
Fax: (432) 229–3653

E-mail: reservations@cibolocreekranch.com
Web site: www.cibolocreekranch.com

**Owner/Manager:** Scott McGehee

**Accommodations:** Guest capacity, 70-plus at 3 separate facilities (El Cibolo, Hacienda La Cienega, La Morita). Inquire about accommodations and availability. Double beds, queen-size beds, king-size beds, and suites with fireplaces, verandas, whirlpool bath, and double showers. The restored forts at 3 separate sites on the ranch carefully adhere to historical accuracy to conform to the architectural style of the late 1800s. Adobe walls, cottonwood beams, and period antiques typify all guest rooms and buildings on the ranch. Traditional Mexican architecture and appointments such as spacious verandas, Saltillo tile floors, tin retablos, and vintage-style lamps.

Rooms have full baths with resort-level appointments, fireplaces in the rooms, down comforters and hand-stitched quilts on the beds.

**Meals:** Cibolo Creek's award-winning menus have been featured in magazines that include *Travel & Leisure, Food & Wine,* and *Gourmet.* Exceptional nouveau-Southwest cuisine and Mexican regional specialties include buffalo rib-eye steaks from Katy, Texas; venison, antelope, and wild boar from Ingram; corn tortillas from south of the Rio Grande; seafood; and pecans from Fort Stockton. Sea bass Veracruz-style and grilled honey-and-chile-glazed quail are just a hint of what delights await. Special needs accommodated with advance notice.

**Activities:** Standard ranch activities and off-site tours augmented by custom-tailored itineraries based on individual requirements and desires. Horseback riding, visits to various ranch attractions and historic sites, excursions to and within Big Bend National Park and Big Bend Ranch State Park, river rafting, evening trip to McDonald Observatory, Chinati Hot Springs trip, vehicle ranch tours, wildlife viewing, cowboy singing by the fireside, educational lectures, shopping in the Mexican border region, and much more. Be sure to take in the unusual Marfa lights, a natural but unexplainable phenomenon of nearby Marfa, Texas (authorities speculate that the lights are caused by static electricity or natural gas upwellings). Exceptional wine cellar and south-of-the border beers.

**Amenities:** This is a full-fledged luxury resort; expect comfy down pillows, rich soaps and bathroom amenities, thick towels, and wonderful appointments throughout the ranch. Spa, available massage therapist, poolside dining or formal dinner service, historical and contemporary library, game room with video and music libraries, and much, much more.

**Special Programs:** No formal children's programs. Best for mature children age 8 and older. Nannies welcome.

**Rates:** $$$$–$$$$$ A la carte activities with moderate prices. Guests may choose to reserve a room, 1 of the 3 forts, or the entire ranch for large parties. Prices vary widely according to accommodations. No minimum stay.

**Credit Cards:** Visa, MasterCard, American Express, Discover, Diners Club

**Season:** Open year-round

**Getting There:** Midland Airport, 212 miles; El Paso, 224 miles; Alpine, Texas, 60 miles. Paved, lighted private airstrip located on the ranch.

**What's Nearby:** Fort Davis National Monument, Fort Leaton, Big Bend National Park, Big Bend Ranch State Park, ghost town of Shafter; Marfa, shopping in Mexico border villages

# DIXIE DUDE RANCH

## Bandera, Texas

Bandera is known as The Cowboy Capital of the World, and once you've stayed at the Dixie Dude Ranch, you'll know why. The Dixie is not simply a dude ranch but rather a working ranch that welcomes dudes. A fine distinction, yes, but an important one, particularly for guests who desire to become immersed in authentic cowboy culture.

Founded in 1901 by William Wallace Whitley, the ranch has been passed down through five generations. The Dixie began welcoming guests in 1937, giving the folks here decades to hone their hospitality to a razor-sharp edge. There's a nice folksiness to the Dixie that will make you feel less like a paying guest and more like a visiting city cousin.

The Dixie is situated on 720 acres in the Texas Hill Country. For those unfamiliar with Texas geography, the area is not the dry desert many imagine but rather a lush, green landscape with abundant water, gentle rolling hills, and stands of live oak and mesquite. It's an enchanting landscape favored by many Texans (who often prefer to explore their huge state rather than take their chances among "the Yankees," a name bestowed on virtually anyone not born in the Lone Star Republic).

The Dixie is tantalizingly close to San Antonio, home to the Alamo and a wonderful mixture of Hispanic and Anglo culture. Plan an extra day to tour the city, and be sure to visit the authentic El Mercado and have lunch along San Antonio's beautiful River Walk. Your sightseeing won't end there, however: Bandera offers the fascinating Frontier Times Museum, there's the Cowboy Artists of America Museum in Kerrville (also a favorite spot for music festivals), Sea World and Fiesta Texas in San Antonio, and seasonal rodeos at many of the nearby towns. Be sure to confer with the ranch activity planner for schedules and events prior to booking your trip.

Back at the ranch there's a broad list of activities. Lots of folks enjoy hunting for fossils and arrowheads, which crop up with regularity but require hawklike eyes to identify. Planned activities include swimming, hayrides, campfire sing-alongs, dancing, and, of course, catch-and-release fishing and daily horseback riding.

The Dixie also has plenty of outdoor recreation facilities, including hoops, a volleyball court, Ping-Pong, horseshoes, and tetherball. An added bonus loved especially by kids is inner tubing in the Medina River, not far from the ranch.

In the evening the Old West comes alive, as cowboy entertainers frequent the spread. Take in a rodeo, enjoy a hayride, sing along to old singin' cowboy standards, and enjoy a trick roper plying his trade. Every night is different, but always captivating and fun.

Texans enjoy a loud, rollicking good time, and the Dixie reflects that spirit. If you are looking for plenty of activities, lots of opportunities for interesting sightseeing, a good horse program, and plenty of evening entertainment, the Dixie will exceed your expectations.

**Dixie Dude Ranch**
P.O. Box 548
Bandera, TX 78003
Phone: (800) 375–YALL (9255); (830) 796–7771

E-mail: cccdixie@hctc.net

Web site: www.dixieduderanch.com

**Owners/Managers:** Clay and Diane Conoly

**Accommodations:** Capacity, 75. 20 total units. Guests can choose from duplex cabins, cottages, lodge rooms, and the 2-story bunkhouse. All accommodations feature private baths, air-conditioning, vented heat. Some include fireplaces. Family rooms with 2 or more beds, as well as rooms for singles or couples.

**Meals:** Served family style and buffet style. Expect Texas cuisine, heavy on beef specialties such as barbecue brisket, as well as pork ribs, fried chicken, all with the expected side dishes. Cowboy breakfast served out on the trail as a special event. No bar; BYOB.

**Activities:** Horseback riding at a slow-to-moderate pace. Swimming, hayrides, campfire sing-alongs, dances, and dozens of recreational games and activities. Catch-and-release fishing, hiking, nature trails. Plan on off-ranch excursions to the lovely Hill Country towns and cities.

**Amenities:** Swimming pool, children's playground and wading pool, shooting range at Bandera Gun Club, seasonal rodeos on-site and in neighboring towns

**Special Programs:** No formal children's program. Kids take part alongside parents and are the parents' responsibility. Babysitting available.

**Rates:** $–$$ full American plan. Daily and weekly rates. Reduced children's rates, group rates; kids under 2 stay free.

**Credit Cards:** Visa, MasterCard, American Express, Discover

**Season:** Open year-round

**Getting There:** Located 55 miles northwest of San Antonio off Highway 173, south of Bandera. Shuttle service available at San Antonio International Airport.

**What's Nearby:** San Antonio (approximately 1 hour); Bandera, The Cowboy Capital of the World with its Frontier Times Museum; water-park attractions in New Braunfels and San Antonio; Lost Maples State Park in Vanderpool; nearby golf and tennis

# FLYING L GUEST RANCH
## Bandera, Texas

When it comes to family vacations, it's sometimes hard to get everyone on the same page. Dad wants to go golfing, but Mom wants to spend time outdoors riding horses. And the kids want to go to an amusement park and play in the water. At the Flying L Guest Ranch, it's possible to do it all—and then some.

A premier resort destination in the central-Texas Hill Country, the Flying L not only boasts of an outstanding guest-ranch property but also a 72-hole championship golf course. Nearby San Antonio features several world-class amusement parks and zoos, along with restaurants, shops, historical sites, and fine dining. And the kids won't get bored on the ranch, as the list of activities for children and adults alike is enough fill up any vacation schedule and leave you with an incomplete "to do" list.

Ideal for singles, couples, extended families, and corporate or church retreats, the Flying L is truly all things to all people. A wide variety of accommodations enables the ranch to custom-fit everyone's needs. Furthermore, the activities schedule is flexible, allowing guests to have as active or leisurely vacation as they like. Let's look at some of the activities the Flying L has to offer.

A whole host of recreational facilities awaits. There are volleyball courts and soccer fields, a softball diamond, shuffleboard, table tennis, swimming in the Texas-size pool, and fishing in either nearby San Julian Creek or Medina Lake. You can also take a mountain-bike ride, a nature hike, or learn the intricacies of cattle roping in the arena. Guests wishing to improve their equitation can opt for private riding lessons, either in the arena or on the backcountry trails in the Hill Country State Natural Area. There are also numerous opportunities for excursions to surrounding Hill Country towns and attractions, so plan for a day or two to see the sights.

Lodging here leans toward resort accommodations rather than traditional and rustic ranch digs. The modern rooms are maintained daily; the suite-style villas include one or two bedrooms and a living room/dining area, plus amenities such as cable TV, refrigerators, full bathrooms, and coffee service. More luxurious suites are also available, as are less-opulent lodging in the bunkhouse, a facility designed to accommodate large groups. With thirty beds, nine bedrooms, and a shared lounge area, the bunkhouse is perfect for group or extended family retreats.

Golfers, especially, will appreciate the Flying L. One of only a handful of ranch resorts offering on-site golfing, the Flying L has its own championship 72-par, 18-hole course, pro shop, driving range, putting green, snack bar, and PGA-certified professional instruction. The challenging courses meander over rolling hills, with plenty of water hazards and native and introduced trees. Still hungry for more golf? The Flying L can arrange for additional tee times at the Woodlake Golf Course in San Antonio.

Other attributes that make Flying L a first-class destination include exceptional meals based on Texas and Southwestern recipes, nightly entertainment, and a climate that is temperate and enjoyable year-round. If you're looking to fit a number of vacations into one location, you won't find many resorts offering the variety and quality that characterizes the Flying L.

---

**Flying L Guest Ranch**
P.O. Box 1959
Bandera, TX 78003
Phone: (800) 292–5134; (830) 460–3001
Fax: (830) 796–8455
E-mail: sales@flyingl.com
Web site: www.flyingl.com

**Accommodations:** Capacity, 140. Guests may choose from suite-style villas with 1 or 2 bedrooms, deluxe suites, or, for groups, the bunkhouse, ideal for extended families, youth groups, or church groups of up to 30 people. Villas include cable TV, sitting room, refrigerator, microwave oven, coffeepot and coffee service, wood-burning stoves, full baths, and wood-burning fireplaces. More spacious deluxe suites include these amenities plus whirlpools and private patio decks.

**Meals:** Menu varies from Southwestern specialties to Mexican dishes to good ol' Texas barbecues (served in a grand buffet fashion outdoors). Special menu items for young cowpokes.

**Activities:** Horseback riding for guests ages 6 and up; separate supervised riding for children 3 to 6. Golf on the ranch's 18-hole championship course; swimming in a heated outdoor pool; tubing at nearby river (extra); 2 lighted tennis courts; recreation area including shuffleboard, table tennis, horseshoes, practice roping, volleyball, soccer, basketball. Mountain biking. Fishing in Julian Creek and Medina Lake. Evening entertainment, local excursion trips.

**Amenities:** Golf-course pro shop, driving range, and putting green; cable TV, wood-burning fireplace and refrigerator in all private rooms; hot tub and private whirlpool baths; daily maid service

**Special Programs:** Supervised children's program for kids ages 3 to 12 (seasonal); activities include pony rides, arts and crafts, fishing, recreational games. Babysitting available.

**Rates:** $–$$$ modified American plan (lunch served separately at additional cost).

Reduced children's rates. Prices include run of the ranch, morning and evening meals, horseback riding, nightly entertainment, supervised children's program. Reduced greens fees for golf. Some off-site activities charged additionally.

**Credit Cards:** Visa, MasterCard, American Express, Discover

**Season:** Open year-round

**Getting There:** 45 miles southwest of San Antonio

**What's Nearby:** San Antonio (approximately 1 hour) with theme parks, shopping, fine dining, historical sites, museums and internationally acclaimed zoo. Hill Country rodeos held throughout spring, summer, and fall; nearby town of Bandera, The Cowboy Capital of the World. Inquire about sightseeing excursions.

# SILVER SPUR RANCH

## Bandera, Texas

"The stars at night are big and bright, deep in the heart of Texas." So goes the popular song that has been a Lone Star State favorite since it was first recorded in the 1940s. Well, deep in the heart of Texas you will find Bandera, the epicenter of the Texas guest ranch business. The Silver Spur Ranch shines brightly among the Bandera guest ranches. It is both a historic guest ranch and also an up-to-the-minute lodging facility, thanks to the remodeling efforts of the new owners, the Walsmith family.

Guests praise the Silver Spur as a friendly place with lots of amenities and

activities, an authentic Texas cowboy feel, good food, and genuine friendliness. Add to that the beauty of the Texas Hill Country, an area that abounds with rushing streams and rivers, dense but compact forests, and a year-round climate that is the most agreeable in the state, and you have the ingredients for a memorable vacation.

The Silver Spur Ranch is for those looking for an inexpensive, friendly place where a family or couple can enjoy the simple pleasures of rural scenery surrounded by friendly folks and quality horses. If you are looking for a spa or gourmet cooking, better pass this one by. If instead you can enjoy spending time with the kids cooking marshmallows over an open campfire, pitching horseshoes, hiking through gentle, peaceful rolling hills, and exchanging a necktie for a cotton bandana and putting up your heels after a fulfilling barbecue dinner, you'll find contentment at this historic Texas dude ranch.

At the center of the Silver Spur is its majestic 14,000-square-foot main lodge made of heavy timbers and river-stone masonry. The vast dining room seats one hundred, and there is a pleasant rock fireplace for the odd chilly evening. There's even a player piano for old-timey entertainment. The lodge features a library of board games and parlor games, including pool and Ping-Pong, as well as a large selection of reading materials. The huge wraparound front porch is simply amazing and a natural place to gather with family or spend a lazy afternoon rocking in the shade.

Recently remodeled, the guest rooms are clean and comfortable, albeit not luxurious. Spacious stone cottages offer a great alternative for larger families. All rooms have air-conditioning, private baths, and color televisions. And if you have a group get-together, there's a bunkhouse that can house as many as eighteen guests, with a nearby guest room for the leader or chaperone.

While the Texas Hill Country can't offer the awe-inspiring mountain scenery of, say, Montana or Wyoming, first-time visitors won't be disappointed. It is simply one of the most relaxing and beautiful places on earth. For many, the words "Texas" and "cowboy" fit like a boot in a stirrup. For those people, a trip to the Texas Hill Country and a stay at the Silver Spur Ranch is a pretty ideal vacation indeed.

## Silver Spur Ranch

A9266 Bandera Creek Road
Bandera, TX 78003
Phone: (830) 796–3037
Fax: (830) 796–7170
E-mail: GNWalsmith@aol.com

**Owners:** Gary and Kay Walsmith

**Accommodations:** Guest capacity, 65. Selection of guest rooms in the stately main lodge and spacious cabins that sleep anywhere from 5 to 8 people. "Bunk Room" sleeps 12–18 and is ideal for youth groups, clubs, and family reunions.

**Meals:** Three hearty meals served family style in the ranch dining room. Special cowboy breakfasts, campfire suppers, and barbecues done "Texas style." Snacks and drinks available throughout the day, but liquor service is strictly bring your own.

**Activities:** A horse-centered guest ranch, the Silver Spur offers daily horseback riding, horsemanship clinics, hayrides and wagon rides, and of course, horseshoes. There are also nature hikes, yard games, bird-watching, barn dances, off-site guided fishing and rafting, nearby golf, and a host of informal and impromptu activities. Occasional visits by western performers and musicians enliven the festivities.

**Amenities:** Massage by appointment; laundry facilities, swimming pool, exercise facilities, game room. The Silver Spur offers small-conference facilities, with or without overnight accommodations. They can also help in planning special events, such as weddings, parties, and reunions.

**Special Programs:** No formal children's programs, although babysitting can be arranged for the very young. Children take part in a variety of activities alongside parents; there are plenty of provisions for kids, however, including table games, a playground with trampoline, volleyball and tether ball, a swimming pool, and special activities. Children ages 6 and older may ride horses, but younger kids can only ride at the wrangler's discretion.

**Rates:** $$ American plan. Price includes 3 daily meals, 2 hours' horseback riding each day, hiking, swimming, and all other ranch activities and amenities.

**Credit Cards:** Visa, MasterCard, Discover. Cash, certified checks, and travelers' checks accepted.

**Season:** Open year-round

**Getting There:** Nearest airport is San Antonio, about 50 miles. It is recommended that guests rent a car there for the trip to Bandera.

**What's Nearby:** Bandera is located about 50 miles south of San Antonio, the Texas city that most reflects the state's Mexican heritage. If possible, plan an extra day to see this lovely city and enjoy its wonderful and famous Riverwalk, the second-most visited attraction in the state behind The Alamo— which also happens to be in San Antonio.

# THE REID RANCH
### Salt Lake City, Utah

The Reid family, Mervin and Ethna, ventured into the Uintah Mountains of Utah looking for a getaway that would provide them with a quiet retreat. When they came upon a remote property recommended by a friend, they knew they had found their place.

Over the years, the Reids have transformed the undeveloped property into a high-desert Shangri-la, perfect for conducting Ethna's seminars for the Exemplary Center for Reading Instruction, which endeavors to improve the teaching techniques of educators. When not conducting these important seminars, the Reids open their ranch to groups and family reunions, providing the perfect site for meetings, team building, and recreation for extended family groups. If you are looking for a place to host a large group, one that offers plenty of recreational opportunities, solitude, and meeting

space, the Reid Ranch could be the ideal haven.

The Reid Ranch is situated at 7,800 feet in the mountains just east of Salt Lake City. This area is resplendent in native wildlife, including deer, elk, moose, bear, beaver, porcupines, and the occasional skunk. It is also a place of great historic folklore. Butch Cassidy and the Sundance Kid were said to hide out in these parts, and Mormon patriarch Brigham Young financed his early settlement in part with revenues from the productive Rhodes Mine, traces of which can still be explored. Fruitland is another intriguing historic artifact: More than a century ago, a land developer lured naive settlers to Duchesne County with pictures of lovely groves of fruit trees and promises of productive farmland, but when the settlers arrived, all they found was sage, cedar, and hard red rock!

Still, the bounty of this land for those who stayed was in the beauty of this semi-arid desert and in the fascinating geology of Utah's spectacular mountains. Said one visitor from South Dakota, the Reid Ranch and its environs compose "one of the seven wonders of the world."

There's plenty to do here, from horseback riding to swimming in one of three heated swimming pools. Guests take part in a variety of outdoor recreational games, including soccer, basketball, volleyball, and tennis. You can practice your archery skills, fish in a stocked pond, or just relax at the ranch spa. The lake provides a rare opportunity to spend a romantic afternoon in a rowboat or canoe. Paddleboats also provide a leisurely lake tour.

Meals are simple but savory. Don't expect gourmet cooking, just good down-home western ranch staples such as steaks and baked potatoes, barbecued chicken and baked beans, and piles of pancakes and ranch eggs for breakfast.

The main appeal of the Reid Ranch is as a group retreat, ideal for plenty of communal bonding. Because the emphasis is on catering to groups, the Reids can accommodate your schedule and goals rather than pigeonholing you into a rigid schedule.

---

**The Reid Ranch**
3310 South, 2700 East
Salt Lake City, UT 84109
Phone: (801) 486–5083; (800) 468–3274
E-mail: greid@reidranch.com
Web site: www.reidranch.com

**Owners/Managers:** Drs. Mervin and Ethna Reid, M. Gardner Reid

**Accommodations:** Capacity, 200+. Groups of 150 or more can reserve the entire ranch. Guests can choose from a number of accommodations ranging from dormitory-style lodging to individual guest suites in the lodge to a private cabin and guest house (both ideal for families). There's even a provision for group campouts. Individual rooms have private baths and beds varying from twins to king sizes. Dormitory-style accommodations in the bunkhouse feature bunk beds and single-sex, locker-room style shower facilities.

**Meals:** 3 meals served daily; a sample menu includes breakfast of ranch eggs, potatoes, toast, and fruit juice; lunch of barbecued chicken, baked beans, potato salad, rolls, and watermelon; dinner of baked ham in pineapple sauce, rice pilaf, carrots and peas, pasta salad, and rolls.

**Activities:** Daily horseback riding, swimming in 1 of 3 pools, archery, beach volleyball, basketball, tennis, softball, fishing, hiking, boating, frisbee golf, and evening campfires

**Amenities:** Conference facilities, spa, lighted sports court, sauna, Reid Ranch Trading Post, wireless Internet access, four telephone lines

**Special Programs:** This ranch caters primarily to groups, including supervised youth groups, corporate groups, and extended families. Single families can also be accommodated.

**Rates:** $ full American plan. As a group-retreat location, the Reid Ranch is designed for communal living and activities. Teen groups, especially, adapt well to the dormitory-style bunkhouse, whereas families may prefer the more private and commodious guest house and cabin or individual rooms in the main lodge. Outdoor camping for as many as 500 guests also accommodated for as low as $41 per day, all inclusive of activities and dining. A real bargain for groups!

**Credit Cards:** Personal and company checks preferred.

**Season:** June through August

**Getting There:** Nearest commercial airport, Salt Lake City (approximately 1 hour's drive). Ground transportation to and from the ranch at additional per-person charge. Reid Ranch is located in Uintah Mountains east of Salt Lake City, off I–40 at the Fruitland exit.

**What's Nearby:** Red Creek Reservoir, an excellent spot for cutthroat trout fishing; Salt Lake City, the Mormon-dominated cultural center of Utah; various resort towns, including Park City; Great Salt Lake, Ashley National Forest, Flaming Gorge Dam, and Dinosaur National Monument

# ROCKIN' R RANCH
## Antimony, Utah

South Central Utah is one of America's most scenic and geologically intriguing areas, and that's a big reason to check out the Rockin' R Ranch. Five National Parks reside within a half-day's drive of this traditional guest ranch, which makes it almost imperative that guests plan on a few extra days of vacation time to explore. Using the Rockin' R as your jump-off point, you can easily reach Bryce Canyon, Zion Canyon, Capitol Reef, Arches, and Canyonlands. Even the Grand Canyon of Arizona is a relatively easy half-day trip from Antimony, a small (168 persons) rural community that hasn't changed much in more than a century.

Of course, its awesome location is just one of the many reasons to visit the Rockin' R. This is truly a great vacation destination, particularly for those looking to visit an authentic working ranch where cowboys still toil to bring in the hay harvest and who know what to do come calving season.

Guests from all over the world come each year to the Rockin' R for its "Old West" authenticity, its friendly service, and its sheer natural beauty. There's no need for clocks and television sets here—your wake-up call is the smell of fresh biscuits, and in the evening the entertainment is likely to be an old-fashioned western band harmonizing cowboy songs that swell out across the rolling meadows. And if you want to really feel at one with the cosmos, all you need do is look out your window into the clear sky to see more stars than you ever thought imaginable.

The Rockin' R Lodge is an impressive statement of frontier optimism. The three-story building and an adjacent structure house guests in thirty-one individual rooms (each with private bath). Some of the upper-floor rooms offer great vistas out over the landscaped grounds through big gabled dormer windows.

The ranch has such a traditional look that Jay Leno sent his emissary, Ross the Intern, there. Over the course of a week, the folks at the Rockin' R transformed the soft city slicker into a ranch hand—well, sort of. Anyway, like most guests, Ross Matthews had a great time becoming acquainted with his inner cowboy.

And that's the main thing here—you really get to take part in the ranch lifestyle. If you wish, you can sign on for the Rockin' R "Cow Camp," where you'll help to drive the ranch cattle between seasonal pastures while working up an appetite for campfire meals served on the trail. Then, in the evening, sit around a blazing fire and swap stories before bedding down under a blanket of stars (or in a tent, if you prefer).

For those who'd rather experience ranch life from the relative comfort of a bunkhouse, The Rockin' R offers pleasant accommodations with the western decor you would expect. Although traditional in their approach, the Black family hasn't overlooked vacationers' desires for modern comforts, outfitting the lodge with overstuffed chairs, a game room, reading room, weight room, gift shop, and more. A nice marriage of frontier hospitality and modern amenities one might find in a modest resort hotel.

Back at the ranch, activities range from riding lessons, hay-wagon tours, and trail riding to more competitive horseback pursuits such as barrel racing, cattle roping, and pole bending (don't worry, you'll be schooled in the fine points of these rodeo activities). You can also stretch saddle-sore muscles with a hike or a swim in the pond. At night, enjoy western dancing, campfire get-togethers, or just turn in early. You will have earned the rest.

---

**Rockin' R Ranch**

10274 South Eastdell Drive
Sandy, UT 84092
Phone: (801) 733–9538
Fax: (801) 942–2680
E-mail: info@rockinrranch.com

**Owner:** The Black Family

**Accommodations:** Guest capacity, approximately 85. Guests stay in the relatively modern guest lodge, built in 1985. Rooms tend to be small but comfortable; each have private baths. There are no televisions or phones in the rooms, but these services are available in the lodge.

**Meals:** 3 meals served daily in the ranch dining room. Expect relatively simple ranch fare, such as roast beef and potatoes, meat loaf, barbecued chicken, etc., and delicious side dishes and desserts. Menu varies daily. All meals served buffet style.

**Activities:** Horseback riding, arena instruction, hayrides, arena competition; tennis courts, basketball, volleyball; fishing in nearby streams and lakes; indoor game room with pool, Ping-Pong; inner-tube float trips in local river; hiking. Sunday offers an excellent opportunity to travel to one of several national parks in the area and sightsee.

**Amenities:** Ranch library, fitness equipment, hot tub, gift shop, conference and group meeting facilities

**Special Programs:** No formal children's program. However, kids may enjoy the ranch petting barn, playground, and a variety of activities planned just for their pleasure. Babysitting can be arranged in advance, at additional cost.

Special "Cow Camp" allows guests to take part in authentic seasonal cattle drives. Guests sleep and enjoy meals outdoors, moving to a new location each day. Inquire for date and costs.

**Rates:** $–$$ American plan. There is no minimum stay, making this the ideal place to visit, spend some time riding and enjoying the many activities, then pushing on to visit some of the great National Parks in the area.

**Credit Cards:** Visa, MasterCard. Personal or traveler's checks accepted.

**Season:** May 15 through September 30

**Getting There:** Rockin' R Ranch is located in Antimony, about 4 hours by car from Salt Lake City, or 4½ hours from Las Vegas. Rental cars available at both airports.

**What's Nearby:** Bryce Canyon, Zion Canyon, the Capitol Reef, Monument Valley, Canyonlands, and Lake Powell are all within a half-day drive. Mountain bikers will want to visit Moab, considered the premier biking area in the desert Southwest.

# STEHEKIN VALLEY RANCH
## Stehekin, Washington

A vast stretch of crystal-clear water surrounded by forests of trees that rise more than 200 feet, casting shadows over a dense underbrush filled with berry bushes, delicate flowers, and thick fern fronds. The central Pacific Cascade mountains are a unique part of the West; here, more than 100 inches of annual rainfall create a landscape that is anything from the Western stereotype of dry, arid deserts.

If you've never been to this part of the country, you owe it to yourself to make a visit. And there are few places finer than the Stehekin Valley Ranch to really get an intimate introduction to the natural beauty of western Washington State. Nestled in a dense forest, the ranch consists of a lovely main lodge with dining room; relax on the porch and enjoy the view of Lake Chelan. For those who've never been to the North Cascades, the immensity of this glacier-fed lake will astound you; it is 50 miles long and 1½ miles wide at its widest point. Its deepest depth is a whopping 1,541 feet.

Roads extend less than halfway to the headwaters of Lake Chelan; beyond these roads, rugged snowcapped peaks rise more than 7,000 feet above the lakeshore, and deep valleys trace the pathway to massive glaciers deep in the heart of the Cascades. The towns of Stehekin and Holden lie at the upper end of Lake Chelan, effectively cut off from automobiles. Everything that locals need—from groceries to fuel to building materials—must be brought by boat.

To get to the ranch, you will need to either take the regular Lake Chelan *Lady Express* shuttle ferry or charter a float plane, an absolutely wonderful way to see this amazing area. Once there, guests can explore on foot, horseback, or in one of the ranch vehicles.

The Stehekin Valley Ranch is not an elaborate place. Rather, it is more like a wilderness camp where guests can relax, enjoy the scenery, take part in a variety of structured activities, or go off on their own and explore. With a maximum of just thirty-four guests, the Stehekin Valley Ranch offers a very personalized approach to customer satisfaction. The pace is your own, not set by somebody else's schedule or expectations.

Horses are one of the best ways to see this lovely country; the Stehekin ranch offers daily horseback rides to scenic Coon

Lake on gentle, trail-wise Fjord (pronounced "fee-ord") horses, a hardy Norwegian breed with a unique and distinctive stripe that runs down the neck and back. These lovely, smallish horses are extremely sure-footed and make for great photo subjects. You'll want to take yours home, but unfortunately you can't.

Naturally, you will want to get out on the water, which is really the best way to see the most country. For additional charge, the Stehekin Adventure Company will take you and yours on a guided kayak tour of Lake Chelan's upper estuary, where you will be able to see native pictographs along the western shore.

For many, the Stehekin Valley Ranch is just the jumping-off point for exploration of the unique beauty of the Cascade Mountains. For others, it is a place to be visited and cherished year after year, like a second home in a very peaceful and secluded place. If you are looking for a wilderness retreat with a laid-back atmosphere and seclusion that's hard to find in the Lower 48, this is indeed the right place for you.

---

**Stehekin Valley Ranch**
P.O. Box 36
Stehekin, WA 98852
Phone: (800) 536–0745; (509) 682–4677
E-mail: ranch@courtneycountry.com
Web site: wwwcourtneycountry.com

**Owners:** Cliff and Kerry Courtney

**Accommodations:** Guest capacity, 34. Guests stay in deluxe cabins, small log cabins and "tent cabins" near the main lodge. The five deluxe cabins each have their own bathrooms plus a queen bed and two twin beds; the newly built log cabins have kitchenettes and bathrooms, a queen-size bed, and a vehicle provided for guests' use. These new cabins offer a chance for independent-minded couples to plan a vacation on Lake Chelan, with the freedom to choose activities on the ranch, create their own meals or dine at the lodge, and generally customize their vacation to suit their whims.

The simplest accommodations, the tent cabins, are framed structures with canvas roofs, screened windows, and kerosene lanterns for light; there are no bathrooms, so guests must use nearby facilities in the main lodge.

**Meals:** 3 daily meals served to ranch guests; breakfasts are the standard fare, with omelets, bacon, hash browns, and hotcakes. Lunch can be enjoyed at the ranch, or request a sack lunch if you are out on the trail or lake. Expect cold sandwiches from the deli bar, hamburgers and salads. Dinner includes homemade breads, fresh vegetables and produce, an ample salad bar, and a main entree from the grill or broiler such as steaks, burgers, vegetarian burgers, fish, and chicken dishes. Be sure to try the homemade pies!

**Activities:** Day hikes, with many choices from easy to strenuous; horseback riding on trail-savvy Norwegian Fjord (pronounced "Fee-ord") horses; Western and English riding lessons; easy mountain biking on Stehekin Valley Road; fishing on Lake Chelan, the Stehekin River, and area streams; river rafting on the Stehekin; sea kayak tours of Lake Chelan; photography sessions; seaplane trips by special arrangement.

In addition to ranch activities, the Courtney family operates one of the oldest and most respected guide services in the Stehekin Valley and North Cascades National Park. They offer pack trips, backcountry horseback riding, tent-to-tent camps, and photography and fishing expeditions. If you have a special backcountry trip in mind, inquire about their outfitting and guiding services.

**Amenities:** This is a remote wilderness ranch; amenities are few.

**Special Programs:** No special children's programs; kids 8 and older can ride horses along with their parents.

**Rates:** $ American plan. Very affordable. Rates include cabin, bedding, towels, all meals, and transportation in the valley. Activities billed separately or as an "Adventure Package." Inquire about the various activity programs available.

**Credit Cards:** Visa, MasterCard. Personal checks and travelers' checks accepted.

**Season:** Open year-round, but realistically, the time to visit is late spring to late fall. Closed December 23 to January 4.

**Getting There:** Out-of-state guests can fly into SeaTac International Airport, south of Seattle, or Spokane International airport. Both are about 180 miles, or 4 hours, via rental car from Chelan.

The only way to get to Stehekin is over water; daily ferrys operate from the town of Chelan, where parking lots allow visitors to park their cars for a fee. A shuttle is provided from the ferry dock in Stehekin to the Stehekin Valley Ranch.

**What's Nearby:** Six local wineries provide vistors with an interesting tour of Washington's prizewinning wines. Pick up a wine tour map at the Lake Chelan Chamber of Commerce. Lakeside Limousine Tours, (509) 470–0333, provides a number of tours, including winery tours.

# ABSAROKA RANCH

## Dubois, Wyoming

Wyoming's Absaroka Range is one of the most spectacular and unspoiled wilderness areas in the Lower 48. Many would argue that this region, less developed by far than the Jackson Hole Valley, although sharing many of the same scenic qualities, is even better for its relative seclusion.

The Absaroka Ranch is a gem of a property, located in the foothills of the Absarokas, overlooking the Dunoir Valley. At 8,000 feet, the ranch offers commanding views of the broad park and pastureland below and the peaks at its back. Wildlife abounds in this region, and your chances are always good of encountering elk, moose, bighorn sheep, eagles, beaver, and the occasional bear. In spring the mountains

explode in a colorful palette of wildflowers, and in summer the region is green, lush, and pleasantly warm without being too hot—a welcome retreat for people from the sweltering East and Southwest. Fall is dedicated to the changing of the leaves, followed by hunting. The ranch works in tandem with Absaroka Outfitters, owned and operated by the Betts family, who also own the ranch. Guests interested in fall big-game hunting should contact the family to plan a special hunt with their licensed and very experienced guides.

This is a small guest ranch, accommodating a mere eighteen guests at a time. Its small size allows for personalized service and a sense of shared adventure with owners Budd and Emi Betts and their family. You'll never feel as though you are being herded from one activity to the next here.

The Absaroka will appeal most to persons seeking a traditional guest ranch. The emphasis here is on horseback riding, fishing, and nature appreciation. Individuals looking for spas and a deep list of activities will be disappointed, but for those who want to put in plenty of saddle time, the Absaroka employs expert wranglers with an excellent knowledge of and appreciation for the Wyoming high country. The ranch is ideally situated for fly fishing; trout species include brown, cutthroat, brook, and rainbow trout. Guided fishing trips to the best, crystal-clear fishing waters of the Dubois area can be easily arranged.

As an outfitter, the Betts family knows the backcountry and welcomes people to explore the wilds on overnight and extended pack trips. This is probably the best opportunity to see lots of wildlife, and you'll enjoy the camaraderie of the campfire. With horses to carry your load, you won't want for any comforts, and you'll sleep soundly in spacious tents pitched in flower-bespeckled subalpine meadows. A memorable trip if ever there was one!

Guests who prefer solid walls will appreciate the rustic but comfortable cabins. Each cabin has two bedrooms and an adjoining bath, ideal for families with teens, and is individually heated. Though there is no formal children's program, the ranch is very family oriented, and its owners will go out of their way to make sure that kids enjoy their stay. A recreation room, children's games, horseback riding, and fun contests on horseback assure that kids won't get bored during their stay.

The Absaroka Ranch is a good choice if you are looking for a peaceful getaway that offers outstanding scenery, good food, good fishing, and personalized care with a family that loves this part of the world and loves sharing it with guests.

---

### Absaroka Ranch

P.O. Box 929
Dubois, WY 82513
Phone: (307) 455–2275
Web site: www.absarokaranch.com

**Owner/Manager:** The Betts Family

**Accommodations:** Capacity 18. 4 total units. Duplex cabins are rustic but comfortable, and ideal for families. Each individually heated cabin has 2 bedrooms with adjoining bath and carpeting. All offer mountain views.

**Meals:** Meals, served in the main dining hall, are of excellent quality, freshness, and variety. Served family style with complimentary evening wine service; otherwise, BYOB.

**Activities:** Horseback riding is the main activity, with several rides of varying lengths available throughout the day. For a backcountry camping experience, inquire about extended pack trips. Guided fishing (mainly fly fishing) and guided nature hikes available.

**Amenities:** Covered porches, main lodge with dining area, recreation room with table games, board games, a foosball table, and jukebox

**Special Programs:** No formal kids' programs, although children are welcome

**Rates:** $$$ full American plan. Group, family, and children's rates available. Reduced rates for return guests at certain times of the season.

**Credit Cards:** None. Personal checks accepted.

**Season:** Mid-June to mid-September

**Getting There:** On U.S. Highway 26/287, 10 miles west of Dubois and 45 miles east of Grand Teton National Park. Daily airline service from Denver International and Salt Lake City to Jackson Hole Airport. Limited air service also available to Riverton, Wyoming.

**What's Nearby:** Jackson Hole, Grand Teton National Park, Yellowstone National Park, and town of Dubois, a friendly western town well worth the visit

# BILL CODY RANCH
## Cody, Wyoming

Wild Bill Cody was an astute businessman who understood and knew how to capitalize on the allure of the West. Cody, Wyoming, is a lot like Wild Bill. Of the many towns in "the Cowboy State," Cody seems best suited to capitalize on its frontier heritage. From its nightly rodeos to its old-time fiddlers' jams, Cody is a bubbling Dutch oven of Wyoming culture—a place where the Old West never got old.

Cody boasts not one but two gateways to Yellowstone National Park. The town also serves as the hub for several loop-tour drives that access five different scenic byways. Poised midway between the park's east entrance and Cody is the Bill Cody Ranch. Fortuitously situated in one of the most scenically awe-inspiring areas in North America, the ranch has been a favorite stop for westward-faring tourists since its opening in 1925. Short of, perhaps, Niagara Falls or the Grand Canyon, you won't find a more appealing site than the towering Sawtooth mountains of this sparsely populated state.

And talk about authenticity—the ranch was at one time owned by a direct descendant of Buffalo Bill himself.

At present, hosts John and Jamie Parsons ride herd on all the ranch details, maintaining a high level of quality and personal atten-tion that has made this one of the best traditional guest ranches in the state. Whether your desire is to fill every minute with excitement or you simply want to kick back on the porch and relax, the Parsons will help to create a personalized itinerary that suits you and your family's desires. Flexibility is the key here. There's no minimum stay or, for that matter, maximum stay. Come for a day, a week, or a month if you like.

Besides the obvious appeal of sightseeing in Cody and Yellowstone, there's plenty to do on the ranch. Horseback riding, naturally. Rides depart at all hours of the day, depending on rider's desires. The wranglers will surprise you with a meal cooked over an open fire or with yarns about local mountain-man and cowboy lore. Groups are limited to about ten riders, ensuring personal instruction if you desire it. Overnight pack trips take you even farther into the wonderful wilderness of the 2.5-million-acre Shoshone National Forest.

Guests also enjoy guided fishing in some of the best waters the West has to offer. Those wishing to raft those same waterways can make arrangements to do so, or just sit by the river with a good book.

Evening entertainment tends toward the informal. One night, a cowboy singer may stop by; on another you'll be treated to a lavish barbecue, or you can simply join your family around the campfire. You'll want to take in the Cody Nite Rodeo, an institution in these parts, and you'll also want to stop in at the Buffalo Bill Historical Center, one of the finest historical and western art collections in the country.

---

### Bill Cody Ranch

2604 Yellowstone Highway.
Cody, WY 82414
Phone: (800) 615–2934; (307) 587–6271
Fax: (307) 587–6272
E-mail: billcody@billcodyranch.com
Web site: www.billcodyranch.com

**Managers:** John and Jamie Parsons

**Accommodations:** Capacity, 65. 14 units. Guests stay in 1- and 2-bedroom cabins with private baths. Comfortable western furnishings and shaded porches.

**Meals:** Meals are served in the main lodge, a restaurant and bar open to the public. Expect ranch-style meals of steak, river trout, and chicken with homemade bread, soups, and salads. Wednesday and Saturday barbecues by the creek. Day lunches available for activities.

**Activities:** Horseback riding is the main activity. Rides go out most hours of the day, with overnight and extended pack trips also available. Guided fishing in area lakes and rivers. Fun family activities and nightly entertainment.

**Amenities:** Hot tub, restaurant

**Special Programs:** Various packages allow guests to choose on-site activities, pack trips, and combination riding/fishing excursions. No formal children's program, although babysitting is available by arrangement.

**Rates:** $$–$$$ Nightly lodging rates with a la carte activities and dining or all-inclusive American plan packages. Prices vary accordingly.

**Credit Cards:** Visa, MasterCard, Discover

**Season:** May through September

**Getting There:** Located midway between Cody, Wyoming, and the east entrance of Yellowstone National Park on the Yellowstone Highway. Commercial airport in Cody, Wyoming.

**What's Nearby:** Cody, a charming western town with many tourist activities, including the Buffalo Bill Historical Museum; Yellowstone National Park, 26 miles west

# BITTERROOT RANCH

## Dubois, Wyoming

Bitterroot is a rider's ranch, run by able horsemen. Rather than simply being a passenger on the trail, you'll really learn to work with and understand your equine partner. Arguably, the ranch offers one of the most advanced trail-riding programs in the country, and the day-to-day riding is augmented by annual riding clinics conducted by some of America's top clinicians. If you are an experienced rider or a novice with a desire to greatly advance your equestrian skills, the Bitterroot is the ideal environment.

The Bitterroot borders the 2.5-million-acre Shoshone National Forest, which in turn abuts Yellowstone National Park. Riders can explore mile upon mile of trails, including the broad plains adjacent to the Wind River Indian reservation. The ranch maintains a herd of 139 saddle horses, ranging from ranch-bred Arabians, quarter horses, Appaloosas, and mustangs. This large herd permits a horse-to-rider ratio of about three to one, which means you'll give out long before the horses do! The ranch maintains its own breeding program and trains its own Arabian horses; among their breeding stock is a Crabbet-bred stallion judged champion foal at the 1985 British Nationals.

Your week begins with an arena demonstration of riding techniques, followed by an evaluation of guests' abilities (a much better criteria for assigning mounts than simply asking guests about their experience). Guides lead riders on short, two- to three-hour rides. Guests may choose from western or English tack, and riding helmets are available and required.

On Tuesday and Thursday, you'll have the opportunity to be videotaped, a helpful way to improve your fundamental riding skills. On Friday, guests compete in a team cattle-sorting event, a great introduction to cattle work. On Saturday, guests take part in an all-day picnic ride. In July, August, and September, you may take part in cattle gathering and herding.

The Bitterroot is owned and run by Bayard and Mel Fox, fascinating individuals with extensive globe-trotting backgrounds. (The couple also owns Equitours Worldwide Riding Holidays.) Bayard is a Yale University graduate who spent years in Europe, the Middle East, and the South Pacific. Mel grew up on a farm at the foot of Mount Kilimanjaro and worked with wildlife in the famous Kenya National Park. Given their multilingual skills

and multicultural backgrounds, you should not be surprised that many of the guests are European or that the cocktail conversation sparkles with fascinating adventures and wry commentary on the world.

Bayard is a particularly avid angler, and when the conversation lags, you can always engage him in a discussion of the local waters. Excellent fly-fishing opportunities abound, both on the ranch and in nearby lakes and streams. The East Fork of the Wind River traverses the ranch, offering roughly a mile of private fishing access. Above the ranch base, the river cuts through a deep gorge that is difficult to access, but well worth the effort if you desire a place where fishing pressure is almost nonexistent and big, strong cutthroat flourish. There are also several small, stocked ponds on the ranch, and numerous fishing holes are accessible via hiking or horseback. Bayard usually goes fishing with guests two or three times a week.

### Bitterroot Ranch
1480 East Fork Road
Dubois, WY 82513
Phone: (800) 545–0019; (307) 455–3363
Fax: (307) 455–2354
E-mail: BitterrootRanch@wyoming.com
Web site: www.bitterrootranch.com

**Owners/Managers:** Bayard and Mel Fox

**Accommodations:** The ranch can accommodate up to 30 people in 12 charming cabins, each with private bathrooms, wood-burning stoves, and electric heat. Cabins are situated on either side of a trout-filled stream for maximum seclusion. Guests gather in the main lodge for meals and relaxing evenings.

**Meals:** A special effort is made with cuisine. Salads come fresh from the garden, ranch-raised beef and lamb are served, and bread is baked in the kitchen. Wine is offered at cocktail gatherings and dinner.

**Activities:** Horseback riding is the primary emphasis; videotaping of riding lessons is available. Special activities include early summer and fall cattle drives, riding clinics with renowned clinicians, and overnight pack trips. Guests looking to spend a lot of time in the backcountry should inquire about extended pack trips into the Yellowstone and Shoshone National Forest. Bayard Fox is an avid fisherman and leads guests on frequent fly-fishing trips.

**Amenities:** Hot tub, video analysis of riding skills, large lodge with stone fireplace, pool table, piano, and extensive video library for guests' enjoyment

**Special Programs:** No children's programs, although children are welcome

**Rates:** $$–$$$ full American plan. Lower weekly nonrider rate available. Reduced rates for children under 16; pack trips at added cost. Minimum stay: half week (3 days riding, 4 nights lodging); one week stay runs Sunday to Sunday.

**Credit Cards:** Visa, MasterCard, Discover. Personal checks and traveler's checks accepted.

**Season:** May 25 through September 30

**Getting There:** 26 miles northeast of Dubois, 80 miles west of Riverton. Airport transfer available from Riverton or Jackson, Wyoming (100 miles east) at added cost.

**What's Nearby:** Dubois

Bitterroot Ranch, Wyoming

# BROOKS LAKE LODGE

## Dubois, Wyoming

Individuals who appreciate the finer things in life will certainly enjoy Brooks Lake Lodge, a premier destination where rustic charm and luxurious elegance go hand in hand. Chosen among America's ten best adventure lodges by *Outside* magazine in 2002, this high-end lodge offers peaceful serenity, superb amenities, and an exceptional staff dedicated to pampering guests.

David Brooks, writing in *Travel & Leisure* magazine, summarized Brooks Lake Lodge well when he described it as "a high-end wilderness experience that marries the refinements of civilization with a reverence for nature."

That reverence for nature is a big part of the Brooks Lake Lodge lore. The lake was first discovered by Bryant B. Brooks in 1889. At the time, the namesake discoverer remarked, "Among the pines glistened a lake . . . what a sight! Where I sat on my horse stretched a broad, peaceful valley. I stood closer that day to nature's heart than ever before."

Brooks Lake Lodge has a long history, steeped in the tradition of the great western lodges that first welcomed guests at the turn of the nineteenth century. Built in the 1920s to serve as a stopover for visitors to Yellowstone, Brooks Lake Lodge (then the Diamond G Ranch) quickly expanded to serve as a vacation-destination dude ranch. Easterners often stayed for weeks or months at a time. Built of logs in the Craftsman style popular during that era, the lodge declined until the 1980s, when new owners refurbished and revitalized this historic property. In 1989 it was designated a National Historic Landmark.

Located in the Shoshone National Forest not far from Yellowstone Park, the lodge is surrounded by the Pinnacle Mountains and the Continental Divide. Brooks Lake, ensconced in the valley, dominates the view north, with nearby Brooks Mountain providing yet another inspiring image.

Guests may choose from a variety of activities best suited to this subalpine environment. Horseback riders are matched carefully to mounts that suit their abilities. A favorite excursion is riding to some of the area lakes and streams to fly fish or simply engage in nature photography. On the trail, you are likely to encounter elk, deer, moose, bighorn sheep, and bald eagles, and at high elevations, the adorable whistling marmot.

Brooks Lake offers a more leisurely fishing experience. Borrow a canoe and paddle out for a few hours of peaceful trolling. And you need not worry that the kids are having a good time; the ranch employs counselors who cook up a full day of fun indoor activities and outdoor adventures.

In the evening, guests congregate in the Tea Room to enjoy conversation and ever-changing entertainment. Local musicians, artists, and craftspeople, as well as special speakers, drop by to delight and enlighten guests.

---

**Brooks Lake Lodge**
458 Brooks Lake Road
Dubois, WY 82513
Phone: (307) 455–2121
E-mail: brookslake@wyoming.com
Web site: www.brookslake.com

**Managers:** George and Theresa King

**Accommodations:** Capacity, 36. 6 lodge rooms, 1 "premier" lodge suite, 5 deluxe cabins, 3 family cabins. All have private baths. Cabins have private porches, wood-burning stoves, and electric heat; 3 family cabins have 2 bathrooms, 2 bedrooms, sitting room, and private porch.

**Meals:** Breakfasts of fresh fruits, home-baked breads, malted waffles; lunch of soups, sandwiches, and pasta dishes; high tea in late afternoon; formal evening dining featuring a 3-course meal of local specialties prepared in gourmet fashion

**Activities:** Fly fishing and lure fishing in Brooks Lake, as well as area streams and lakes with professional guide (equipment provided); scenic mountain trail rides; guided wilderness hiking; overnight and extended pack trips at additional cost; evening entertainment. Winter cross-country skiing on tracked trails, snowmobiling, snowshoeing, dogsledding, ice fishing.

**Amenities:** Full-service, 3,000-square-foot spa with workout room, dry sauna, 10-by-17-foot outdoor Jacuzzi, 2 treatment rooms. Game/card room; opulent lodge with guest rooms and common areas, furnished with antiques, paintings, and sculptures by Wyoming artists; full bar; comfortable outdoor furniture and shaded porches; recreational equipment and fishing tackle available.

**Special Programs:** Children's coordinator and children's program with guided and supervised daytime activities such as hiking, canoe trips, horseback riding, arts and crafts. Evening activities, too. Children 7 and older may ride horses.

**Rates:** $$$$ full American plan. Children's rates; reduced winter rates. 3-day minimum stay in summer.

**Credit Cards:** Visa, MasterCard, American Express, Discover

**Season:** Summer, mid-June to September; winter: late December to mid-March

**Getting There:** The area is served by major airlines to the Jackson Hole, Riverton, and Idaho Falls airports. If driving to the lodge from Jackson Hole, proceed north on Route 191/26/89; at Moran, turn east on Route 26/287. If driving to the lodge from Dubois, Lander, or Riverton, follow Route 26/287 west. From both east and west, there is a USFS Recreational Area sign for Brooks Lake. There you will turn onto Brooks Lake Road. The lodge is 5 miles away.

**What's Nearby:** Jackson Hole, approximately 60 miles west; Dubois, approximately 23 miles east; Yellowstone National Park, approximately 65 miles northwest; Grand Teton National Park, approximately 40 miles west

# CM RANCH
Dubois, Wyoming

Dubois and its surrounding environs might be called the epicenter of dude ranching in Wyoming, and perhaps even North America. There are scores of dude ranches in this area, all touting the scenic splendors and isolation that makes this part of Wyoming extra special.

The CM Ranch is one of the oldest and most venerated guest ranches here. The property first opened in 1927, and it is

CM Ranch, Wyoming

listed with the National Register of Historic Places. In its way, the CM set the standard for dude ranches and continues to define just what a great dude ranch can and should be.

Situated in a peaceful, secluded valley at the mouth of Jakey's Fork Canyon in the Wind River Range, the ranch shares a border with the Shoshone National Forest and the Fitzpatrick Wilderness Area, permitting guests access to a seemingly endless network of trails and some exceptional fishing waters. (Incidentally, the CM also owns 4 miles of stream on Jakey's Fork, giving guests the chance to fish for native and introduced trout species on a managed and low-pressure waterway.)

During the day you can ride, swim, picnic, participate in activities, or just relax with a book. Evenings are occupied with square dances and cookouts, softball games, horseshoes, and volleyball on the lawn. Every week, a local photographer presents a slide show, and there's an evening dedicated to cowboy poetry and music.

The CM strives to provide an environment for families but also welcomes singles and couples. Here, nobody will feel like the odd man out; a broad mix of clients and the friendly staff (experienced horse instructors and college students, mainly) ensures that you will find suitable people to share in your adventures. And if the idea of vacationing with kids doesn't appeal to you, the ranch hosts adults-only weeklong sessions in early fall.

The look of the ranch is old school, with actual chinked-wall log buildings down at the corrals. The logs for the ranch buildings were cut up in the valley and hauled to the current site by teams of horses and wagons. The scathed pine logs give the interiors a warmth that's hard to beat, and the various lodging houses and guest rooms have been tastefully updated to suit modern standards of comfort. Guest houses, for instance, include large modern kitchens, washers and dryers, and electric heat.

Guests looking to rough it, however, can opt for an extended pack trip into the Wind River Mountains. After reaching the base camp at Moon Bay, riders can take forays into the Fitzpatrick Wilderness, enjoying the high-alpine scenery of Simpson and Alice Lakes, or take a journey to the Continental Divide to see Gannett Peak, the highest mountain in Wyoming, and Three Rivers Mountain, where rainwater splits and divides to form the headwaters of the Columbia, Missouri, and Colorado Rivers.

One of the most fascinating aspects of the CM is the bands of striated rock that make up its broad valley geology. The strata of rock here are a virtual storybook of the earth, displaying three billion years of development. Here, you can see leaf imprints, along with shell and dinosaur fossil deposits amid the cake-layer-like formations—an extraordinary place for casual geologists or anyone with a curious and inquisitive nature.

This is a great old-time ranch with modern appointments and a wonderful staff. It's no wonder that it has been a favorite for more than seventy-five years.

---

**CM Ranch**
P.O. Box 127
Dubois, WY 82513
Phone: (800) 455–0271; (307) 455–2331
Fax: (307) 455–3984
E-mail: cmranch@wyoming.com
Web site: www.cmranch.com

**Managers:** Mike and Kass Harrell

**Accommodations:** Capacity, 60. Well-built older cabins with modern appointments line the Jakey's Fork stream that runs through the property. Above the main ranch are more modern log houses well suited to larger families and groups. Cabins have 1, 2, and 3 bedrooms with old-timey log furniture, wood-burning stoves, and large porches. The larger houses will accommodate up to 6 guests: These have 2 or 3 bedrooms and a living room; 2 feature fireplaces, and the third, Hardie House, has a woodstove.

**Meals:** Guests dine together in the main lodge. Made-to-order breakfasts and feature such items as homemade granola and fresh fruits, omelets, sourdough pancakes, and fresh-baked breads. Lunch is served buffet style and mainly taken on the shaded outdoor porch. Dinner, served family style, includes savory fare such as game hens and poached salmon. Vegetarian dishes are available, and special diets can be accommodated with advance notice.

**Activities:** CM's horse-riding program emphasizes exhilarating trail rides with small groups (average size, 6 persons). Weekly all-day picnic rides to Whiskey Mountain, home of the largest herd of bighorn sheep in North America. Pack trips into the Wind River Range. Fly fishing on private stream as well as gold-medal waters near the ranch and high-mountain lakes. Catch-and-release encouraged. Swimming in heated outdoor pool. Hiking. Evening dances, slide shows by area photographer, outdoor games such as softball, volleyball, and more. Cowboy entertainers. Weekly arena gymkhana game on horseback; breakfast and picnic rides.

**Amenities:** Outdoor heated pool; well-appointed cabin homes available with indoor kitchens, stone fireplace or woodstove. Recreation room ideal for reading and games, Ping-Pong table, small library, and geology study room.

**Special Programs:** Supervised riding for kids 5 and older. The ranch strives to create a variety of activities for children and teens, including explorations of Native American petroglyphs, visits to a local fish hatchery, lawn games, Ping-Pong tournaments, and overnight campouts. Pack trips offered as part of the ranch vacation package or as a separate vacation. Inquire for pack-trip-only rates.

**Rates:** $$–$$$ full American plan. Reduced rates for nonriders and children. All-inclusive except for fishing-guide services and fishing-tackle rental.

**Credit Cards:** Visa, MasterCard. Personal checks preferred.

**Season:** Mid-June through September

**Getting There:** The area is served by major airlines to the Jackson Hole, Riverton, and Idaho Falls airports. Inquire for specific directions to the ranch.

**What's Nearby:** Yellowstone National Park, Grand Teton National Park, Jackson Hole, Whiskey Mountain (home to the largest herd of bighorn sheep in North America), float trips on the Snake River. Dubois, a small western town, includes 2 museums devoted to regional history.

# EATONS' RANCH
## Wolf, Wyoming

It all began here. Well, sort of. In 1879 the Eaton brothers—Howard, Willis, and Alden—established a horse-and-cattle ranch in Medora, South Dakota, and almost immediately began to welcome their friends from the East. Some stayed all summer. Eventually, the visitors began underwriting the costs of their visits, and the dude-ranch industry was born.

One of the "dudes" was a neighboring ranch owner, Teddy Roosevelt. Roosevelt extolled the virtues of life out West, and the Eatons' place grew as more and more people flocked to the area. In 1904 the brothers decided to move their outfit to Wyoming, a state with greater scenic grandeur and more varied terrain for horseback riding. They found the ideal setting along Wolf Creek, not far from Sheridan.

Eatons' Ranch, which has remained in the family's hands for a century, is now operated by the brothers' third-, fourth- and fifth-generation descendants. And, not coincidentally, many of the people who come here are the third-, fourth- and fifth-generation descendants of people who sought out the Eatons' western hospitality decades ago.

The ranch is a good-size outfit capable of hosting 125 guests in fifty-one individual cabins. It's also home to a sizable herd of horses (about 200), providing everyone with a fresh mount. You'll need one to explore the roughly 7,000 acres of riding land, enough so you'll scarcely have to cross your old tracks the entire week. If that's not enough, you can head up into the Bighorn Mountains west of the ranch. The Eatons take an active interest in their community, hosting a number of popular celebrations in nearby Sheridan throughout summer. These events include a roping tournament, the Eatons' Ranch Cup, a cowboy/dude golf tournament, a "Calcutta" cowboy auction, and team-roping contest. If that's not enough, there are also several rodeos and the wonderful Don King Days Celebration (a roping, bronc riding, and polo tournament held at the Big Horn Equestrian Center), which is a social highlight attended by local folks each September. You'll scarcely be able to plan your vacation without overlapping a true Western celebration in which the Eatons have a hand!

Back at the ranch, you'll find more than enough activities to satisfy your interests. Drop your fishing line in Wolf Creek, take a hike, spend some time quietly observing native deer, elk, and bighorn sheep, golf on one of several local courses, or simply relax by the heated outdoor pool. You won't have to worry about the kids, as a whole day's worth of activities await them at Howard Hall (although babysitters, available at extra charge, are encouraged for the very youngest children). Activities range from arts and crafts to scavenger hunts to afternoons at the pool. There are also horseback rides for The Mosquito Fleet, kids age six and older, along with nature hikes, movies, and marshmallow roasts.

For the adults, the Eatons host a weekly cocktail party, as well as bingo nights, country-western dancing, and an exciting team-roping competition for local cowboys held throughout summer. That, and the aforementioned rodeo and western events in town, will seldom leave you time to rest and reflect, but if you are so inclined, the ranch maintains a modest library for book readers.

## Eatons' Ranch
Wolf, WY 82844
Phone: (800) 210–1049; (307) 655–9285
Fax: (307) 655–9269
E-mail: info@eatonsranch.com
Web site: www.eatonsranch.com

**Owner/Manager:** The Eaton Family

**Accommodations:** Interestingly, many of the cabins here were built by pioneering guests, and the structures were usually named for their builders. Talk about a working vacation! In some cases these cabins still have actual iceboxes, which are still cooled by huge blocks of ice delivered aboard a vintage Model A pickup. Of course, they also have modern comforts, including private bathrooms. This ranch may be old, but you won't have to live entirely in the nineteenth century!

**Meals:** Meals served in ranch dining room. Western dining includes made-to-order breakfasts with eggs, meats, etc., plus healthful alternatives such as fruits, cereals, muffins. Lunch varies from buffets to barbecue cookouts. Dinner includes 2 nightly entrees, with choices of beef, poultry, fish, and pasta. Saturday-night barbecue by the creek. Special dietary needs accommodated with advance notice.

**Activities:** Horseback riding is the mainstay here; Eatons' is one of the few dude ranches that allow solo riding, once a guest has demonstrated proficiency. Twice-daily rides, pack trips, picnic rides, and arena instruction available. Fishing in Wolf Creek, swimming in the heated pool. Game room, hiking, nature observation, trips to Sheridan (extra cost), special events.

**Amenities:** Coin-op laundry, ranch store, coffee shop

**Special Programs:** Children's programs with supervised activities. Arts and crafts, scavenger hunts, pool parties, planned kids' rides. Babysitting at additional cost.

**Rates:** $$–$$$ full American plan. Reduced rates for children, nanny rates. Rates vary according to room availability. Applicable rates will be clearly stated at the time of your booking.

**Credit Cards:** Visa, MasterCard, Discover

**Season:** June through October

**Getting There:** The Sheridan Airport is served by United Express Airlines out of Denver. Shuttle to ranch at no added charge. Other airports: Billings, Montana (2 hours), Casper, Wyoming (2½ hours)

**What's Nearby:** Yellowstone Park, ½-day drive; Little Big Horn National Monument, Fort Kearny, Tongue River Canyon, Whitney Gallery of Western Art, Buffalo Bill Museum in Cody

# FLYING A RANCH
## Pinedale, Wyoming

We all love kids, right? Well, sometimes we'd also love an escape from their frenetic energy, too. If kids (either yours or someone else's) aren't part of your vacation plans, you might want to check into the Flying A Ranch, an adults-only guest ranch located in the beautiful Wyoming mountains just south of famous Jackson Hole.

Nestled in the Gros Ventre and Wind River Ranges, the Flying A offers an elegant guest-ranch vacation for discerning adults and older teens (at least sixteen years of age). To give you just a taste, guests are housed in seven luxurious log cabins, each completely renovated with designer decors and modern luxury conveniences such as kitchenettes complete with coffeemakers, wine goblets, and cooking ware. The floors are solid oak, the furniture is made from hand-hewn pine, and the flannel sheets, overstuffed pillows, and luxurious bed coverings are sumptuous and cozy. You'll think you walked right into an L.L. Bean catalog!

The ranch sits in the middle of a grassy park, giving guests a wonderful view in every direction. You'll be able to enjoy glorious sunrises and sunsets, with views of woodland animals and grazing horses filling up the hours in between.

The ranch doesn't operate on rigid schedules. You can fill every minute of your day or work at elevating relaxation to a fine art. For riding enthusiasts, the Flying A offers shorter half-day rides or more rigorous full-day outings. Each guest is assigned his or her own horse for the duration of their stay, so you won't spend each day adjusting to a new mount. By week's end, you may not want to part with your new friend.

If you'd like a change of pace, the ranch also offers guided hikes and mountain-biking tours in the Bridger-Teton National Forest, which surrounds the ranch. And by all means, pick up a pole and spend a morning or afternoon fishing. The ranch provides equipment and fly-fishing lessons for both beginning and experienced anglers. (Owner Keith Hansen is an avid fly fisherman and is happy to share his passion with guests.)

In addition to these common guest-ranch activities, you can also take a mountain bike for a ride, go on a guided nature hike, play volleyball, horseshoes, or join fellow guests in a game of cards. The ranch staff also can help plan and facilitate day trips to Green River, Waterdog Lake, Grand Teton National Park, or Jackson Hole. There's also the popular Mountain Man Rendezvous, held on the second weekend in July, and the Mountain Man Museum in Pinedale.

Befitting an adults-only ranch, the cuisine here appeals to mature tastes. The menu encompasses everything from western staples such as grilled steaks to south-of-the-border specialties to Italian pastas. Lunch is more than a simple sandwich; it's a healthful and hearty meal. And the morning ranch breakfasts will get your motor running.

The Flying A is a great alternative to the typical family ranch and truly a place to get away from it all, including those beloved but noisy kids.

---

## Flying A Ranch

771 Flying A Ranch Road
Pinedale, WY 82941
Phone: (800) 678–6542; (307) 367–2385
Fax: (605) 336–8731
E-mail: flyinga@wyoming.com
Web site: www.flyinga.com

**Owners/Managers:** Debbie and Keith Hansen

**Accommodations:** Capacity, 14. 7 cabins. Cabins feature living rooms, fireplaces, private baths, kitchenettes, and decks with mountain views. All are furnished with handmade pinewood furniture, designer bedding and window coverings, and solid oakwood floors.

**Meals:** All meals served in the main dining room. Before-dinner appetizers served in the ranch saloon. Expect excellently prepared meals featuring ranch and continental cuisine. Be sure to take home a copy of *From the High Country of Wyoming,* the Flying A Ranch cookbook, featuring 350 favorite recipes served on the ranch. Some favorites include Kraut Top Chops, Spinach Lasagna, Oriental Chicken Casserole, and the humorously named Fowl Thing.

**Activities:** Unlimited horseback riding, evening hayride, mountain biking, hiking, swimming, fly fishing, guided hikes, volleyball games, horseshoes, local excursions to favorite sites in and around Jackson Hole

**Amenities:** Hot tub, luxurious guest cabins, fly-fishing equipment, private covered porches, elegant main lodge and dining room, guest saloon (BYOB)

**Special Programs:** Adults-only guest ranch (unless your party rents the entire ranch)

**Rates:** $$$$ full American plan. Prices vary according to cabin. Off-site activities not included.

**Credit Cards:** No credit cards. Cash, personal checks, and traveler's checks only.

**Season:** Mid-June to early October

**Getting There:** Nearest airport, Jackson Hole. Transportation to and from the ranch at additional charge. Inquire for specific directions to the ranch, a 1½-hour drive.

**What's Nearby:** Jackson Hole, Grand Teton National Park, Yellowstone National Park

# GOOSEWING RANCH

## Jackson Hole, Wyoming

As the gateway to the Yellowstone and Grand Teton Parks, Jackson Hole, Wyoming, is the epicenter of guest-ranch vacationing in North America. If one acknowledges that this is the area that sets the standard, then the Goosewing Ranch sets the gold standard.

This is an exceptional place. A working ranch reborn as an isolated retreat deep in the Gros Ventre River Valley, the Goosewing marks the entry to a protected, pristine wilderness. The valley is host to spectacular game: elk, moose, mountain sheep, antelope, bear, eagles, geese, cranes, and more. The Gros Ventre River cuts through the ranch, providing habitat to native cutthroat trout and an excellent opportunity for anglers.

The Goosewing is a four-season vacation ranch, nearly as popular and appealing among winter guests as summer vacationers. Skiers enjoy the proximity to world-famous Jackson Hole Winter Resort, as well as the on-site cross-country and snowshoeing trails. Snowmobiling adds another element of winter fun, with guided tours through Yellowstone National Park and the backcountry surrounding the ranch.

Come spring, the Rockies come alive with fields of wildflowers, gushing streams, and fresh, green growth across the meadows. This is an especially good time to visit for photographers, bird-watchers, and amateur naturalists.

Summer, of course, is vacation time for families. Typically, guests choose from a variety of activities that include horseback riding, fishing, nature hikes, bike riding, swimming, and trips to Jackson to sample its quaint shops. A favorite day trip involves a ride to Sportsman Ridge, where one can visit the cabins and corrals of the mountain men who used this as a base camp for their explorations. Young children often stay "back at the ranch," mastering their skills as riders and future rodeo cowboys.

Should you have a special desire to see a rodeo, visit Jackson, take a rafting or float trip, an overnight pack trip, or a photography class with a professional, the ranch activity manager will be happy to help you make special arrangements.

Goosewing Ranch is small and relatively isolated, even by Jackson Hole standards. With a capacity of about thirty, one becomes instantly familiar with other guests and the small staff. Its small size makes it ideal for family reunions—the staff can lavish families with special attention not found at large resorts. The cabins are wonderful, with a distinct western feel and decor. The Mountain Man Cabin, for instance, is a lovely log-cabin design, with a decor of heavy pine-log furniture and the trophy pelts of a variety of game species native to the area. The Cowboy Cabin, with its decorative ropes and old leather tack, has the feel of a real cowboy bunkhouse, although, admittedly, one that is far cleaner and well-kept than ones where most buckaroos have ever slept!

Of the many ranches in the Jackson area, this is one the author is particularly fond of. Its combination of a wonderfully secluded location, tasteful decor, exceptional dining, reasonable and affordable prices, and a wide choice of seasonal activities make it a great choice for an unforgettable vacation.

© Goosewing Ranch

Goosewing Ranch, Wyoming

## Goosewing Ranch

P.O. Box 4084
Jackson Hole, WY 83001
Phone: (888) 733–5251; (307) 733–5251
Fax: (307) 733–1405
E-mail: info@goosewingranch.com
Web sites: www.goosewingranch.com;
www.yellowstoneexplore.com

**Owner:** François Corrand

**Accommodations:** Capacity, 30. 8 cabins
and 1 larger "family lodge," many of them
themed (Cowboy Cabin, Trapper Canyon,
Fishing Cabin, etc.). Log interiors with
heavy pine furniture and western decor and
artifacts. Daily maid service, private bathrooms, laundry facilities available.

**Meals:** An eclectic seasonal menu typifies
dining at the Goosewing. Cookouts, trail
lunches, wine cellar and bar (additional).
Special diets accommodated with advance
notice.

**Activities:** Horseback riding, mountain biking, fishing, sightseeing visits to Jackson,
swimming, horseshoes, Yellowstone Park
tours, rafting and float trips, wagon rides,
photography. Winter snowmobiling, snowshoeing, cross-country skiing.

**Amenities:** Hot tub, billiard room, swimming pool, large lodge with massive stone
fireplace, plush guest robes and linens, airport transportation

**Special Programs:** Children's program with
riding lessons, target practice, roping, and a
variety of supervised activities

**Rates:** $$–$$$ full American plan.
Reduced off-season rates, children's
rates, package rates. Inquire about winter

snowmobile package rates, shorter and longer stays.

**Credit Cards:** Visa, MasterCard, American Express. Traveler's checks, personal checks, and cash accepted.

**Season:** Summer: June 1 to October 5; winter: December 15 to March 31

**Getting There:** Located 1 hour from Jackson Hole Airport. Connecting flights to Jackson through Denver International and Salt Lake City Airport. Airport shuttle available; call for specific driving directions.

**What's Nearby:** Jackson, Grand Teton National Park, Yellowstone National Park, Jackson Hole Ski Area, Grand Targhee Ski Resort

# GROS VENTRE RIVER RANCH
## Moose, Wyoming

When he was president, Bill Clinton was enchanted with the Jackson Hole region of Wyoming. It's not hard to understand why. The area has a rich history dating back to its earliest days as a fur-trapping region all the way up to its present-day status as a world-renowned vacation destination. With its unsurpassed scenic beauty, winter skiing, exceptional dining, world-class shopping, and President Clinton's favorite diversion, golf, Jackson is truly a premier place to experience the West.

Needless to say, there are a lot of exceptional guest ranches in the Jackson Hole. Gros Ventre River Ranch is among the best of the best. The ranch is a mere 18 miles south of Jackson, 45 miles south of Yellowstone National Park. Its proximity to the Grand Teton mountains means that guests enjoy exquisite mountain views regardless of whether they are out on the trail, hip-deep in a fishing stream, or just kicking back and watching the sunrise from their cabin porch.

There is a simple beauty to this ranch. For example, the cabins and guest lodges, which include traditional log interiors and exteriors set off with rustic pine furniture, are pleasingly arranged amid stands of aspen and pine trees. Secluded, yet close to the action of the Main Lodge and situated so as to afford guests stunning mountain views and the Gros Ventre River.

Don't expect to lounge around a luxurious pool or get a facial and sauna in a spa. This is, first and foremost, a riding ranch. Remember, simplicity is the key here. If water is your thing, you can take a bracing dip in the river or relax in the privacy and relative luxury of your private bath.

That said, this ranch is very comfortable and accommodating. Dining takes place in the beautiful log cabin–style Main Lodge, where guests are welcome to browse about the collection of western art and sculpture prior to meals. The dining is top-drawer, featuring entrees such as prime rib, rack of lamb, grilled chicken, and mountain trout. Breads and desserts are home-baked, and vegetables and fruits are fresh and wonderfully prepared.

Guests will enjoy riding through exceptionally scenic sections of the Teton National Forest and designated wilderness areas. Groups are arranged by riding skill and limited to eight riders per guide. Riders who wish to meander easily through fields of wildflowers, stopping often for photo opportunities, will find other riders of similar interests. Those who prefer a fast-paced, ground-covering ride are as easily accommodated.

Fishing is a big draw at Gros Ventre. The ranch has excellent Orvis fishing tackle on hand for guests, and there is great fishing in its own stocked ponds and on the Gros Ventre River. Guests wishing to visit some exceptional local waters (including the Snake River) may also coordinate with a ranch activity director to take part in off-ranch guided fishing excursions.

Gros Ventre, of course, serves as the ideal base camp for forays into Jackson (you'll want to visit the town square, with its elk-antler arches and its wonderful art shops) as well as Yellowstone National Park. A weekly rodeo held in Jackson is a favorite activity for ranch guests and something you won't want to miss. And golfers, don't forget to take along your clubs; the Jackson Hole Golf and Tennis Club is just 14 miles away. You may even find yourself sharing the course with a certain famous Arkansas politician.

---

**Gros Ventre River Ranch**
P.O. Box 151
Moose, WY 83012
Phone: (307) 733–4138
Fax: (307) 733–4272
E-mail: info@grosventreriverranch.com
Web site: www.grosventreriverranch.com

**Owners:** Karl and Tina Weber

**Accommodations:** Capacity, 40. Guests are housed in duplex-style log cabins and larger duplex guest houses. All rooms are carpeted, electrically heated, and have private baths and porches. Cabins are rented by the "half," with each half consisting of a private bedroom and bath, with either a king bed or two twins. Log lodges are more like suites, with a bedroom, private bath, and living room, wood-burning stove, kitchenette, and a private deck with a view of the Tetons. Families of 4 or more can rent an entire log lodge, or it can easily be shared by 2 couples.

**Meals:** 3 meals served each day, with complimentary wine service with dinner. Meals range from rack of lamb to fresh mountain trout to prime rib. All meals feature home-baked breads and desserts. Evening barbecue cookouts to break up the evening routine. Box lunches available to guests taking off-site excursions.

**Activities:** Excellent horse-riding program, with a herd of close to 100 ensuring a good match and a fresh mount for each guest. Helmets, boots, and hats available for riders. Rides take place in the Grand Teton National Forest. Fishing in stocked ponds, local streams; off-site guided fishing available. Hiking and nature observation with guest naturalist. Canoeing. Mountain biking. Trips to Jackson, Yellowstone. Golf, tennis, and weekly rodeo competition.

**Amenities:** Beautiful log-cabin lodge with recreation room (pool and table tennis), large guest lounge with western art and sculpture, low guest-to-guide ratio, cabin porches, laundry facilities, airport shuttle

**Special Programs:** No children's programs, although children are welcome. Riders must be at least 7 years old (arena pony rides for young children). Special activities for kids include scavenger hunts, recreational games, movie night, and special kid-size fishing equipment. No day care or babysitters, although some staff may take babysitting assignments during their off hours.

**Rates:** $$$–$$$$ full American plan. Children's rates, off-peak rates. Rates include lodging, all meals, riding, use of ranch facilities, and airport transfers from Jackson Hole.

**Credit Cards:** None. Cash, personal checks, and traveler's checks welcome.

**Season:** May 25 through October 12

**Getting There:** 18 miles outside Jackson; closest airport in Jackson. Airport transfers available. Inquire for driving directions.

**What's Nearby:** Jackson, Wyoming; Yellowstone National Park, Grand Teton National Park

# HEART SIX RANCH
### Moran, Wyoming

The Heart Six began in the late 1800s as a trapping hideout for Dick "Beavertooth" Neil. Local lore holds that Beavertooth would don his snowshoes and walk backward over great distances to throw nosy game wardens off his trail. At present, Beavertooth Neil's dance hall, built in the 1920s, makes up part of the main hall at this Jackson Hole institution, the Heart Six.

The Heart Six dates from the early 1900s, a time of major settlement in the Jackson Hole region, coinciding with the creation of Yellowstone National Park. At one time, a stagecoach ran past the ranch, enabling folks to go on up to Yellowstone to see its amazing sights. Now the stage is gone, but folks still enjoy the Heart Six as a keyhole to the Yellowstone, away from the congestion and the madding crowds.

The ranch is owned by the Harris family, who purchased the property in the 1980s. It was and remains their dream to create a place where guests enjoy this beautiful slice of North America and vacation amid the lore and legends of the Old West.

At daybreak, you'll awake to the sound of wranglers gathering the saddle-horses and the smell of breakfast cooking in the lodge. Standing on your porch, you can see the sun coloring the majestic Grand Teton, which rises to the formidable altitude of 13,770 feet—a sight you will not forget.

Getting your day under way involves choosing from a grand array of activities. You can, of course, explore the ranch and the Bridger-Teton National Forest on horseback. The ranch takes great pride in its horse herd, which includes mustang horses adopted from the Bureau of Land Management's wild-horse-adoption program. That's right, you may be paired off with a genuine mustang! (It's okay; they've been tamed for guests and enjoy your company.)

You may wish to float the famous cataracts of the Snake River or fish along the meandering banks of the Buffalo River, which cuts through the ranch. A tour of Yellowstone will certainly be on your agenda, if not immediately, then at some time during your stay, so be sure to take a camera.

As the afternoon winds down, you can find a quiet place to read or if you are still feeling energetic, take a ride on a mountain bike or a hike on the numerous trails. And after dinner, you will enjoy the activities and evening entertainment taking place on the ranch.

As a change of pace, you may also choose to take part in an overnight pack trip, spending a night underneath the stars much as ol' Beavertooth surely did many times during his forays into trapping country. The lure of the high country is strong, what with its beautiful wildflowers in spring and early summer and cool summer afternoons perfect for riding and hiking. After a few days in the hills, you may be ready for a good scrubdown, a clean, fresh shirt and jeans, and a trip to Jackson for the weekly rodeo, a favorite of tourists and locals alike. Stop in the many western boutiques for a new pair of riding boots (yours may be scuffy due to all the riding) and a genuine cowboy hat.

It's tough to beat the natural beauty and the charm of the Jackson Hole region of Wyoming, and at the Heart Six, you'll become an instant part of this historic region of "The Cowboy State."

---

**Heart Six Ranch**

P.O. Box 70
16985 Buffalo Valley Road
Moran, WY 83013
Phone: (888) 543–2477; (307) 543–2477
Fax: (307) 543–0918
E-mail: info@heartsix.com
Web site: www.heartsix.com

**Owners:** Brian and Millie Harris

**Accommodations:** Capacity, 50. Guests stay in modern but rustically fashioned cabins. Cabins vary from 1 to 3 bedrooms. All have electric or gas heat; many have woodstoves as well.

**Meals:** 3 hearty ranch meals served daily. Standard dinner fare includes steak, seafood, chicken, homemade pies and cakes, and a variety of American dishes, selection of beers, wines, and mixed drinks.

**Activities:** Summer activity focuses on horseback riding, hiking, mountain biking, canoeing, and river-float trips. Horseback rides take place in the morning and afternoon, with all-day rides also available. For a true wilderness experience, ask about extended pack trips into the Bridger-Teton National Forest and the Teton Wilderness. Trips vary from 3 to 10 days and offer excellent opportunities for wildlife observation and high-country fly fishing and lake casting. In winter, the Heart Six Ranch offers a wide variety of guided snowmobile tours, ranging from 1-day trips to 2-, 3-, and 5-day custom-package tours. Explore Yellowstone National Park or powder bust along the Continental Divide Trail. Combination packages are available, with 1 or 2 days in Yellowstone and the Continental Divide and a day off from snow machining to experience Jackson and the National Elk Refuge and Wildlife Museum. Winter guests may also enjoy cross-country skiing, snowshoeing, and downhill skiing at the world-renowned Jackson Hole Winter Resort.

**Amenities:** Spacious main lodge with stunning mountain views

**Special Programs:** Supervised children's activities for kids 3 and older. Younger children are their parents' responsibility. Babysitting at additional cost, when available.

**Rates:** $$–$$$ full American plan. Children 3 to 5, half price; no charge for kids 2 and under.

**Credit Cards:** Visa, MasterCard

**Season:** Open year-round

**Getting There:** Nearest airport, Jackson, 35 miles. Ranch is northeast of Jackson on Highway 26. Transportation available from Jackson.

**What's Nearby:** Jackson, with museums, nightlife, restaurants, and shopping; Yellowstone National Park

# HF BAR RANCH
## Saddlestring, Wyoming

Among the oldest guest ranches in America, the HF Bar Ranch has served generations of "westerning" vacationers. Founded in 1902 by physician Frank O. "Skipper" Horton, the ranch still reflects his philosophy that a vacation should test unused muscles and stimulate the mind.

"A vacation doesn't mean slumping," Horton liked to say. Couch potatoes, take note. A visit to this wonderful historic ranch will present plenty of physical challenges and lots of opportunities to experience new things. Never fired a shotgun? The HF Bar employs certified sporting-clay instructors to teach you gun safety and help you achieve proficiency on any range. Never ridden a horse? The staff of cowboys and cowgirls will pick out a gentle mount, match you to the proper saddle, and help in your progression from greenhorn to seasoned hand (expert riders will also be suited to responsive mounts). And if you want to truly "get away from it all," you can partake of an extended stay in Willow Park, where you'll sleep beneath the stars, enjoy meals cooked over an open fire, and enjoy the peaceful serenity of this outstanding high-mountain camp, just like the mountain men of days past.

There is a delightful blend of the old and the new at the HF Bar. Moms and dads can work out with yoga instructors, and kids will certainly enjoy plenty of fun times in the heated outdoor pool. You can also take a mountain-bike tour or try the challenge course—a group activity requiring teamwork and the overcoming of physical and mental challenges.

Of course, you can also opt for more traditional guest-ranch activities, including fly fishing (guides available at added cost), hiking, hayrides, and cookouts. One definite advantage of this sprawling, 9,000-acre working ranch is that it encompasses 15 miles of private fishing water along Rock Creek, ensuring that you'll be casting in lightly taxed waters, where catch-and-release is the order of the day. There's even a fly-fishing shop on-site.

Since you'll probably discover muscles you never knew you had, the ranch provides many soothing options to get you feeling relaxed again. A certified massage therapist is available, as well as a reflexologist. Afterward, settle in for a movie with the kids (the ranch maintains an extensive video library) or gear up for a wide range of evening entertainment.

Built in the heyday of early guest ranches out West, the HF Bar has a pleasing rustic feel and look that belies its modern appointments. Each cabin is unique and unusual, a reflection of their having been built to meet the growing needs of the facility and of its guests. You'll want to inquire about availability and types of accommodations, as guest houses vary considerably. Chances are, there is one ideal for you, your friends, or family members. You won't find telephones and televisions in the cabins, however; HF Bar is committed to socializing, away from the beckoning of modern communications. (Bring a cell phone or use the ranch phone if need be.)

With a century of service to guests, the HF Bar draws upon a deep well of experience when it comes to making folks happy. The ambience combines the best of the ranch's traditions while adding nice modern touches to make sure that every guest's needs are met. It's the perfect place for an active and engaging vacation.

---

### HF Bar Ranch

1301 Rock Creek Road
Saddlestring, WY 82840
Phone: (307) 684–2487
Fax: (307) 684–7144
E-mail: hfbar@wyoming.com
Web site: www.hfbar.com

**Owner/Manager:** Margi Schroth

**Accommodations:** Capacity, 125; 35 individual cabins. Guests are lodged in cottages with a living room, open fireplace, private bath, and outdoor porch. Cabins vary widely in size, from 1 to 7 bedrooms and 1 to 3 bathrooms.

**Meals:** Guest meals are served 3 times daily to the call of a clanging dinner bell. All food is prepared fresh, with home-baked breads and dessert items. Complimentary morning coffee or tea in your cabin. Expect hearty, filling fare. Outdoor cookouts feature a huge, river-rock grille. Children's menus and a Kids' Buffet Bar at every meal. Special diets accommodated on request.

**Activities:** Excellent horse program with more than 220 horses, ensuring the correct mount for each rider. Daily rides in the morning and afternoon plus all-day "long rides." Riding lessons available upon request. Guided and unguided fishing (inquire about guided trips with HF Bar's sister company, Rock Creek Anglers). On-site Orvis fishing shop. Remote pack trips to Willow Park, a particularly fine fishing and hiking location (mid-June to early September). Shooting range with expert instruction (additional charge). Hiking, mountain biking, "challenge course," swimming pool, yoga classes, bird hunting.

**Amenities:** Heated pool, exercise and fitness studio, fishing shop, massage therapy, reflexology therapist

**Special Programs:** Children's program includes nature hikes, Frisbee golf, scavenger hunts, overnight camping trips, face painting, visits to the petting zoo, arts and crafts, and more. A children's director coordinates daily activities.

**Rates:** $$–$$$ full American plan. Children under 5 free; special nanny rates. In addition to living accommodations and meals, rates include use of a saddle horse and all ranch facilities. The only extra expenses normally incurred are for personal laundry, beverages, purchases in the Ranch Store, sporting-clay shooting, and instruction or fishing services from Rock Creek Anglers. Occasionally, special-event preparation fees may be charged.

**Credit Cards:** No credit cards accepted. Cash, traveler's checks, or personal checks only.

**Season:** Mid-June to mid-September

**Getting There:** Located 35 miles south of Sheridan

**What's Nearby:** Sheridan, King's Saddlery Western Museum

# LAZY L & B RANCH

## Dubois, Wyoming

It would be nearly impossible to find more interesting and varied riding terrain than what's available at the Lazy L & B Ranch. The property is surrounded by three distinct mountain ranges—the Absaroka, Wind River, and Owl Creek Mountains—and is bordered by the 50,000-acre National Elk Refuge, national forest, and the Wind River Indian Reservation. Guests explore everything from lush river bottoms to the sparse plateaus and "Badlands" formations of the Indian Reservation to forested mountain trails leading to wide-open, high-alpine meadows and breathtaking mountain vistas.

A rider's paradise? Indeed. But there's more to the Lazy L & B than just exceptional scenery. This is a family-run outfit, where hospitality is the word of the day. Owners Bob and Lee Naylon have more than a quarter century of experience in the western-hospitality field, and the couple takes a very hands-on approach to guest ranching. Whether you come with family, friends, or by yourself, you'll fit in comfortably and be "gathered up" by the Naylons and their staff.

Like most traditional guest ranches, the emphasis here is on riding, fishing, and hiking. The ranch accommodates anglers with several stocked ponds and access to numerous rivers, namely the East Fork, Wiggins Fork, Bear Creek, and Wind River. You can also take an icy-cold dip in the river after a hot day on the trail; if you prefer a little warmer waters, try the solar-heated pool or luxuriate in the Jacuzzi, not far from the river's banks.

Children aren't left out of the action here. There's a supervised kids' riding program for those over age four that includes equestrian safety and basic riding instruction. Kids also participate in a wide variety of recreational games and arts and crafts, and they can help feed the horses or visit with the farmyard animals. On several evenings during the week, the children join the ranch wranglers at the cookouts or at the dining table, giving parents a little "quiet time" alone.

The main lodge has an inviting fireplace where guests can relax and enjoy a good book from the library or meet for parlor games or formal entertainment such as cowboy-poetry performances or cowboy singing.

Visitors looking for a wilderness adventure may wish to inquire about the Bear Basin Wilderness Camp, the center of the ranch's pack-trip program. From this base camp high in the Washakie Wilderness, guests are able to explore timbered canyons and high-mountain passes (as high as 11,000 feet in elevation). Camps are limited to eight guests, so the feeling is intimate.

You'll sleep in large and comfortable tents outfitted with wood-burning stoves, cots, and sleeping pads. But if you wish, you can always sleep under the stars, like the mountain men of old. Guests can book these wilderness trips as an inclusive vacation or add the trips onto their stay at the main ranch. In addition, there are special fall big-game hunting trips and fishing camps. Ask about bow hunting, as the ranch takes great pride in its guides' abilities at calling in the elk.

This is a small, friendly place that offers one of the finest horse programs in the guest-ranch business. If you are looking forward to plenty of riding with excellent mounts and very capable guides who share your passion for seeing varied and compelling wilderness areas, this could be for you.

**Lazy L & B Ranch**
1072 East Fork Road
Dubois, WY 82513
Phone: (800) 453–9488; (307) 455–2839
Fax: (307) 455–2849; (760) 387–9123
(winter)
E-mail: ranch@lazylb.com
Web site: www.lazylb.com

**Owners/Managers:** Bob and Lee Naylon

**Accommodations:** Capacity, 35. Guests are housed in individual cabins tucked amid cottonwood trees along the banks of a river. Cabins are furnished in traditional western decor and include refrigerators, private bath or shower, electric heat, and porches, some with mountain views.

**Meals:** Western ranch-style meals featuring homemade breads and desserts, buffet breakfasts, tailgate lunches, sit-down dinners, and outdoor barbecues

**Activities:** The Lazy L & B features an excellent riding program emphasizing small, guided groups. Guests are paired with horses for the week, and if you get along, you'll form a bond with your personal mount; if not, you can always switch. There are fast horses for riders who like to go fast, slow horses for those who like to go slow, and, as Bob likes to say, "For those who don't like to ride, we

have horses that don't like to be ri' Fishing, recreational games, mountain... ing, swimming in the river or in a heated pool, hiking, and rifle shooting. Evening entertainment featuring western performers, hayrides for children, barbecues, and trips to Dubois for evening dances.

**Amenities:** Pool, Jacuzzi, library in main lodge, shooting range, remote wilderness camp

**Special Programs:** Children's program features riding lessons, games, arts and crafts, special dining sessions with ranch wranglers, hayrides, petting zoo, and a special barbecue. Inquire about Bear Basin Wilderness Camp pack-trip vacations and seasonal hunting trips.

**Rates:** $$$ full American plan. Special children's rates. Nannies stay free when caring for 2 or more young children.

**Credit Cards:** Visa. Personal checks preferred.

**Season:** Late May through August

**Getting There:** Nearest airport, Jackson (approximately 70 miles). Driving directions available. Shuttle service, $100 per vehicle, each way.

**What's Nearby:** Dubois, Grand Teton and Yellowstone National Parks

# LOST CREEK RANCH & SPA
## Moose, Wyoming

An upscale resort ranch for the discerning traveler: This about sums up Lost Creek, a small but opulent facility, located a mere stone's throw from historic Jackson, and the gateway to Yellowstone National Park. This

outstanding property has received rave reviews from numerous sources, including several major travel and dining magazines.

This popular luxury resort and spa books one year in advance, so you'll have to plan well ahead if you hope to visit. But for those of you who manage to book a trip, the rewards are great. The ranch offers a cornucopia of activities, ranging from the normal guest ranch staples—horseback riding, hiking, and park tours—to the types of things found only in the world's finest spas: massages, sea-salt body scrubs, facials, yoga classes, and strength training.

## Visiting Jackson Hole

On the arts front, the small town of Jackson has more than thirty galleries that display a vast array of artistry, from traditional western works to contemporary pieces. Photography and painting are among the most prevalent art forms, but sculpting, particularly bronze work, is also commonly seen in Jackson's many galleries.

The National Museum of Wildlife Art, founded in 1987, is home to the nation's premier public collection of fine art devoted to wildlife. Its vantage point on a butte overlooking the National Wildlife Refuge provides incredible views of the mountain known as Sleeping Indian, as well as wildlife in both winter and summer.

Each summer the Grand Teton Music Festival presents an eight-week season of orchestral and chamber music performed by the resident company of 200 professional musicians from many of the nation's finest orchestras. Special winter concerts are also scheduled. Concerts are held in the 740-seat Walk Festival Hall, which is acclaimed for its intimacy and superb acoustics. Walk Festival Hall is located in Teton Village, just 12 miles northwest of the town of Jackson.

The Spa at Lost Creek includes a heated swimming pool, an oversize hot tub, tennis courts, and a wide variety of spa treatments. Guests can order from a spa menu that includes seaweed and mineral wraps, mud masks, and manicures and pedicures. Spa treatments are billed separately from the general charges.

The ranch lodge is sumptuous and luxurious, with lovely custom furniture, tasteful furnishings, and original artwork. The oversize, lovely guest cabins are fully appointed with modern conveniences befitting a luxury hotel. Double-room cabins include living rooms and gas fireplaces, and all cabins include refrigerators, coffee service, one or two full baths, a porch, daily maid service, and personal laundry service.

Meals are prepared to an extremely high standard. All meals are prepared from fresh, seasonal ingredients. Two delicious entrees are served with the evening meal, and note that wine service is also available.

As one might expect of such a top-drawer facility, Lost Creek welcomes an international clientele. The young staff members often come from foreign countries as well, helping to bridge any language gaps that may exist.

---

**Lost Creek Ranch & Spa**
P.O. Box 95
Moose, WY 83012
Phone: (307) 733–3435
Fax: (307) 733–1954
E-mail: ranch@lostcreek.com
Web site: www.lostcreek.com

**Managers:** Mike and Bev Halpin

**Accommodations:** Capacity, 50. 10 luxurious cabins; 1-bedroom or 2-bedroom/2-bath cabins with refrigerators, coffeemakers, gas heat. Larger cabins have living rooms, kitchenettes, and gas fireplaces.

Nightly turndown service, twice-daily maid service, courtesy laundry service.

**Meals:** Expect gourmet preparation of all meals, fresh seasonal ingredients, fresh-baked goods, accommodation of special diets. Wine list, beer service. Separate children's seating, if desired.

**Activities:** Riding program with excellent instructors personalized to individual needs. Rides divided by riding ability and further divided into small groups of 8 or fewer. Other activities include guided or unguided hiking, swimming, tennis, float trips on the Snake River, shooting sports, Yellowstone Park and Grand Teton National Park. Nearby golf and guided fly-fishing trips.

**Amenities:** Full-service spa including facial treatments, manicures and pedicures, body treatments, fitness center, exercise classes, and more. Spa activities not covered in guest lodging price.

**Special Programs:** Supervised daily children's program for kids 6 to 13. Recreation room, activities, daily horseback riding, cookouts.

**Rates:** $$$$$ modified American plan. All meals and ranch activities, except spa activities, are included in the price. 1-week minimum. Off-season and group rates. Children under 5 are free.

**Credit Cards:** American Express. Personal checks accepted.

**Season:** Late-May through mid-October

**Getting There:** Courtesy pickup from Jackson Hole Airport. Rental car suggested for sightseeing trips.

**What's Nearby:** Yellowstone National Park, Grand Teton National Park, National Elk Refuge, town of Jackson

# MOOSE HEAD RANCH

## Moose, Wyoming

With its spectacular view of the Tetons, Moose Head Ranch is a postcard-perfect place to "get away from it all." Even more so when one considers that the Moose Head is a privately owned property uniquely situated in the middle of Grand Teton National Park, which gives ranch visitors an unprecedented opportunity to explore the popular park and yet have a peaceful and secluded retreat from which to enjoy the adventure.

Said one many-time visitor, "The owners are always there and know everything there is to do in Wyoming, and it's a pleasant place to just read and watch the scenery . . .

the cabins are rustic, but we love them; that's Wyoming to us."

Moose Head Ranch, which was homesteaded in 1923, passed into the hands of the Mettler family in the late 1960s. At present, the ranch is run under the capable guidance of Louise Mettler-Davenport and her husband, Kit Davenport. Louise enjoys a hands-on approach with guests, visiting with them when they arrive to help plan out a fun-filled and exciting week's adventure.

There are a number of activities that you won't want to miss. Trips to Yellowstone, of course, are de rigueur, but Louise can also suggest various hot spots for visiting in nearby Jackson, scenic routes winding up into the Tetons, and a trip to the famous Elk grounds, where Boy Scouts in the Jackson area fund their entire year's program with the annual collection of elk horns shed by the resident herds.

Moose Head is a fine place for family vacations, as the approach taken here is very family oriented. Children and their parents spend most of their time together, riding or fishing or taking hikes. Riders looking for fast gallops through open meadows might want to look elsewhere, as the pace of riding here tends to be slow, unless everyone in the family is an accomplished horse rider. Even then, the emphasis is on nature appreciation and contemplation, not on mad, exciting dashes.

There is no specific children's program or separate mealtimes for kids. If you are like most busy modern families, you'll probably welcome the ample amount of shared time you'll get to spend with your kids.

Kit is an avid fisherman and is a patient and willing instructor. You'll be able to participate in fly fishing on the ranch, which has ponds stocked with fat, healthy trout, thanks to the ranch's catch-and-release philosophy. You may not take home a trophy fish, but you can take home the photos to prove your own particular "fish tale."

Nearby, you will find exceptional golf courses, tennis facilities, and white-water rafting. The Davenports and their capable staff can help you plan any number of adventures or cultural events. One you won't want to skip is the weekly rodeo held in Jackson, featuring area cowboys and even wranglers from many of the guest ranches throughout the region. Afterward, stop in at the Million Dollar Cowboy Bar, just off the main park in Jackson, and peer at the hundreds of silver dollars that were set into the unique bar. Get there early, and

you may even get to sit in a genuine cowboy saddle. Right next door, you'll also find one of the best hamburger shops in Wyoming—and perhaps even the entire West!

---

## Moose Head Ranch

P.O. Box 214
Moose, WY 83019
Winter address:
3100 Welaunee Road
Tallahassee, FL 32309
Phone: (307) 733–3141 (summer);
(850) 877–1431 (winter)
Fax: (307) 739–9097
Web site: www.wyomingdra.com/moosehead

**Owners/Managers:** Louise and Kit Davenport

**Accommodations:** Capacity, 44. Guests stay in 14 modern log cabins nestled among pine and cottonwood trees. The cabins lack room phones or TVs but are hardly spartan. You will enjoy private baths, electric heat, and in-cabin coffeemakers and refrigerators; you can also relax on your own porch.

**Meals:** 3 meals served daily. Breakfasts cooked to your order, picnic lunches and buffet lunch service, and gourmet evening meals featuring 4 daily entrees. BYOB.

**Activities:** Twice-daily horseback rides and all-day rides. Hiking, fishing in the Snake River and in stocked ponds (equipment and flies available); tennis, golf, and river rafting off-site. Outdoor recreational games and parlor games available.

**Amenities:** Library, airport shuttle, in-room refrigerators and coffeemakers; beautiful grand lodge, with a huge porch resplendent in overflowing flower boxes and lounge furniture for relaxing

**Special Programs:** No formal children's program, although children of any age are welcome

**Rates:** $$$–$$$$ full American plan. Minimum 5-night stay. Special rates for children 6 and under.

**Credit Cards:** No credit cards. Traveler's checks and personal checks or cash only.

**Season:** Early June to mid-August

**Getting There:** Nearest airport, Jackson (18 miles). Airport shuttle to ranch available.

**What's Nearby:** Jackson Hole Valley, National Elk Refuge, Yellowstone National Park

# PARADISE GUEST RANCH
## Buffalo, Wyoming

You set up high expectations when you name a place Paradise, but in this case, this Wyoming guest ranch meets them.

The name wasn't simply chosen, but rather given to the ranch by visiting friends of founder Dr. Gordon Meldrum, whose father had homesteaded the ranch at the foothills of the Bighorn Mountains. Dr. Meldrum often invited friends to join him on the ranch, where riding and seasonal hunting were the order of the day. Many friends remarked that the beautiful mountain meadow where the original homestead was situated was "a paradise on earth." And, naturally, the name stuck.

Meldrum and his wife, Mabel Lee, formally opened the ranch to guests around 1905, with the property passing into Mabel's capable hands in 1911 upon the doctor's passing. She operated the ranch capably and successfully until 1927, when it was sold to the nearby Horton's HF Bar Ranch (also featured in this book).

Eventually, it was sold to a colorful cowboy character named "Wyoming" Jack O'Brien. O'Brien became well known in these parts as a cowboy entertainer among the dude ranches, and he eventually went on to make recordings and perform on radio shows. He saved enough salary to buy the ranch, then passed it off to an industrious woman, who followed in Mabel Lee Meldrum's pioneering spirit. Finally, the ranch was purchased in 1981 by Apache Oil, which went to great pains to restore the property to the pristine condition it now enjoys.

This is an informal ranch, with a whole host of traditional guest-ranch activities and features. Nestled in the heart of the Big Horn National Forest, the ranch provides an ideal place for riding, hiking, and fishing. A large swimming pool with comfy lounge furniture is a great respite from the dusty trail, one that might have been welcomed by Butch Cassidy and the Sundance Kid, who holed up not far from here (one of the finales of any visit is a hike into the red-rock canyons to explore their one-time hideaway).

This is an exceptional place for naturalists. Spring brings carpets of wildflowers, woodland birds, and a huge variety of wildlife, including elk, deer, coyotes, badger, beaver, fox, antelope, and birds of prey. Naturalist guides will help you find and identify the flora and fauna.

A rec hall is perfect for prone-to-be-bored kids, and dad or mom can shoot billiards or play Ping-Pong or board games. Need a cowboy hat? The original homestead now serves as a general store, where guests can pick up a few cowboy mementos. Active recreationists will find many outdoor games in which to compete. And the recently added fly shop is the place to fill holes in your tackle box.

Individuals looking for true outdoor adventure can sign up for backcountry pack trips into the Cloud Peak Wilderness. The Frying Pan Lake Camp is a 12-mile ride from the ranch, and the lake there provides a great place for fishing. (An enormous trout-rearing pond, fed by spectacular Rock Creek, assures that even the rank amateur won't get skunked.)

Incidentally, Paradise offers some intriguing special programs, including adults-only weeks and special women's-riding weeks that cater to individuals with out-of-the-mainstream vacations. Singles, couples, and adventurous women will find themselves as welcome as families at the Paradise Guest Ranch.

---

**Paradise Guest Ranch**
P.O. Box 790
Buffalo, WY 82834
Phone: (307) 684-7876
E-mail: fun@paradiseranch.com
Web site: www.paradiseranch.com

**Owners/Managers:** Clay and Leah Miller

**Accommodations:** Capacity, 70. Guests stay in 18 luxurious 1-, 2- and 3-bedroom cabins equipped with fireplaces, kitchenettes, washers and dryers, and outdoor porches with meadow views.

**Meals:** Meals are served in the main dining hall, convenient to the lodging cabins. 3 meals served family style each day plus covered chuckwagon meals outdoors, cookouts, and "gourmet night." French Creek Saloon serves up cocktails, wine, and beers and also serves as a gathering point for talent shows, square dancing, and general socializing.

**Activities:** Horseback riding features small groups (8 or fewer) with capable riding instructors/guides. Numerous rides of varying length go out throughout the day, allowing you to ride briefly or at length. Families can ride as a group, or children can ride separately. Special lunch-on-the trail ride is a favorite. Some cattle-work and team-penning events held for guests. Swimming in a large, heated outdoor pool. Outdoor recreational games include volleyball, badminton, and horseshoes. Indoor rec room with billiards, Ping-Pong, and board games. Hiking and fly fishing are popular pastimes. Inquire about backcountry pack trips to Frying Pan Lake Camp.

**Amenities:** Heated pool, gift shop, fly-fishing shop, indoor Jacuzzi, deluxe rooms with many amenities not typical at most guest ranches

**Special Programs:** Great children's program for kids of all ages. Special teen socials and overnight camping trips. Women's weeks feature extensive riding programs, ranch-cooking classes, wine-tasting parties, fishing, and more just for the gals. Backcountry pack trips also available.

**Rates:** $$–$$$ American plan. Reduced rates for kids 12 and under; kids 2 and under stay free if accompanied by a nanny. Reduced off-season rates, discounted family week, special ladies' dates. Off-peak rates will save you considerable money.

**Credit Cards:** None. Personal checks accepted.

**Season:** Late May to October

**Getting There:** Nearest airport in Sheridan, 45 miles north. Ranch is 16 miles west of Buffalo. Commuter flights from Denver to Sheridan. Transportation available from the Sheridan airport.

**What's Nearby:** Sheridan, a very western town with restaurants and shopping, museums, and rodeo events

# THE RED ROCK RANCH
## Kelly, Wyoming

The Red Rock is a small, family-oriented ranch situated in a secluded valley of the spectacular Jackson Hole Valley. At the end of a long, winding road that follows the sinuous contours of the Gros Ventre River, the ranch is set back in a pleasant open meadow of the Gros Ventre Mountains, surrounded on all sides by the Bridger-Teton National Forest.

With a capacity of only twenty-five guests, the Red Rock Ranch gives one the feeling of participating in an intimate family retreat. Guests stay in quaint, clean, and comfortable cabins outfitted with traditional woodstoves. A large log cabin–style lodge is an inviting place to socialize or to simply relax, and great home-style meals are also served here.

Activities at the Red Rock are traditional. The horse program is at the center of most daily action, but guests may also take time out to fish and swim. A beautiful outdoor pool offers an inviting temptation to simply "take a day off" and read the newest hot summer novel. In the evening, barbecue meals along the banks of the river offer a pleasant diversion, and guests regularly join in sing-alongs of old western standards sung by a guitar-strumming cowboy entertainer. After supper, kids and adults alike can enjoy the recreation room, which

features an antique Brunswick pool table built in 1892.

A traditional cattle ranch that was homesteaded in the 1890s, Red Rock Ranch is named for the colorful red cliffs and rock formations characteristic of this area. Since 1974, the ranch has been owned and operated by the MacKenzie family, who enjoy sharing their western life with the guests. Although Red Rock is a family-friendly resort most of the season, the MacKenzies set aside certain weeks just for adults. If you are a couple without kids or simply need a break from the children, you may wish to explore that option.

A tidy ranch layout gives the ranch a pleasant and clean appearance and facilitates activities. The cabins are neat little log units with new rooms, sitting porches, a sitting room, refrigerator, and hitchin' racks. The names for each cabin are taken from Indian tribes, and the furnishings have an old-timey Western style.

Overflowing flower boxes give a nice, cheerful ambience to these very private lodgings. The cabins are arranged in a horseshoe configuration that surrounds the main lodge, where most of the after-hours activity takes place. It's a short walk to the pool area, which is the place to be after a hot day on the trail. Guests wanting to soak their saddle-sore bodies can take a dip in the eight-person hot tub, then follow that up with a refreshing cool-off in the pool.

Of course, the ranch's proximity to Jackson is the main reason guests come here. Day trips to the Yellowstone and to Jackson are musts for first-time visitors, but seasoned returning guests often find that they'd rather spend every moment of their vacation on the ranch. It's such a peaceful and lovely place that this sentiment is an easy one to understand.

---

### The Red Rock Ranch
P.O. Box 38
Kelly, WY 83011
Phone: (307) 733–6288
Fax: (307) 733–6287
E-mail: redrockranch@onewest com
Web site: www.theredrockranch.com

**Owner/Manager:** The MacKenzie Family

**Accommodations:** Capacity, 25. Guests stay in individual log cabins named for North American Indian tribes. Cabins have 1 or 2 bedrooms, sitting room, porch, electric heat, a woodstove, and twin- and queen- or king-size beds. A few have sofa sleepers for extra children. Daily maid service.

**Meals:** 3 daily meals, all carefully prepared by the ranch chefs. Separate children's dinner seating. Breakfast cookouts and end-of-week evening barbecue.

**Activities:** The horse program includes half-day and full-day rides through the scenic country that surrounds the ranch. On the day of arrival, guests are schooled in horse safety and handling before heading out on the trail. Weekly kids' gymkhana (games on horseback) in the arena. Fishing in area streams and local guided fishing, by arrangement. Outdoor recreational games, evening dances in the dance hall. Float trips on the Snake River may be arranged.

**Amenities:** Outdoor pool with large hot tub

**Special Programs:** Children can be watched while parents ride and during the adult dinner hour. Youth wranglers will guide children on horseback rides and will oversee children during a midweek campout. Nannies are encouraged for guests with small children.

**Rates:** $$$ full American plan. Reduced rates for children under 12; children under 2 are free.

**Credit Cards:** None. Cash, traveler's checks, or personal checks only.

**Season:** June through September

**Getting There:** Nearest airport, Jackson Hole, approximately 30 miles. Airport pickup available at additional charge.

**What's Nearby:** Yellowstone National Park, Grand Teton National Park, Jackson

# RIMROCK DUDE RANCH

## Cody, Wyoming

Since 1956, the family-owned-and-operated Rimrock Dude Ranch has provided a traditional guest-ranch experience to small groups of guests. Many return season after season, drawn by the ranch's scenic beauty and the friendly service of owners Gary and Dede Fales. Among its guests have been American ski racer and Olympic champ Tommy Moe and President George H. W. Bush!

Of course, you don't have to be a celebrity to visit the Rimrock. In fact, the very reasonable, all-inclusive rates make this ranch a very good choice for families that have to stretch every vacation dollar.

With a rather small guest capacity (thirty-eight), the daily program follows a fairly predictable yet accommodating schedule. Guests arrive on Sunday, easing into the "vacation mode" and meeting the ranch staff during the evening picnic dinner. On Monday, wranglers work with guests to find just the right horse for each person's skills and temperament, and saddles are fitted. An afternoon ride follows lunch, and the evening kicks off with cowboy entertainment. Each day follows this sort of prescribed routine.

Highlights of the week include a trip to the Cody Nite Rodeo, a white-water rafting trip, and an all-day ride to Table Mountain (some guests opt for a less taxing half-day ride). On Friday, everyone heads to Yellowstone National Park to tour Yellowstone Lake and the Geyser Basins, to view the abundant wildlife, and, of course, to witness the eruption of Old Faithful Geyser. (Guests who've already toured the park may decide to visit nearby Cody or simply spend the day horseback riding.)

The week closes with a ranch rodeo with plenty of games on horseback, along with a sumptuous prime-rib dinner. Guests get a chance to entertain the staff during the concluding talent show.

The ranch is neat, quiet, and lovely, with authentic chinked log-cabin architecture and naturalistic landscaping that is very congruous with the native environment. The ranch swimming pool is a welcome amenity for parents with children. Individuals who like fishing can work the private pond—no license required. Serious anglers may hire a local guide and fish some of the fine trout waters for which northwest Wyoming is famous. The ranch's prime location in the Absaroka Mountains puts it midway between Cody, a frontier town founded by Buffalo Bill Cody, and the east entrance to Yellowstone National Park. You'll be afforded ample opportunity to visit both of these fascinating tourist destinations.

Guests wanting to travel off the beaten path should inquire about wilderness pack trips, a specialty of the Rimrock. A limited number of these special pack trips are scheduled each season. The ranch's proximity to the East Gate of Yellowstone National Park makes it an ideal location to see the famous park when it is not overrun with tourists. Snowmobile tours offer an easy way to cover some serious ground and take in many of Yellowstone's most famous sites. Rimrock's guides spend most of the year working in the rugged Yellowstone area and are knowledgeable in the history and natural wonders of the park. Don't overlook the opportunity to visit during the winter season, when the schedule is tailored to the interests of the guests and the adventure of visiting a western dude ranch is distinctly different from during the summer months.

---

**Rimrock Dude Ranch**
2728 Northfork Route
Cody, WY 82414
Phone: (307) 587–3970
Fax: (307) 527–5014
E-mail: fun@rimrockranch.com
Web site: www.rimrockranch.com

**Owners/Managers:** Gary and Dede Fales

**Accommodations:** Capacity, 38. 9 log cabins from small (suitable for a couple) to large, ideal for big families. Cabins include private baths and daily maid service and are located along both sides of Canyon Creek, a small stream bisecting the property.

**Meals:** All meals served family style in the ranch dining room, except for frequent barbecues served throughout the week. Basic, hearty American dishes and typical ranch fare.

**Activities:** A fairly structured week, but with numerous options, will satisfy almost any visitor. Horseback riding, trailside cookouts, barbecues, trips to Cody Nite Rodeo, softball games, Yellowstone Park or Cody, Wyoming trip, fishing, river rafting, swimming, hiking, ranch rodeo event.

**Amenities:** Swimming pool, ranch shuttle service, kids' rec room

**Special Programs:** None

**Rates:** $$$ full American plan. Reduced rates for children, varying by age. Prices do not include taxes, gratuity, and park use fees.

**Credit Cards:** Visa, MasterCard as deposit. Personal checks on balance of payment.

**Season:** June through September

**Getting There:** Located midway between Cody, Wyoming, and the east entrance to Yellowstone National Park. Most guests fly into Cody. Ranch shuttle from airport available.

**What's Nearby:** Cody, founded by Buffalo Bill Cody, site of the Buffalo Bill Cody Historical Center; Cody Nite Rodeo. Also, Yellowstone National Park.

# R LAZY S RANCH

Jackson Hole, Wyoming

---

A prime location virtually on the skirts of the Teton Mountains, just a stone's throw from internationally famous Jackson Hole Winter Resort, would be enough to attract many to the R Lazy S. But when you couple superlative location with a top-drawer staff (there are roughly two guests to every one staff member) and throw in a broad and flexible menu of activities, you have

the recipe for an exceptional guest-ranch experience.

The 325-acre ranch abuts the south boundary of Grand Teton National Park, with the scenic Snake River to the east and the soaring Tetons to the west. During trail rides and hikes, you'll trek through pine and fir forests that give way to subalpine meadows lush with wild grasses and native wildflowers, finally arriving at craggy alpine basins. Once there, you may see whistling marmots greeting the rare visitor, and if you peer closely into the crystal-clear lakes, you might spy trout on the prowl for insects.

Sound too good to be true? Read on. Back at the ranch, the facilities are first-rate without being pretentious or stuffy. The guest cabins are individually distinctive, offering a variety of floor plans to accommodate families or groups of different sizes. All have full baths and are heated, and most have sitting rooms or a living room with fireplace. After a quick washup following a day of activities, guests relax in the main lodge, where most meals are served. The lodge looks out over the Jackson Hole Valley, often described as one of the most scenic areas of the West. Be careful sitting by the huge stone fireplace in a big comfy chair—you might just nod off to sleep and miss the night's exceptional dinner!

We're quite keen on the mix of activities at the R Lazy S. The traditional guest-ranch activities are all there, but there are a few added extras that are equally inviting. Once a week, for instance, guests are invited to try waterskiing at a nearby lake (for persons not familiar with the West, waterskiing is something rare in these parched parts). You can also try your hand at rock climbing, a natural in these parts. There are two nearby championship golf courses ideal for duffers—golf balls are known to fly noticeably farther in the thin mountain air.

Of course, the town of Jackson offers numerous possibilities, from cultural events to county fairs to the popular weekly rodeo contest. You can also visit lots of western art galleries (there are close to thirty in this rather small town), and no visit would be complete without a stopover to see the Silver Dollar Bar at the historic Wort Hotel.

Although the ranch is generally family oriented, in fall during the height of fly-fishing season, the ranch becomes the providence of adults-only. Guests looking for a more mature experience and who have an interest in improving their fishing skills will want to inquire about the fall adults-only season.

Given its proximity to Yellowstone National Park, the Jackson area is the epicenter of the guest-ranch industry in North America. Given its long-standing tradition of serving guests, the R Lazy S stands as one of the finest of the area's many guest-ranch destinations. A long list of repeat customers is testament to the quality and attention to detail that characterize this fine establishment.

---

## R Lazy S Ranch

P.O. Box 308
Teton Village, WY 83025
Phone: (307) 733–2655
Fax: (307) 734–1120
E-mail: info@rlazys.com
Web site: www.rlazys.com

**Owner/Manager:** The Stirn Family

**Accommodations:** Capacity, 45. Guests stay in 14 log cabins featuring 1, 2, or 3 bedrooms, most with sitting rooms or living rooms and fireplaces. All have 1 or 2 bathrooms. Teen dorm with bathroom accommodates 4, either boys or girls.

**Meals:** 3 meals served daily plus outdoor barbecue cookouts and trailside lunches. Western-style home cooking, served buffet style or family style. Separate seating for children and teens. BYOB.

**Activities:** Horseback program with arena instruction for riders of all abilities. More than 80 horses allow wranglers to custom-fit their guests. Other activities include fly fishing with instructors or guided fly fishing (extra). Numerous rivers, lakes, and streams, on-site and off-site, from which to choose. Weekly fishing clinic for anglers. Float trips on the Snake River, off-site golf and tennis. Waterskiing weekly on Jackson Lake. Swimming hole and inner-tubing in nearby river. Warm-spring pools in the Jackson Hole Valley. Evening activities include talent shows, slide shows, dances, hayrides, recreational games such as softball and volleyball. Excursions to Jackson and the Yellowstone National Park (private car or rental encouraged).

**Amenities:** Superb lodge with valley and mountain views, a massive fireplace and a rec room. Teen "bunkhouse." Outdoor recreational games area; on-site laundry facilities.

**Special Programs:** Children 7 and older. Children's riding program in which kids ride separately from parents, if desired. Separate children's dining.

**Rates:** $$–$$$ full American plan. Minimum 1-week stay. Inquire about guided fishing trips.

**Credit Cards:** None. Personal checks preferred.

**Season:** Mid-June through September

**Getting There:** Located 1 mile from Teton Village, approximately 12 miles west of Jackson, Wyoming. Nearest airport: Jackson.

**What's Nearby:** Teton Village, Jackson; Yellowstone National Park

# 7D RANCH

## Cody, Wyoming

Originally opened as the Dewey Riddle Ranch, for its original owner, the 7D gained its current name when it was purchased in the late 1950s by the Dominick family: Dr. DeWitt "Doc" Dominick, his wife, Lee, and their five children. At present, the ranch is still owned and operated by the Dominicks, who have passed the operation down through successive generations.

From the original log cabins to the Molesworth furniture in the Main Lodge, this place exudes an old-timey vibe that will help connect you to the past. (For readers unfamiliar with the Molesworth name, Thomas Canada Molesworth was a Cody furniture maker whose work graced many of the best guest ranches, hotels, and private homes in the West.) Persons looking to visit a classic and timeless western guest ranch little changed since the heyday of the postwar 1950s western-vacation craze owe it to themselves to visit the 7D.

The folks at the 7D are horse lovers, and they will take extra care to instruct you and to fit you to a complementary horse. For guests who wish to really improve their riding skills, arena riding lessons are available—and encouraged—throughout your weeklong stay. Even the most expert rider is likely to gain some valuable new insights during his or her stay. An exhibition on horse training, given in the ranch's training-specific round pen, is fascinating, even to guests who haven't had much experience with horses.

Like many guest ranches in the Cody area, the 7D prides itself on offering great fishing. The Sunlight River cuts through the property, offering a great "first time" experience for novices who will find it easy to catch the small brook trout. Below Sunlight Falls, rainbow and cutthroat trout abound for anglers willing to go a little bit afield to stalk these larger and more challenging species. Furthermore, the ranch staff includes a full-time fishing guide, who can demonstrate some of the better spots on nearby rivers and lakes throughout the region.

Guests wishing to hike can head out in virtually any direction and attain awe-inspiring vistas without completely exhausting themselves. But for those who crave a true peak experience, the ranch can help you to devise an all-day climb leading to one of the many summits surrounding the property.

In the evenings the 7D schedules diverse and fun entertainment. There are lawn sports, roping instruction, lectures on the wild species of the region, cowboy singers and storytellers, square dances, a Native American sweat lodge, campfires, and the thrilling Cody Nite Rodeo. You'd have to work hard at being bored!

In addition to its regular dude-ranch program, the ranch also offers wilderness pack trips and fall guided hunting trips.

All in all, this is a ranch with lots of family character and tradition. The Dominick family's excellent stewardship has helped to retain the vintage personality of the place and allows guests the chance to step back in time to a less-hurried time.

## 7D Ranch

P.O. Box 100
Cody, WY 82414
Phone: (307) 587–9885; (888) 587–9885
Fax: (307) 587–9885
E-mail: 7Dranch@wyoming.com
Web site: www.7dranch.com

**Owner/Manager:** The Dominick Family

**Accommodations:** Capacity, 32. 11 cabins shaded in Aspen groves. Cabins vary in size from 1 to 4 bedrooms and feature wood-stoves, full bathrooms, and charming western decor. Daily maid service and laundry facilities available.

**Meals:** Meals are served family style in the main dining hall. Food is of superb quality, including such staples as 7D ranch-raised beef, fresh-baked breads, and crisp salads with vegetables from the ranch garden. Weekly "cowboy breakfast" on the trail and outdoor barbecue are signature experiences of any 7D visit.

**Activities:** Horseback riding includes full- and half-day rides, limited to small groups of similar abilities. Excellent preride instruction. Great fishing, either in ranch ponds, the ranch river, or guided fly fishing (extra). River rafting, wildlife viewing, mountain biking, local sightseeing, cattle drives, overnight campouts.

Special backcountry pack trips from 2 to 7 days (inquire for details). Skeet-shooting range, basketball court, horseshoes, roping lessons, and volleyball. Evening activities include expert speakers whose topics range from wild animals to geology; evening square dances, Indian sweat lodge, sing-alongs, campfires with marshmallow s'mores, and lawn games.

**Amenities:** General store, laundry facilities, youth rec room

**Special Programs:** Excellent children's program includes full-time counselors and riding instructors, hikes, and organized activities for kids ages 6 to 12. Backcountry pack-trip vacations, fall hunting trips, and special September adults-only weeks.

**Rates:** $$$ full American plan. Children's and off-season rates. Minimum 1-week stay.

**Credit Cards:** Visa, MasterCard (3 percent service charge added). Personal and traveler's checks only.

**Season:** Mid-June through mid-September

**Getting There:** Nearest airport in Cody, 50 miles from the ranch, and in Billings, Montana. Ranch shuttle available.

**What's Nearby:** Cody, a charming western town founded by Buffalo Bill Cody. Be sure to explore the Buffalo Bill Cody Historic Center and Museum.

# TA GUEST RANCH
## Buffalo, Wyoming

When Earl and Barbara Madsen purchased the TA Ranch in 1991, their first thought was to continue operating it as a traditional cattle outfit. But as restoration of the Victorian-era ranch buildings progressed, they recognized that this property was simply too wonderful not to share it with others.

Currently, the TA stands among the finest traditional historic ranches in North America. You won't find swimming pools and a posh spa facility on the TA, just lovingly kept facilities and gracious hosts who enjoy providing a taste of the West as it was more than a century ago.

Each of the buildings has been faithfully restored to its 1800s-era origins, right down to the period wallpaper. The TA has fifteen sleeping rooms, which will accommodate up to thirty guests. Each guest room has a private bathroom, but no phones, televisions, or clock radios to disturb you. (You can, however, reconnect to the modern world with televisions, VCRs,

and Internet access provided for the guests' use and enjoyment.)

This place overflows with local history. While at the TA, you can see the reminders of itinerant cowboys who carved their initials and names into the barn's old pinewood doors. If you examine the barn more closely, you'll also discover bullet holes from a gunfight that took place here in 1892! As the story goes, a group of cattle barons set out to control the Powder River area. Their intention was to hunt down the small, independent ranchers of the region and chase them out. Events didn't follow their plan, however. When word got out among Johnson County residents, the hunters became the hunted. The rapacious cattlemen were pinned down at the TA Ranch, where the gun battle ensued. (You can learn more about this intriguing tale during your visit.)

If you're looking for more outlaw history, the bank robbers Butch Cassidy and the Sundance Kid once hid out in this country, and you can take an off-ranch hike to their famous Hole-in-the-Wall, where they would escape the pesky Pinkerton detectives. This tour will also take you to an authentic buffalo jump and to a place where Indian artists drew pictographs on the rock walls. You'll have tales to tell your friends for months to come.

Folks who like to ride and are concerned about the pokey nose-to-tail trail rides common to many guest ranches will be pleased to learn that the TA follows a different path. Guests are taught the essentials of riding safety and etiquette and carefully matched to horses that suit their riding skills. You'll be able to ride across vast open meadows, through creeks, over canyon passes, and along ancient Indian trails—a liberating experience for both rider and horse. Guests interested in cattle work can pitch in alongside the wranglers to gather and move the herd, check fences, water holes, and salt licks.

Guests looking for alternate trail transportation can head out on a mountain bike (if you can't bring one, the staff can help get you mounted). Trails vary from mild to wild, with the beautiful Bighorn Mountains providing the perfect backdrop for an enervating ride.

What's intriguing about the TA Ranch is that the owners, Earl and Barbara, have taken great pains to retain its authenticity and history. They've even helped to create a foundation to provide for the research and illumination of the ranch's rich history and the history of the region. True western-history buffs, as well as just plain folk looking for an authentic western getaway, will appreciate all the work and care evident in all details of the TA Guest Ranch.

## TA Guest Ranch
P.O. Box 313
Buffalo, WY 82834
Phone: (800) 368–7398; (307) 684–5833
Fax: (307) 684–5663
E-mail: taranch@trib.com
Web site: www.taranch.com

**Owners/Managers:** Earl and Barbara Madsen

**Accommodations:** Capacity, 30. Guest rooms are integrated into several historic properties on the ranch. All buildings have been carefully renovated and are decorated with authentic antiques, as well as more modern furnishings such as kitchenettes with microwave ovens, coffeemakers, and refrigerators. Guests dine in the Cook House, a restored homesteader's cabin, which, in addition to the dining room, includes 2 bedrooms that make an ideal family suite.

**Meals:** Nouveau Western-style ranch cuisine. Breakfasts include oven-baked goods such as caramel-pecan rolls, banana-walnut muffins, and buttermilk biscuits with homemade jams. These are followed with egg dishes, breakfast burritos, ranch fries, breakfast cereals, and fresh fruits. Lunch is similarly robust, with sandwiches, salads, and desserts. Dinner is a truly special occasion. Menu items vary, but a typical weekly menu may include prime rib, Basque pasta, boneless pork chops, and country-fried chicken. You'll enjoy crisp garden salads, side dishes, and toothsome desserts.

**Activities:** Daily activities focus on horseback riding, hiking, mountain biking, fishing, and tours of nearby attractions. Golfing at 3 nearby championship courses. Local rodeos. Living-history presentations that bring to life the Native American culture and the Western history of this region of

Wyoming. A variety of outdoor and indoor recreational games including horseshoes, volleyball, roping practices, and board games.

**Amenities:** This is an authentic historic property, where amenities such as pools and such would seem out of place. That said, it is like stepping back into the Old West, but with all the rough edges sanded off. A big main lodge with a wide porch invites guests to relax with a book from the ranch library. Wet bar for socializing and a study for quiet reading and relaxation.

**Special Programs:** No children's program. Rambunctious youngsters probably won't feel as at-home as more quiet children. Children are their parents' responsibility and should be at least 8 years old if they will be riding horses. Nannies encouraged for younger children.

**Rates:** $$$ full American plan. Rate includes room, 3 meals, snacks, horseback riding, and all ranch activities, as well as a scenic day tour throughout the Powder River Basin, reservoir or stream fishing, and more. Stay a day, a week, or a month. Reduced rates for kids 11–15 and children 5–10; children under age 4 are free.

**Credit Cards:** Visa, MasterCard

**Season:** May through October

**Getting There:** Nearest airport in Sheridan, 45 miles. Ranch is located 13 miles south of Buffalo on Highway 196.

**What's Nearby:** Historical attractions include Custer Battlefield, the Oregon Trail, and the famous Hole-in-the-Wall hideout of Butch Cassidy's gang. Rodeo events in Buffalo, as well as shopping, dining, museums.

# T CROSS RANCH
## Dubois, Wyoming

Once you cross under the main gate that greets newcomers to T Cross Ranch, you'll have left the modern world behind and magically stepped back into the Old West. Ahead lies the rugged and preternaturally beautiful Absaroka Mountains, whose secrets you will soon begin to learn. The historic ranch buildings are nestled in a quiet, secluded meadow back-to-back with the Shoshone National Forest, part of the contiguous public lands that connect northwestern Wyoming to the Yellowstone National Park, the Grand Teton Wilderness, and tens of thousands of acres of forest lands.

Hosts Mark and Gretchen Cardall represent the fourth generation in this family-owned and -operated guest ranch and outfitting business, passing on a tradition of western hospitality. Their two children, Kameron and Ethan, help out in the day-to-day operations, ensuring that the tradition will continue for years to come. The buildings on the ranch were handcrafted in the 1920s and 1930s from the native lodgepole pine, lending the perfect ambience to this mountain escape. Inside the guest cabins, the lodgepole furniture ties you to the outdoor theme, while Indian rugs and western artifacts serve to remind you (not

T Cross Ranch, Wyoming

that you could forget) that this is indeed the real West. Don't worry that you'll have to fuss with nineteenth-century outhouses or draw water from the horse corral; the plumbing is modern, with full showers and plenty of hot water.

The main lodge is likewise folksy and rustic, with lots of Wyoming cowboy charm. Far from austere, however, the lodge is wonderfully comfortable and cozy, with its massive stone fireplace and its spreading veranda. Guests tend to congregate here to socialize before and after the lavish meals, to swap fish stories, and to tell tales of their day's adventures.

And there will be plenty of stories to tell. T Cross owns sixty head of horses, all handpicked for their mountain savvy and calm dispositions to handle the roughest country as unstintingly as they will travel across a broad, grassy meadow. Each guest (beginning with kids as young as six) is assigned his or her own horse for the duration of the stay. Once properly mounted, guests can choose from half-day to full-day rides that wind through groves of aspen trees and pine and fir forests and that offer spectacular views of the Washaki Wilderness. Keep quiet and be attentive, and you'll likely encounter wildlife ranging from slow-moving porcupines to dashing coyotes. There's a fair share of elk, deer, and moose to see, too.

In 2005 T Cross established the Washakie Wilderness camp in Five Pockets, one of the most beautiful subalpine meadows in the Absaroka range. It offers a place to really get into a wilderness setting of magnificent beauty. Five mountain streams converge here to form the headwaters of Horse Creek. In addition to the camp, T Cross offers a limited number of guests the opportunity to take part in progressive pack trips through the Wind River Mountains and Washakie Wilderness through breathtaking high-mountain passes. Those looking for a truly extraordinary backcountry experience can't go wrong with either adventure.

In addition to riding, you will enjoy fishing in picturesque Horse Creek, where brook trout and mountain whitefish abound. An annual stocking program has also added rainbow and cutthroat trout to the species list, but you'll have to play catch-and-release, for the benefit of the other guests—not to mention the fish!

---

**T Cross Ranch**
P.O. Box 638
Dubois, WY 82513
Phone: (307) 455–2206; (877) 827–6770
Fax: (307) 455–2720
E-mail: tcrossranch@wyoming.com
Web site: www.tcross.com

**Owners:** Mark and Gretchen Cardall

**Accommodations:** Capacity, 24. 8 cozy log cabins tucked into the pine trees. Cabins feature Indian rugs, handcrafted log furniture, down quilts, woodstoves or fireplaces, hot showers, and individual porches.

**Meals:** Hearty and filling ranch cuisine with a touch of elegance. Cook will prepare your freshly caught trout. Breakfast and dinner rides. BYOB happy hour every evening in the lodge.

**Activities:** Horseback-riding program with half- and full-day rides conducted at the walk, trot, lope, and canter as well as "the wild ride," for experienced horsemen. Arena instruction, gymkhanas, perhaps some cattle work. Inner tubing, hiking, horseshoes, rock climbing, rifle range, volleyball games, overnight campouts, lake and river fishing. Inquire about backcountry wilderness pack trips and guided fall hunting. Evening entertainment with local cowboy poets and musicians, square dances, campfires, and cookouts.

**Amenities:** Jacuzzi hot tub, gift shop, main lodge with grand stone fireplace, large porch, and western artifacts

**Special Programs:** Children 6 and older ride with "youth wranglers." Gymkhana games on horseback, tepee cam, and innertubing for kids and teens.

**Rates:** $$$ full American plan. Rates prorated in the off-season (anytime but July and August) for shorter stays.

**Credit Cards:** None. Personal or traveler's checks only.

**Season:** Mid-June to late September

**Getting There:** Nearest airports are in Jackson and Riverton. The ranch can arrange ground transportation from either airport, or you may rent a car. Dubois has a private airport with a 5,000-foot blacktop runway for private and charter flights.

**What's Nearby:** Dubois, Yellowstone National Park, Grand Teton Park, and Wind River Indian Reservation

# TRAIL CREEK RANCH BED AND BREAKFAST

## Wilson, Wyoming

For some people, the idea of a structured guest-ranch vacation is a little, well, claustrophobic. For those who want to explore western Wyoming on their own schedule, the Trail Creek Ranch, located just minutes from Jackson and within easy driving distance of Yellowstone National Park, is the perfect retreat.

A unique bed-and-breakfast, Trail Creek is situated in a lush valley, surrounded by groves of aspen, pine, and green meadows that support the resident horse herd. Its 280 acres offer ample elbow room. It's a great place to recharge your batteries. And it's easy to enjoy a sumptuous country breakfast before heading out to explore the Jackson Hole region.

Great recreation is what the original owner, Elizabeth "Betty" Woolsey, had in mind when she purchased the property in 1942. The captain of the first U.S. women's Olympic ski team, Woolsey discovered the ranch's main lodge while skiing in the wonderful dry-powder snow that made this region so famous for skiing. The ranch proved equally appealing in summer, when cool weather and wonderful views made it a natural place for outdoor activities.

Woolsey passed away in 1997, but not before creating a conservation agreement that prevents the 280-acre ranch from development. Now the ranch is run by Margaret "Muggs" Schultz, who has been at the ranch for more than fifty years, and Alex Menolachino, a young woman who has been with Trail Creek for most of her adult life. Alex and her husband, Mike, are raising their family in this little slice of paradise.

A working ranch since 1946, Trail Creek has always enjoyed an international clientele, as well as Americans "in the know." Guests congregate in the main lodge, with its comfortable living room and dining room. Mornings are spent over a leisurely breakfast featuring homemade pastries, fruits, and the wonderful creations of the resident chef. At the end of the day, guests return to enjoy the sunset on the large covered porch, and impromptu cocktail parties often arise (there's a bar, but you'll need to bring your own liquor, wine, or beer).

For vacationers wishing to head directly for the hills to enjoy mountain biking, hiking, or some other local activity, sack lunches can be ordered. There's horseback riding on the ranch, as well, at added charge. This is an "a la carte" experience, more than an all-inclusive guest-ranch visit. The folks at Trail Creek Ranch will offer their assistance and advice in finding perfect activities to suit your vacation wishes and your activity level, whether that means guided fly fishing in a local river or shopping for new shoes in Jackson's posh shops!

You can, of course, also relax for the day on the ranch itself. There's plenty of native wildlife for early risers to observe, including moose, elk, coyotes, and birds. Wolves and bears have also been sighted, though they are not easy to come by—thank goodness!

The ranch also features a heated swimming pool with views of the pasture and the rustic barn. This is the kind of place independent explorers will love—their own special ranch retreat in the heart of Jackson Hole, one of the great recreational destinations in North America.

**Trail Creek Ranch Bed and Breakfast**
P.O. Box 10
Wilson, WY 83014
Phone: (307) 733–2610
Fax: (307) 733–2610
E-mail: TrailCreekRanch@msn.com
Web site: www.jacksonholetrailcreekranch
.com

**Owners/Managers:** Muggs Schultz and
Alexandra Menolachino

**Accommodations:** Capacity, 25; 12 in winter. Guests stay in a number of cabins ranging from small units suitable for couples to
large family-size, multiroom cabins. Prices
reflect accommodations rather than the
number of guests. Winter guests enjoy 3
meals per day with their accommodations.

**Meals:** Breakfast of homemade pastries and
baked goods, fruits, and hearty ranch breakfasts. Sack lunch available by request and
at added charge.

**Activities:** Horseback riding, hiking, mountain biking, swimming in the outdoor pool.
The staff will assist you in making off-site
plans that take advantage of the many
activities in the Jackson Hole region.

**Amenities:** Lovely guest cabins, each with a
unique design and appeal. The Suite, for

example, has antique twin-size beds, wonderful artwork, full bath with tub. The Ritz
is a 2-bedroom cabin with living room and
fireplace, kitchenette, queen-size bed in
the master suite, twin beds in the loft, and
extra sleeping space in the living room.

**Special Programs:** No children's program or
scheduled activities, although young guests
are welcome.

**Rates:** $$$ European plan, bed-and-
breakfast. 3-day minimum stay in summer.

**Credit Cards:** Visa, MasterCard. Personal or
traveler's checks accepted.

**Season:** June to September 30. Winter
accommodations (February to March) for 12.

**Getting There:** Located near Wilson, on the
Teton Pass northwest of Jackson. Most
guests fly into Jackson, Wyoming, or drive
in private cars. Airline shuttle service to
Jackson from Denver International Airport
and Salt Lake City. Inquire for specific
directions to the ranch. Rental car or pri-
vate vehicle for local sightseeing and activi-
ties are strongly recommended.

**What's Nearby:** Jackson Hole region, includ-
ing the famous Jackson Hole Ski Area,
Grand Teton National Park, Teton Village,
and Jackson. Yellowstone National Park,
Grand Targhee Winter Resort

# TRIANGLE C RANCH
Dubois, Wyoming

A first-class ranch in a spectacular setting
with innovative programs and dozens of
activities. What more could you want in a
ranch vacation?

The Triangle C Ranch is a great place to
"get away from it all" without forsaking

creature comforts or being too far from the
action. The main lodge is a big, gorgeous
8,000-square-foot log building with a wrap-
around pine deck and is backed by a huge
rock escarpment that gives it a postcard
aspect. Kick back in The Moose Room

Triangle C Ranch, Wyoming

© Bob Woodall/FocusProductions.com

Lounge, where a towering log ceiling and a huge stone fireplace provide the perfect frame for the massive moose head that presides over the goings-on. And in the unlikely event that the ranch proves too small for you, you can head into Dubois with the other guests for a night of dancing or take in the attractions of Jackson, including an authentic cowboy rodeo.

Just an hour from Jackson Hole and Yellowstone National Park, the Triangle C is perched on a bluff overlooking the Wind River, with views of the Absaroka Range. An ideal spot for photographers!

There is a nice mix of traditional and contemporary activities. You can learn the ancient art of archery with an instructor (bow and arrow provided), travel back in time with the mountain men and learn

how to shoot a black-powder rifle and throw a tomahawk, or take a guided canoeing trip.

Guests who like more contemporary outdoor sports can schedule a tee time at the nine-hole course in Dubois. Or they can make a day of it and try the Arnold Palmer–designed championship course in Jackson Hole. Rafting is another option, and many guests choose to take a scenic float trip down the Snake River (whitewater raft trips are also available with area outfitters, at additional charge). Mountain biking on the ranch is another popular pastime.

The Triangle C is owned and operated by the Garnick family, which has been involved in the Wyoming guest-ranch business for more than three decades. They take great pride in their ranch and have striven to help it retain its heritage (the ranch was established in 1909), while providing it with modern comforts and genteel frontier elegance. The recently added Pinnacle Cabins, for instance, are two-story log complexes with king and queen suites, fireplaces, and Jacuzzi bathtubs. Each has a different theme—Indian, Trapper, Cowboy, and The Ranch House. The lodge features the Tie Hack Bar, whose polished knotty-pine bar, old-timey furniture, and artifacts seem to have been lifted from a Clint Eastwood western. This is truly a showcase property!

Although the Triangle C is very kid-friendly, twice a year the ranch is turned over to fun-seeking single adults. Each spring and fall, singles converge on the ranch for these special "country singles weeks." Dine and dance in Jackson Hole, tour the Yellowstone Park, go floating on the Snake River, fish, hike, bike—and perhaps meet the cowboy or cowgirl of your dreams!

---

**Triangle C Ranch**
3737 Highway 26
Dubois, WY 82513
Phone: (800) 661–4928; (307) 455–2225
E-mail: info@trianglec.com
Web site: www.trianglec.com

**Owner/Manager:** The Garnick Family

**Accommodations:** Capacity, 50. Guests stay in original 1920s log cabins and in the new Pinnacle Cabins. Take your pick, from rustic tradition to modern comfort. The Pinnacle Cabins are 2-story log complexes, each decorated around a western theme; the original cabins are set in the woods and vary from honeymooner suites to double bedrooms with bunk beds for the kids.

**Meals:** The Triangle C's resident chef, Sallie, serves up fresh, healthful ranch fare.

Sallie has been cooking homemade goodies at the Triangle C for several years, baking homemade breads and specialty desserts. Prime rib, trout almandine, and Cornish hens are just a few of the dinner entrees. Breakfast rides, old-fashioned picnics on the deck, and barbecue ribs and New York steaks at the campfire cookout. Special diets can be accommodated with advance notice.

**Activities:** Summer dude-ranch activities include horseback riding, mountain biking, hiking, canoeing, black-powder shoot and tomahawk throwing, archery, campfire cookouts, scenic float trips on the Snake River, Yellowstone tours, fishing, pack trips (inquire for details), and more. Winter snowmobiling, snowshoeing, cross-country skiing, alpine skiing. Fall hunting trips and fishing trips.

**Amenities:** Conference rooms with computers, copiers, Internet access; 2-table pool parlor, home theater, library, dining room with 65-person capacity, Tie Hack Saloon, archery and shooting ranges, guest laundry, hot tub

**Special Programs:** Twice-annual "singles weeks" for adult singles. Included are trips to Jackson and Dubois, hiking, riding, rafting, social events. The youth programs are among the best in the country, with a complete naturalist program, a teen program, and a children's program. Typical teen activities include cookouts, horseback riding, personal watercraft riding on Brooks Lake, dances, mountain-bike rides, and more. A great place for kids of all ages to make new friends and learn new, confidence-building skills.

**Rates:** $$ full American plan. Reduced children's rates, off-season rates, and nonrider rates. Some off-site activities are extra.

**Credit Cards:** Visa, MasterCard, American Express. Personal and traveler's checks accepted.

**Season:** Open year-round. Dude ranch (spring and summer), hunting and fishing (fall), snow-sports activities (winter)

**Getting There:** Located 18 miles west of Dubois, 65 miles north of Jackson. Nearest airports: Jackson, Dubois, Riverton. Ranch shuttle available; rental cars or personal transportation recommended for guests wishing to take part in off-site activities such as golfing.

**What's Nearby:** Dubois, Jackson Hole, Yellowstone National Park

# TRIANGLE X RANCH
## Moose, Wyoming

A true all-season ranch, the Triangle X is a great place to visit whether you are planning a summer getaway or a winter vacation. This is an authentic working ranch where haying, branding, and raising livestock are the order of the day, but this doesn't mean it's all work and no play.

Guests enjoy everything from horseback riding to river-float trips to square dancing and barbecue cookouts. The winter schedule includes cross-country skiing, snowmobiling, snowshoeing, and off-site alpine skiing at the famous Jackson Hole Winter Resort.

The Triangle X is situated in the heart of the Grand Teton National Park, offering guests mountain views and backcountry wilderness unsurpassed anywhere in the Lower 48. The ranch has been the pride and joy of the Turner family, who have welcomed adventurous guests through four successive generations. The Triangle X is the only dude ranch concession still in operation within Grand Teton National Park.

Around 1928, J. C. Turner of the Triangle X Dude Ranch moved dovetailed logs from neighbor John Fee's partially completed homestead cabin to the Triangle X Ranch, where the logs were used to form the first ten courses of Turner's new barn. This historic landmark still distinguishes the property.

One of the Turner family's specialties is backcountry pack trips in the Grand Teton and the south Yellowstone wilderness areas. The Turner family has been in the outfitting business their entire lives and represent one of the most respected and experienced teams in the industry. They know where to find wildlife, how to make guests comfortable and safe on the trail, and, most important, how to show guests a really good time! Vacationers looking for a backcountry adventure or a superb Wyoming hunting trip will definitely want to inquire about this year's offering for extended wilderness pack trips and guided hunts led by these outdoor experts.

Persons looking for a somewhat more "civilized" trip will want to find out more about a proper ranch stay. Ranch vacationers stay in generous one-, two-, and three-bedroom log cabins with indoor plumbing (sometimes a luxury on a real working ranch), polished wood floors, and attractive western-motif interiors. You'll have a postcard-perfect view of the Teton Range from the comfort of your covered porch.

The Triangle X also serves as the perfect place for "river rats," people who thrive within earshot of the rushing rapids and burbling brooks. That, of course, means river rafters and anglers. If you're looking for both scenic beauty and exciting adventure, you'll want to get on the list for a rafting trip on the Snake River. Next to horseback riding, it's the favorite activity at the Triangle X.

Anglers will find themselves in a piscatorial paradise. The Jackson Hole area has literally hundreds of miles of streams and numerous lakes where you can pursue a variety of trout species. The ranch can provide you with a raft and guide for a day of float fishing, or they'll show you some of their "secret spots," which they've ferreted out over a lifetime of fishing the region.

For those individuals looking for a traditional western guest ranch with a wide variety of summer and winter activities, a true working-ranch atmosphere, a congenial staff, and unsurpassed views, the Triangle X is the ideal choice.

---

**Triangle X Ranch**
2 Triangle X Road
Moose, WY 83012
Phone: (307) 733–2183
Fax: (307) 733–8685
E-mail: trianglexranch@wyoming.com
Web site: www.trianglex.com

**Owner/Manager:** The Turner Family

**Accommodations:** Capacity, 75. Guests stay in 1-, 2- and 3-bedroom log cabins, each with bathroom and covered porch. Spectacular views!

**Meals:** Meals are served in the main dining room of the lodge. Dinner service is elegant western, with elk-horn chandeliers and linen tablecloths. The ranch owners tout their four-star cooking staff, which mixes up the menu but always serves up home-made breads, fresh vegetables and salads, and exceptional main entrees. Outdoor cookouts and trail-ride cookouts are a big part of the ranch dining experience. Chil-

dren dine in a separate seating except on family nights.

**Activities:** Fundamentally a riding ranch, the Triangle X maintains an extensive trail-riding program with mountain-savvy horses. Riders of all abilities will be matched to appropriate mounts. The riding here is especially scenic, and you are likely to encounter numerous native animals, so be sure to take a camera in your saddlebag. Backcountry wilderness pack trips (4 days to 2 weeks) where guests can rough it in established camps with sturdy sleeping tents. Fall wilderness hunting camps. Guided fishing in area lakes and streams. Snake River float trips. Winter snow-mobiling, cross-country skiing, snowshoeing, and alpine skiing at several nearby ski areas. Evening excursions to Jackson, where dancing, dining, shopping, and melodrama can be found. Nighttime rodeo action near town. Evening "social," square dances, local history lecture, cowboy singing and folklore.

**Amenities:** Ranch gift shop, ranch transportation to and from airport, old-fashioned swimming hole

**Special Programs:** Children 12 and under take part in the Kiddie Wrangler program of supervised riding, arts and crafts, swimming trips, and more. Summer backcountry pack trips, winter activity packages, guided fishing and hunting trips.

**Rates:** $$ full American plan. Off-season rates, pack trips, winter rates available. 1-week minimum stay in summer.

**Credit Cards:** None. Personal or traveler's checks accepted.

**Season:** May to November, mid-December to April

**Getting There:** Nearest airport, Jackson (25 miles). Located near Teton Village, north of Jackson.

**What's Nearby:** Jackson, Yellowstone National Park

# UXU RANCH

## Wapiti, Wyoming

Anyone looking for an authentic western ranch vacation with modern refinement will feel right at home at the UXU, one of the most graciously furnished and loveliest guest ranches to be found in this book. Ranch owners Grant "Tuff" Flaharty, Heidi Flaharty, and Ray Flaharty all bring extensive business experience and decades of time spent in the hospitality and ranching businesses to the UXU, a landmark property in the original Old West guest ranch town of Cody.

Grant rose to the heights of corporate America, eventually becoming president of a $125 million company. Having traveled the world, he decided to go back to his family ranching roots. The UXU has given him a place to live his dream of providing down-home hospitality, raising horses, and riding to his heart's content—and also to dabbling in his passion for creating full-course fine-dining meals paired with carefully selected wines. The result is a refined guest ranch experience for people desiring the most of the Wild West—without the rough edges.

The Flahartys could not have picked a more attractive property to live out their guest ranching ambitions. The UXU Ranch is an eleven-cabin property not far from the borders of Yellowstone National Park on a stretch of highway once described by Teddy Roosevelt as "the most scenic 52 miles in the United States."

The UXU has a colorful history. As local lore has it, the ranch was bought by an estranged husband, whose wife lived just down the road. To vent his feelings, he named it the "U (expletive) U" so that he could let his ex know his feelings each time she passed by. But Forest Service officials didn't take kindly to a swear word being used within the boundaries of the Shoshone National Forest, and so the ranch became the "UXU."

Since taking over this longtime western guest ranch, the Flaharty family has kept the decor authentic; the main lodge area is adorned with the worn hats of true ranch hands and gracefully aged kitchen ware, the log cabins are exquisite in a rustic fashion that is comfortable, spotlessly clean, and cozy. True cowboys never had it this good! Keeping much of the ranch's original Old Hickory furniture, the previous owner contracted furniture designer J. Mike Patrick of Cody, Wyoming, to create some whimsical western furniture reminiscent of the style of the famed furniture maker Thomas Molesworth. Patrick built beds, mirrors, ottomans, sconces, night tables, and dressers. The furniture is replete with Chimayo cushions and carved images of moose, fly fishermen, and cowboys.

The Flahartys are definitely hands-on owners. They join guests each evening at the dinner table, sharing conversation and stories over gourmet nouveau-western cuisine.

And while the accommodations are great, a visitor isn't likely to spend a lot of time admiring them, for the UXU Ranch is all about experiencing Wyoming's rugged, beautiful landscape. It's said that the best way to see a ranch is on horseback, and the UXU accommodates its guests with an excellent horse program. In addition to guided rides, guests enjoy guided fly fishing in area creeks and rivers, mountain biking, river rafting, guided trips to the Yellowstone, and a trip to the Buffalo Bill Historical Center in Cody and the Cody Nite Rodeo. The ranch hot tub overlooks the Absaroka Mountains, and there's an underground sauna for guests who need to relax tense muscles. Golfing and shooting are nearby at the Cody Shooting Complex.

The UXU has been reviewed in dozens of magazines, from travel publications to food magazines, daily papers, and architectural digests. One thing reviewers never seem to tire of is the two scenic outdoor showers in the Hollister Log Cabin, which were moved piece by piece and then rebuilt on the property. If you stay, be sure to ask about the unique, and some would say heavenly, plumbing.

---

## UXU Ranch

1710 Yellowstone Highway
Wapiti, WY 82450
Phone: (800) 373–9027; (307) 587–2143
Fax: (307) 587–7390
E-mail: uxuranch@aol.com
Web site: www.uxuranch.com

**Owners:** Grant and Heidi Flaharty and Ray Flaharty

**Accommodations:** Capacity, 34. 1- and 2-bedroom traditional log cabins. Daily maid service.

**Meals:** Host Heidi Flaharty presides over the western-style gourmet cuisine. Special dietary requests honored with advance notice. "Honor" bar with more than 40 wines.

**Activities:** Horseback riding with instruction, guided fishing, hiking, mountain biking, river rafting, guided Yellowstone trips, visits to the Buffalo Bill Historical Center and the Cody Nite Rodeo. Softball games, nearby golf and skeet shooting.

**Amenities:** Sauna, hot tub, rooms complete with bathrobes and bath supplies, cabins with private porches and swings, daily maid service, meeting rooms for conference/business meetings

**Special Programs:** Children's program for kids over 6 includes horseback riding, archery, and games.

**Rates:** $$$$–$$$$$ full American plan. Rates based on accommodations; the most luxurious and expensive, the Hollister Cabin, is $6,100 for the first adult and $1,075 for each additional person. Reduced children's rates, off-season rates.

**Credit Cards:** Visa, MasterCard. Personal checks and traveler's checks accepted.

**Season:** June 1 to September 27

**Getting There:** Guests fly to Cody, Jackson, or Billings, Montana. Inquire about special rental-car rates or use the free ranch shuttle service.

**What's Nearby:** Yellowstone National Park, Cody, and Jackson Hole, Wyoming

# CANADA

# BREWSTER'S KANANASKIS GUEST RANCH AND GOLF RESORT

### Banff, Alberta

With Banff National Park at their backs, the Brewster family began accommodating tourists on its ranch operation in 1923. Missy Bagley Brewster recognized that the family's homestead on the shores of the Bow River would be an ideal place for people to rest and stay on their way to Banff. The venture met with fabulous success, and over time the Brewster family was able to greatly expand its ventures. Now, along with the guest ranch, the Brewster properties include a nine-hole mountain golf course with spectacular Mount Yamnuska rising up in the background and Brewster's Mountain Lodge in Banff (another great place to vacation).

This is a spectacular part of Canada, rivaling its stateside equal, Jackson Hole, Wyoming, as a gateway to a fantastic national park. Brewster's location in Kananaskis is less than an hour's drive from ultramodern Calgary, a cosmopolitan city with a wonderful, laid-back Western ambience. Less than half an hour's drive west of Kananaskis lies Banff National Park, with its soaring mountains, crystalline lakes, and dozens of recreational opportunities. Travelers who've never visited Alberta owe it to themselves to vacation here. And with the strong U.S. dollar making a Canadian vacation a relative bargain, there's never been a better time for those who live south of the border.

The ranch is a landmark property with 2,000 acres of forest mixed with wide-open pastures and cool, pleasantly shaded glades. Horseback riding, of course, is the main activity. Expect expert guidance and instruction from the staff. Half-day rides satisfy many guests, but if you don't mind waking up saddle sore the next day, the full-day ride to the ridge of Mount Yamnuska offers a splendid and unforgettable overview of this especially scenic area. You may even get to play a game of polo with guests on your own ranch-raised thoroughbred!

Vacationers looking for even more adventure should inquire about mountain pack trips. These rides take guests over the historic Horse Drive Trail, which the Brewsters have used for more than a century while driving horses to and from winter pasture. You'll ride to one or both of the ranch's cabin camps, which provide a much more comfortable place to lay one's head than the camp tents provided by most outfitters.

Back at the ranch, guests can enjoy swimming in the Bow River (an icy experience, but nice on a hot summer afternoon). Those who prefer their water hotter can take a relaxing dip in the fifteen-person whirlpool.

Other activities include hiking amid the wildflowers and wild berry bushes, hayrides, canoe trips, singing songs and sharing stories around the campfire, and fishing for cutthroat trout and Dolly Varden in the lakes and streams adjacent to the ranch.

An especially good time to visit is July, when the annual Calgary Stampede comes to town. Founded in 1912, the rodeo boasts of being "the greatest show on dirt," and, indeed, it is. Stampede Park is a vast area of agricultural displays, horse shows, carnival midways, and commercial exhibits. Be sure to check on the dates if you plan on a July vacation.

The Brewster properties are bustling places, but the flexible schedule allows visitors to do as much, or as little, as they wish.

---

### Brewster's Kananaskis Guest Ranch and Golf Resort

Box 2606
Banff, Alberta T1L 1C1
Canada
Phone: (800) 691–5085; (403) 673–3737
Fax: (403) 673–2702
E-mail: kgr@brewsteradventures.com
Web site: www.brewsteradventures.com

**Owner/Manager:** The Brewster Family

**Accommodations:** 60-person capacity. 33 cabins and chalets located on the banks of the Bow River. Rooms feature aromatic cedar interiors, full shower/bath, antique furnishings, and daily maid service.

**Meals:** Wholesome foods served family style on long tables. The eggs, butter, cream, milk, meat, and vegetables are strictly fresh. Fresh fruits in season. Homemade breads a ranch specialty.

**Activities:** Horseback riders are assigned their own horses and "rigs" (tack). Rides near the ranch lead to high-mountain vistas or through the foothill country on the Stoney Indian Reservation. Several all-day trips take place throughout the week, with evening campfire cookouts and beautiful sunsets. Gathering the horse herd is a favorite "special" activity for willing guests. Pack trips and overnight rides also available.

Fishing in local lakes and streams; Calgary Stampede trips; visits to local Native American reservations with cultural events and native crafts; golf at the ranch's 9-hole mountain course (soon to be 18 holes). Evening and off-time activities include reading in the library, pool playing, and parlor games.

**Amenities:** Recreation room, library, piano, golf shop with power carts and club rentals, snack bar

**Special Programs:** No special kids' programs, although there are plenty of family activities that kids can take part in with their parents. Children must be 7 years of age or older to ride horses. Ideal for conference groups, weddings, and large family gatherings, a barbecue pavilion allows as many as 300 guests to be seated. Inquire about special packages: Romance package, Spikes'n'Spurs golf and riding package, women-only group get-togethers, Corporate Getaway Days.

**Rates:** $$ modified American plan. Breakfast and dinner included in the daily lodging rates. Box lunches available by request. Activities such as golf, overnight pack trips, and horseback riding are charged separately. Be sure to inquire about packages, such as the Spurs'n'Spikes golf and riding package, as well as rafting, canoeing and other activities.

**Credit Cards:** Visa, MasterCard, American Express. Traveler's checks accepted.

**Season:** June through September

**Getting There:** 28 miles east of Banff National Park, approximately 45 minutes west of Calgary just off the Trans-Canada Highway. Nearest airport: Calgary.

**What's Nearby:** Calgary, Lake Louise, Banff, and Banff National Park

# THE HOMEPLACE RANCH

Priddis, Alberta

When the only people living in Alberta's western foothills were the Stoney and Sarcee Indians, they referred to the area as "Paradise." If your idea of paradise is one of timbered forests, lush green pastures, blue, blue skies, and wonderful seclusion, then the Homeplace Ranch is paradise indeed.

A small ranch with a capacity of only fourteen guests, the Homeplace lives up to its name. Guests feel like family, and a stay here is guaranteed to make you good friends with the ranch owners, the MaKenny family.

Homeplace Ranch operates year-round and is a genuine working cattle ranch. Located just a half-hour south of Calgary, the ranch lies at an elevation of 4,900 feet (1,500 meters) in the foothills of the snow-capped Canadian Rockies. The ranch is surrounded by thousands of acres of federal forest lands that harbor a wide variety of wildlife species including bears, deer, coyotes, various birds of prey, elk, and many more. Small group rides virtually ensure that you will see plenty of critters large and small during your stay.

Guests stay in the main lodge or coach house in private rooms, each with its own bathroom and shower. A common western-style living room and the main dining room are where guests and ranch employees tend to congregate and socialize.

After a filling breakfast, riding is the usual order of the day at the Homeplace. Each guest is assigned a horse for the week, with a careful pairing of rider skills to the horse provided. Safety and a good rapport with your horse are stressed, and guests are welcome to join in the early-morning grooming and saddling of their mount, if they so desire. Most of the horses were born and raised right here on the ranch, and their familiarity makes them steady and reliable mountain horses no matter their breed.

After riding, guests gravitate toward the Jacuzzi bath or head to the creek to cool their feet. The ambitious can also hike the many local bridle paths and trails or try their hand fishing for grayling and rainbow trout in the nearby streams. Seasoned anglers will want to explore the world-renowned Bow River, a trophy trout-fishing destination just twenty-five minutes from the ranch. Weekends offer a number of entertaining diversions such as rodeos, polo games, and the urbane but still very western nightlife and fancy dining in Calgary, a modern and delightful city much like Denver.

If your vacation goals include "playing cowboy," you can ask to join the resident cowboys and spend time checking cows and "circle riding" the ranch. If you want to squeeze in some sightseeing, the Homeplace can serve as your base camp to explore Banff, Calgary, and the Head Smashed in Buffalo Jump. Equestrians will want to check out Spruce Meadows, a world-class show jumping facility located just south of Calgary and a mere 20 kilometers east of Homeplace. There, you'll see top-drawer jumping horses, western stock horses, and perhaps catch a polo match. (Ask about special Spruce Meadows event packages, as well as the Calgary Stampede Days rodeo packages.)

The staff will be happy to help you plan and coordinate such excursions, and if this

The Homeplace Ranch, Alberta, Canada

is your desire, it is recommended that you bring or rent your own car (Budget Car Rentals at the Calgary Airport offers reduced rates to ranch guests, so be sure to ask). Golfers can arrange tee times at the Winter Green Country Club, just 7 miles from the ranch.

---

### The Homeplace Ranch
Site 2, Box 6, RR 1
Priddis, Alberta T0L 1W0
Canada
Phone: (403) 931–3245
E-mail: mac@homeplaceranch.com
Web site: www.homeplaceranch.com

**Owner/Manager:** The MaKenny Family

**Accommodations:** Capacity, 14. Guests are housed in individual rooms in the main lodge and the coach house. Guest rooms have individual bathrooms and showers.

**Meals:** Typical ranch fare served family style in the main lodge. Guests dine with employees. 3 daily meals, plus snacks, coffee, and fresh cookies always available. Steak cookouts (at least one a week).

**Activities:** Horseback riding is central to ranch activities; careful matching of horse and rider plus experienced wranglers to teach guests ensures a safe and enjoyable experience. Due to small group rides, guests do not follow a prescribed nose-to-tail type of trail riding but are encouraged to master the walk, trot, and canter where appropriate. Cattle work may be available to guests expressing an interest. Instruc-

tion with written evaluation available. Trout fishing on the ranch, trophy fishing in nearby Bow River with outside outfitter, informal recreational games, nearby golf. Winter alpine skiing nearby and cross-country skiing and snowshoeing on the ranch. Inquire about rodeo excursions to the famed Calgary Stampede and special events at Spruce Meadows.

**Amenities:** Jacuzzi bath, comfortable guest lounge in the main lodge, tepee site for overnight campouts, and lots of artifacts, photos, and memorabilia that highlight this ranch's almost 100-year history

**Special Programs:** No formal children's program, although children over 7 are allowed to ride.

**Rates:** $$ full American plan. 3-, 5-, and 7-day packages. Inquire about the various special-event packages centered around the Calgary Stampede Rodeo and the events at Spruce Meadows. Early in spring, the ranch offers a trail-clearing expedition in which guests help prepare the trails for summer riding; this trip involves lots of riding and plenty of good, outdoor work, as well as extended rides into the high country to gather cattle.

**Credit Cards:** None. Personal checks accepted.

**Season:** Open year-round

**Getting There:** 30 miles south of Calgary off Route 22. Shuttle service from the airport available at additional cost.

**What's Nearby:** Banff National Park, Calgary, and Spruce Meadows

# CHILCOTIN HOLIDAYS
# GUEST RANCH

## Gold Bridge, British Columbia

Chilcotin Holidays Guest Ranch is a wilderness experience like no other, short of a visit to Alaska. Located in the southwest corner of Canada, Chilcotin's 2,000-plus square miles of guide territory is virtually a wildlife preserve. Here, you can encounter hundreds of species, from mountain goats to moose, deer, bighorn sheep, and even grizzly bear. (Don't worry, the guides know how to safely manage wildlife encounters.)

Due to a unique outfitting arrangement, the ranch has almost unprecedented outfitting rights to this huge chunk of mountain territory that ranges from lowland Douglas fir forests up to the delicate alpine tundra, where visitors encounter unusual wildflowers and vegetation that grows only in these isolated islands of high-alpine land. The ranch is run by Kevan Bracewell and Sylvia Waterer, whose experience encompasses all facets of guest-ranch operations, adventure travel, tourism, and resource management (Sylvia actually has a postgraduate degree in the latter two fields of study). Since 1990, they've made it their goal to use their diverse skills to create the ultimate "once in a lifetime" adventure experience for their guests.

At the center of this philosophy are guest participation and involvement. On a ride, you may take part in counting wildlife for population studies or collect grizzly hair from a rubbing tree, which will later be used for genetic testing to study the migration and habits of the native bears. You'll be passively and actively learning about the fascinating ecosystem of this region of North America.

Located on the leeside of the Coastal Mountain Range, the ranch is situated in a "rain shadow," which means that the dreary days the Pacific Northwest is known for aren't a problem here. Typically, the summer weather is warm and sunny, whereas in winter the skies are often blue, with just enough precipitation to make cross-country skiing and snowmobiling pleasurable. Another benefit of this idyllic, dry climate: very few bugs!

*Chilcotin* is an Indian name that means "People of the Blue Water." Glaciers in the region give the lakes throughout the territory a pleasing turquoise color. In the past, the area was a trading region where inland tribes met with coastal Indians, and some of your riding adventures will likely take you over the old trade routes. You may also encounter signs of a thriving gold mine, now abandoned. At one time, this area was one of the richest gold-producing areas of British Columbia.

Carrying you to these historic sites are Chilcotin's unusual Mountain Cayuse horses, a mixture of breeds that creates a horse well-suited to the rugged mountain environment. These horses have great stamina, strength, and energy but are also gentle and capable of carrying anyone from the most seasoned rider to young children taking their maiden horseback rides.

The Chilcotin Ranch offers guided fishing, wildlife viewing, wilderness guide training hikes, pack trips, and mountain bike trips. Winter adventures include snowmobiling and cross-country skiing. Guests are matched by abilities, interests, and ages. Families, for example, are matched with families, and not with single adults. More

Chilcotin Holidays Guest Ranch, British Columbia, Canada

© Chilcotin Holidays

experienced individuals (avid hikers, for instance) will not be put with novice outdoorsmen. This attention to detail makes a Chilcotin Holidays trip truly special.

---

**Chilcotin Holidays Guest Ranch**
Gun Creek Road
Gold Bridge, British Columbia V0K 1P0
Canada
Phone: (250) 238–2241
Fax: (250) 238–2274
E-mail: adventures@chilcotinholidays.com
Web site: www.chilcotinholidays.com

**Managers:** Kevan Bracewell and Sylvia Waterer

**Accommodations:** Capacity, 18. Ranch guests stay in the 2-story ranch house, which has 9 comfortably furnished guest rooms. Shared baths, daily maid service.

Adventure guests stay in the permanent base camps in either log or tent cabins, some with heating and bathroom facilities.

**Meals:** At the ranch or on the trail, you'll be surprised and pleased by the appealing and creative cuisine. Unlimited fresh fruits and vegetables, home-baked goods, and hearty main courses such as candied salmon, barbecued ribs, tomato salad with balsamic vinegar and olive-oil dressing, chickpea and spinach salad, baked cookies, and oatmeal squares. Sumptuous!

**Activities:** A low guest-to-guide ratio allows Chilcotin Holidays to focus on education as well as guest safety. Groups are matched by ability, age, and family groups. All-inclusive adventure packages include such activities as daily riding, riding lessons, guided hiking, mountain-biking tours, fishing, gold panning for kids, horse-logging demonstrations, horseshoe-throwing competitions.

Additional activities include pack trips (often teamed with ranch stays) and mining-town tours. Winter activities include ice fishing, horse-drawn sleigh rides, target shooting, horseback riding, wildlife viewing, cross-country skiing, and snowmobiling.

**Amenities:** The ranch building is comfortably simple. Rooms have feather duvets; big, soft pillows; and queen and double beds.

**Special Programs:** Most trips involve prescribed activities or "adventures," as the ranch literature refers to them. Choose from a number of formal adventure packages and participate in numerous informal activities that take place on the ranch and on the trail.

**Rates:** $$$–$$$$ full American plan. Inquire for package specifics and rates. Bring 6 or more, and the person who organized the trip pays nothing.

**Credit Cards:** Visa, MasterCard. Traveler's checks and cash accepted.

**Season:** Open year-round

**Getting There:** Ranch shuttle service available from Vancouver. Nearest airport, Vancouver. Drive time is approximately 4½ hours.

**What's Nearby:** This is an isolated ranch destination; good dining and shopping in Whistler, British Columbia, about 2 hours south.

# ECHO VALLEY RANCH & SPA
## Jesmond, British Columbia

Echo Valley Ranch & Spa is a premier facility; you'll find its equal, but none better in North America. This unique destination spa and guest ranch welcomes guests to a superb sanctuary, healthy dining, world-class spa services, and a diversity of year-round outdoor adventures. Echo Valley is not your ordinary ranch; there is a certain "East meets West" flavor here that is reflected in such things as Thai stretching classes and "Thai night," where the cuisine and dancing reflect the resort's proximity and relationship to the Pacific Rim. An unusual—but intriguing—change of pace!

The ranch was the dream of resident owners Norman and Nanthawon Dove, who purchased the property in 1995. The 160-acre property is augmented by 10,000 acres of leased cattle land and a seemingly endless wilderness owned by the Canadian people. Despite being "in the middle of nowhere," the ranch has a menu of activities that rivals that of any guest ranch described in this book. Here's a quick, but certainly not exhaustive, list.

Daily horseback riding, riding lessons, and clinics; guided hiking; natural history walks; white-water river-rafting trips; 4 x 4 tours; gold panning; fly fishing, spinner, and bait fishing in local lakes and streams; "flight" seeing trips; spa treatments, and Thai stretching class.

Spa enthusiasts will especially appreciate the Baan Thai spa, a traditional Thai house and pavilion designed by famous Thai architect Dr. Pinyo Suwankan. Full-time resident aestheticians and spa therapist offer a complete array of health-spa services. The facilities include beauty and massage salons, exercise equipment, outdoor hot tub, sauna, steam rooms, and showers, hydrotherapy-treatment room, and a heated indoor pool. Daily Ruessn dat ton, meditation, and fitness classes (seasonal—inquire about availability).

As you might have guessed, this is an adult-oriented destination, with an age floor of thirteen years. From mid-July to early August, the age restriction is removed, and more kid-friendly activities and family-oriented events are available. You can, of course, book the whole ranch for a family reunion or other get-together, and you can bring young children.

The evening entertainment is every bit as diverse as the daily activities. There are weekly cookouts with live music performances, Native American drumming, chanting, and dancing. On Thursday guests enjoy Thai night, with an authentic Asian dinner and instruction in dancing.

On quieter nights, guests may enjoy a big-screen television with VCR and DVD, or satellite programs. You can join in karaoke, dancing, billiards, shuffleboard, darts, or board games, or just find a quiet place to read the newest best-selling novel.

The ranch riding program is pretty special. The ranch uses Tennessee walking horses, stately animals known for their ground-covering stride and Cadillac-smooth ride. If you've never ridden one, you will be amazed at how quickly and easily they move, and you may find yourself less sore at day's end, too! (For those riders who wish, there are also a few horses of traditional western breeding, such as quarter horses.)

It's hard to imagine a ranch that offers so much. You'll simply have to go there and see it for yourself. This is a great property, a place where the Far East meets the Old West, thanks to the wonderful owners who have realized their dreams of an inviting and truly special guest ranch.

---

### Echo Valley Ranch & Spa
P.O. Box 16
Jesmond, British Columbia V0K 1K0
Canada
Phone: (250) 459–2386
Fax: (250) 459–0086
E-mail: info@evranch.com
Web site: www.evranch.com

**Owners/Managers:** Norman and Nanthawon Dove

**Accommodations:** Capacity, 40. 2 deluxe lodges, 4 cabins, a traditional Baan Thai (Thai house). The Dove Lodge is a log-cabin structure with 6 guest bedrooms, all with large baths and great views. This is the centerpiece of the ranch, where guests meet for meals and games or to dip in the outdoor hot tub. The Lookout Lodge has 9 large bedrooms, all with baths; 4 rooms feature lofts; all rooms feature porches or balconies. The Baan Thai complex features traditional Thai architecture. A penthouse suite with teak furniture from Thailand is the "jewel" of the property. Across from the suite is the Baan Thai Spa. Additional cabins include 1- or 2-bedroom floor plans, with sitting areas and private bathrooms; some have private Jacuzzi hot tubs.

**Meals:** Full-time professional chef Kim Madsen prepares lavish gourmet meals. Emphasis is on healthful foods (real organic foods are used extensively), including wild mushrooms, herbs, and berries. Special diets accommodated with advance notice. Wines and beers available.

**Activities:** Riding, riding lessons, white-water rafting, nature hikes with naturalists, lake and stream fishing, airplane tours. There are two complete spas, with a broad assortment of spa services, both traditional and Taiwanese.

**Amenities:** Conference facilities with audio equipment, computer networking, and Internet access; separate "breakout" rooms. Baan Thai Spa with in-house spa service providers; luxurious rooms with typical resort amenities; satellite TV and media room; guest recreation room, hot tubs, heated pool, and more.

**Special Programs:** Kids under 13 are welcome from mid-July to early August; otherwise, kids must be 13 or older. Groups of 20 or more can "book the ranch" and bring along younger children.

**Rates:** $$$ full American plan. Prices vary depending on packages chosen. Special themed events include culinary weeks, hiking, basics of fly fishing, learn to ride, and more. Inquire for dates. Check the ranch literature for detailed descriptions of the different package offerings.

**Credit Cards:** Visa, MasterCard. Personal checks and traveler's checks accepted.

**Season:** Open year-round

**Getting There:** Nearest airport: Kamloops, British Columbia. Private airstrip on the ranch. Located 270 miles north of Vancouver, 100 miles from Kamloops.

**What's Nearby:** This ranch is situated in the heart of the Canadian wilderness.

# SPRINGHOUSE TRAILS RANCH
## Williams Lake, British Columbia

Many people enjoy the freedom of trailer and car camping in summer. Springhouse Trails Ranch is one of a handful of guest ranches with its own campground, enabling the gypsy camper the chance to enjoy a dude-ranch vacation in their own home-away-from-home. In addition, this Canadian guest ranch offers the more traditional cabins as well as apartment-type lodgings.

The campground is the full-service type, with full hookup RV sites, bathrooms, showers, and laundry facilities. There is even a trampoline for kids!

Flexibility is the rule at Springhouse Trails. Campers can take advantage of the relatively inexpensive camping rates (especially affordable for residents of the United States, given current exchange rates). Vacationers looking for accommodations can rent rooms by the night or as an American plan package that includes lodging and two- or three-meal-a-day options. Activities such as horseback riding can be paid for a la carte or as part of an inclusive package that includes lodging, horseback riding, three daily meals, and use of all ranch facilities. This level of flexibility makes Springhouse Trails Ranch appealing to people who wish to stay for a night, a week, or a month—an arrangement that's hard to find at most guest-ranch destinations.

The ranch is located in British Columbia's Cariboo Mountains at an elevation of 3,000 feet. The forests have abundant stands of pine and fir, which give the air a refreshing and clean scent. Broad, open pasturelands and glades invite lots of exploration on horseback. Guided riding is informal, with lots of opportunities to range out and explore the surrounding wilderness and lots of opportunities for family vacation photos.

The property was revitalized by Werner and Susi Moessner, a German couple who left Stuttgart in the late 1970s in search of land. They opened Springhouse Ranch to guests in 1980 and developed quite a clientele of European guests who appreciated the bilingual nature of the ranch as well as the excellent German cuisine that was mixed in with the more standard western ranch meals served in the dining room. At present, the ranch is run by the Moessners' daughter, Eve, and her husband, Herbert Winkler, in the tradition of their family.

Springhouse Trails Ranch is situated near a small lake amid open pastures and rolling hills. Activities are informal, with horseback riding, hiking, and nearby fishing being the principal draws. A nearby bird sanctuary is an ideal place for nature observation (be sure to bring along a pair of binoculars and a guidebook to Western birds). Casual lake fishing is also a popular pastime, so plan to bring along a rod and tackle if that interests you. Guests wishing to play a round of golf or work on their tennis swing can take advantage of public facilities in nearby Williams Lake. River-rafting excursions may also be arranged through Chilko River Expeditions, which has a good relationship with the folks at Springhouse Trails.

A flexible schedule also leaves time to explore several nearby gold-rush towns (this area of British Columbia once formed the heart of a major gold rush) and a chance to take in local rodeos or take an airplane tour of this lovely region of the West. Your hosts will be glad to help you coordinate excursions, and be sure to inquire about upcoming community events and celebrations such as the Williams Lake Stampede Rodeo.

## Springhouse Trails Ranch

3067 Dog Creek Road
Williams Lake, British Columbia V2G 4X2
Canada
Phone: (250) 392–4780
Fax: (250) 392–4701
Web site: www.springhousetrails.com

**Owners/Managers:** Eve and Herbert Winkler

**Accommodations:** Capacity, 40. Guests are housed in rustic, individual log cabins with kitchens and in apartment-style guest rooms in 2 large lodges. Also available is a full-service campground with a dozen RV spaces with hookups and laundry and shower facilities.

**Meals:** Guests dine in the lodge's main dining room/restaurant. The menu is a mix of standard western ranch items as well as German specialty items such as schnitzel. Weekly outdoor barbecues. Full bar.

**Activities:** Horseback riding, hiking, fishing, informal outdoor games and recreation. Nearby golf, tennis, and river-rafting excursions (extra). The Williams Lake area offers many opportunities for sightseeing, so be sure to plan accordingly.

**Amenities:** RV campground with full hookups for 12 vehicles; restaurant with bar; children's playground

**Special Programs:** No special kids' program, although children are welcome.

**Rates:** $–$$ Packages with full American plan and horseback riding. Children's rates.

**Credit Cards:** Visa, MasterCard, American Express

**Season:** May to September

**Getting There:** Located 11 miles southwest of Williams Lake; 6 hours northeast of Vancouver by car. Airport service to Williams Lake via Vancouver International Airport.

**What's Nearby:** Williams Lake, with golf, tennis, and seasonal rodeo events

# THREE BARS
# CATTLE & GUEST RANCH

Cranbrook, British Columbia

Located on the western side of the Canadian Rockies, Three Bars Cattle & Guest Ranch shares much in common with the guest ranches located in the land of its southern neighbor, Montana. Persons familiar with the Glacier National Park will find themselves right at home in this beautiful stretch of Canadian backcountry. The summer weather here is moderate and mild, with clear, cold mountain streams, wide-open pastures and parklands, and forests that run to the far horizon.

Amid all this natural splendor is a handsome, modern log lodge with peaked-roof awnings and a broad, inviting front porch that emphatically says, "Relax—you're on vacation." Whether your idea of time off means relaxing with the latest *New York Times* bestseller or taking a soothing trip down the mild St. Mary's River, the Three Bars is a great place to find your bliss.

As an actual cattle ranch, the Three Bars promotes an excellent riding program. The ranch boasts of more than ninety riding horses, which works out to two horses per guest. That makes matching every guest to an appropriate horse quite easy and ensures that no horse in need of a little time off is pressed into service. Your horse will be yours for the week, but on the off chance that you don't get along, another will be ready to step up and become your new pardner.

With so many mounts, the riding is unlimited at the Three Bars. Take off for a few hours or spend the entire day in the saddle, going deep into the endless system of trails. After a couple of days in the saddle, guests may opt for the "fast ride," where they get the opportunity to do some trotting and galloping during a ground-covering guided tour. (Guests who are really avid and enthusiastic horsemen will want to inquire about special "horsemanship" weeks.)

Riding lessons are available in the arena to help newcomers attain sufficient proficiency in the saddle and to review the essential points of safety on horseback. Even children get in on the action, with riding programs for kids as young as seven years. There are daily activity programs and a Junior Wrangler riding program for kids, too.

The nearby St. Mary's River is not only a good place for a float trip but it's also a Blue-Ribbon trout habitat ideal for anglers. Just a short walk from the ranch, the St. Mary's is the ideal place for first-timers and fly-fishing veterans alike. Basic fishing tackle is available at the ranch, or you can bring your own custom carbon-fiber fly rod. If you require a guide, the ranch will be happy to help you find a local outfitter who knows all the best spots. For the less demanding, a stocked pond in Cranbrook provides a great place to spend time fishing with the kids. The ranch will be happy to outfit you with spinning rods and a local map.

The Three Bars is fairly upscale, with a nice complement of amenities such as an indoor pool, outdoor hot tub, and tennis court. Children will enjoy the children's play area and petting zoo, and everyone seems to have fun playing volleyball and pitching horseshoes.

The Three Bars is home to the Beckley family—Jeff, April, and their two sons, Tyler and Jesse. The Beckleys love sharing their rural western lifestyle with guests, and it shows in everything they do.

---

### Three Bars Cattle & Guest Ranch
9500 Wycliffe Perry Creek Road
Cranbrook, British Columbia V1C 7C7
Canada
Phone: (250) 426–5230
Fax: (250) 426–8240
E-mail: info@threebarsranch.com
Web site: www.threebarsranch.com

**Owner:** The Beckley Family

**Accommodations:** Capacity, 40. A fairly upscale facility, with modern guest cabins featuring private entrances, sun chairs, log furniture, queen-size beds, full private baths, and sitting areas. Linens and bath and pool towels provided; daily maid service. Inquire about the different cabin floor plans, which vary to accommodate a variety of family situations.

**Meals:** Western ranch meals, predinner cocktail hour. Special diets with advance notice.

**Activities:** Horseback riding with expert instruction, ideal for guests who want to learn. Guests join in cattle driving, when needed. Guided hikes, fishing in St. Mary's River. Weekly float trips during the spring and early summer runoff. Swimming, tennis, hiking, mountain biking. Nearby golf.

**Amenities:** Hot tub, indoor swimming pool, tennis court, lounge, media room (TV, VCR, DVD, etc.), meeting rooms for conferences, high-speed wireless Internet, fitness center. Nearby golf, downhill skiing, and helicopter tours (additional).

**Special Programs:** No formal kids' programs, although children over 6 may ride on supervised rides with wranglers. Babysitters available.

**Rates:** $$ full American plan. Reduced spring and fall rates; stays shorter than 7 days available. Reduced children's rates.

**Credit Cards:** Visa, MasterCard. Personal or traveler's checks accepted.

**Season:** May through September. The ranch is available October through May for conferences.

**Getting There:** Courtesy shuttle from Cranbrook Airport provided. Three Bars is located between Cranbrook and Kimberly in the southeastern corner of British Columbia. Canadian Airlines and Air Canada offer regional airport services with connections to Vancouver, British Columbia and Calgary, Alberta. Drive time from Spokane, Washington, is 4 hours; from Calgary, 5 hours via Banff National Park. Request a map for specifics.

**What's Nearby:** Glacier National Park (east of the ranch, in Montana) and Waterton National Park, in Alberta; also, Banff National Park (2 hours north) and Calgary. Nearby Cranbrook, British Columbia, hosts an annual rodeo. Step back in time and visit the gold-rush days at Fort Steele, a restored Canadian Mounted Police outpost, located just a few minutes away from the ranch.

# MEXICO

# RANCHO LAS CASCADAS

San Agustin Buenavista, State of Mexico

Cowboys and men on horseback played as big a role in the development of Mexico as they did the American West. In fact, the earliest horsemen in the Americans were the Spaniards, who used horses to colonize the Spanish territories and whose *vaqueros* (Spanish for "cattle hands") introduced the equipment and much of the vocabulary used by America's cowboys.

Opened in 2004, Rancho Las Cascadas pays tribute to that heritage. Swiss owner Ursula Wiprachtiger runs her operation with typical Swiss efficiency while embracing the local culture of the area, extending her love of and fascination with Mexico to her guests. Her passion is infectious.

Rancho Las Cascadas will appeal to singles, couples, and families looking for more than just healthful outdoor recreation, horseback riding, and fine dining. It offers a true cultural experience. Guests can expect to visit a number of nearby villages and farms, where the residents are for the most part untainted by throngs of tourists. Agriculture is still practiced in traditional ways, and Mexican handicrafts and artisans abound at the local markets, where you can pick up pottery and handmade jewelry and other handicrafts at ridiculously low prices.

If you plan carefully (Ursula can help here), your vacation may coincide with one of the many village fiestas. These rich festivals often include dances, musical performances, special foods, fireworks, and much more. Other special events include horse exhibitions that draw upon the ancient traditions of Spain and Mexico, and the famous "Dia de Los Muertos," when Mexicans celebrate the memories of their deceased ancestors.

Colorful folkloric presentations are a regular part of the activities at Rancho Las Cascadas, including dance performances organized by a former member of Mexico City's renowned Ballet Folklorico and musical performances by local guitar maestro Jesus Gonzalez Magallanes.

Horseback riding is a particular passion of Ursula and her staff. The ranch maintains its own herd of quarter horses and quarter horses crossed with criollos, a compact native horse bred throughout Mexico. The horses here are trained in the respectful traditions of "horse whisperers," which results in responsive, spirited mounts that are nonetheless tolerant of novice riders. Ursula or one of her assistants accompanies every group ride, keeping firm control over the conduct of riders and ensuring a safe trip. But that doesn't mean a tedious head-to-tail journey; riders will learn to competently handle the occasional trot and ground-covering canter as part of their equestrian education. The experience is ideal for advanced riders who appreciate quality horses, but suitable for riders of all abilities.

With more than 7,000 acres to roam in the valley, trail ride terrain includes everything from open grassland savannahs to small climbs up rolling hills and rocky descents into heavily wooded ravines and across gentle streams. Rides can last several hours to all day, and many trips take riders to local villages and areas of natural wonder.

Certainly, a vacation in Mexico isn't for everyone. Having a friendly group of competent innkeepers and guides who speak a variety of languages, including French, German, and English as well as Spanish,

Rancho Las Cascadas, Mexico

certainly helps one to overcome cultural and linguistic barriers. The Rancho Las Cascadas is a guest ranch and more: It is a place to experience another culture while enjoying the comforts that one might find at a top-notch American or European bed-and-breakfast. The lovely setting amid a land rich in cultural and natural attractions makes a trip to this rural inn more than just a vacation. It's an adventure.

---

### Rancho Las Cascadas

54280 San Francisco Soyaniquilpan
San Agustin Buenavista, Estado de Mexico
(Note: it is best to contact the ranch via the Internet or by phone.)
Phone: 0052 55 1070 2080

E-mail: uschi@ranchomex.com
Web site: www.ranchomex.com

**Owner:** Ursula Wiprachtiger Schreyer

**Accommodations:** Guest capacity, 12. Guest houses and guest rooms built by skilled stone masons, with authentic Mexican tile floors and decorated with Mexican country handicrafts. A wonderful ambience! All 6 rooms have private bathrooms with showers and amenities, and purified water to drink. Patio rooms open to the courtyard and fountain; deluxe patio rooms, open to the courtyard, are larger and include individual sitting areas. Two freestanding cabins, the Casa Luna and Casa Sol, provide maximum privacy and their own shaded porches.

**Meals:** 3 daily meals prepared. Menus include regional Mexican recipes and

European cuisine, reflecting the heritage both of the ranch and its Swiss owner, Ursula. A sample dinner menu might include cold avocado soup, a savory chicken in a spicy chocolate "mole" sauce, and a refreshing lime sorbet. Special dietary needs honored with advance notice. All beverages included: beers, wines, and cocktails.

**Activities:** Rancho Las Cascadas offers not merely the chance to ride horses but to experience the culture of Mexico. Ride through open fields and see Mexican farmers working the land in traditional fashion; visit Mexican villages and ancient haciendas; see the area waterfalls "Cascadas" that give the ranch its name; visit the studio of a local, noted painter and perhaps take a class with the master; visit a secluded swimming hole fed by the cascading falls. Enjoy a special trip to Tula and its famous Toltec ruins, pyramids, and amazing ancient statues. Visit a local town with Spanish colonial architecture and spend a few hours visiting a traditional "market day" in the town plaza.

Day rides typically include a picnic lunch; expect to be schooled in proper equitation while riding the well-bred horses— expect to travel at the walk, trot, and canter. In the evening, enjoy Mexican folk music performed by master musicians or a folkloric dance performance.

**Amenities:** Swiss owner Ursula maintains the operation with the traditions of a Swiss innkeeper; despite its very rural locale, Rancho Las Cascadas is surprisingly modern in its amenities. Coffee and tea service in the morning, shower compliments in the bathrooms, dinner served on fine china with crystalware, a fully stocked bar, TV with DVD player, computer access, a whirlpool, children's toys, washer and dryer, and mobile phone communications service are a short list of the many amenities.

**Special Programs:** Children are welcome for those who rent the whole ranch, but there is no formal kids' program. Given the large cultural components of visits and the long hours in the saddle, Las Cascadas is best suited to well-behaved, mature children and teens.

**Rates:** $$ American plan

**Credit Cards:** Visa, MasterCard, American Express, Discover. Other payments: PayPal, money transfer.

**Season:** Open year-round

**Getting There:** Located 50 miles north of Mexico City. Airport transfers to the ranch from Mexico City International Airport can be arranged at extra cost.

**What's Nearby:** Tula, with its ancient Toltec ruins, is a must-see. Visits to local communities where you will enjoy a variety of cultural activities are a planned part of any visit. Visit the old Hacienda of Tandeje, built in 1695. Weekly market in Jilotepec.

# INDEX

# ABOUT THE AUTHOR

Gavin Ehringer's writing has appeared in dozens of equestrian and Western-lifestyle publications, including *Cowboys & Indians, America's Horse, New Country,* and *Western Horseman.* He is the author of the Western Horseman book *Rodeo Legends* and coauthor of *Rodeo in America,* published by the University of Kansas Press. In addition, he has contributed to several guidebooks about ski resorts in his home state, Colorado, and a guidebook to Aspen, Colorado.

Before embarking on a writing career, Ehringer worked as a wrangler at several guest ranches in Colorado, including the award-winning C Lazy U Ranch, which is featured in this book. He also apprenticed on working cattle ranches throughout southern Colorado.